COOKING WITHOUT BORDERS

ANITA LO

COOKING

WITHOUT

BORDERS

with CHARLOTTE DRUCKMAN

photographs by LUCY SCHAEFFER

STEWART, TABORI & CHANG

NEW YORK

CONTENTS

CHAPTER ONE

INTRODUCTION

In every mouthful of food lie hints of history—personal and global. This book is a collection of those stories and recipes. It provides a window onto world cuisine from a contemporary American perspective; it's also a portrait of my life as a working chef. I have always been and remain a chef who cooks. Most nights of the week I can still be found behind the line at *annisa*, expediting, cooking, and plating: It is where I am most at home.

I was brought up in the suburbs of Detroit, Michigan, with parents who had both emigrated from Asia. My father was from Shanghai and walked out of China at the beginning of the Cultural Revolution. My mother was from Malaysia; her family was part of a large population of people from the Fujian province who had immigrated to Kuala Lumpur and who, both linguistically and nationally, continue to define themselves as Chinese. When she arrived in the United States, her first stop was Tennessee, where she received her pre-med degree. My parents met in San Francisco—she was interning at the same hospital where my father was a doctor. They both worked long hours as practicing physicians.

Our household was international. My father died when I was three and I grew up mostly with my stepfather, who came from Denver, Colorado, but spent much of his life in New England, teaching at both Harvard and the Rhode Island School of Design. His extended family had emigrated from Germany, and my siblings and I were raised on German nursery rhymes and visits to our *tanta ancien* in the Fatherland. My parents' long work hours both afforded and required the presence of a nanny. Over the years, a variety of women lived in our home, and brought the tastes of their ancestry with them. The food smells of the American South, Mexico, and Eastern Europe all broadened my family's appetites.

A Hungarian Catholic nun, Sister Elizabeth Angel, stayed with us longest and had the most influence on me emotionally. She also left her mark culinarily. Growing up, my favorite meal was her chicken paprikash, a rich stew made with plenty of fragrant sweet paprika and sour cream and served with her handmade dumplings.

For me, family time together was defined by our moments at the table, where my parents shared their heritage through the meals they provided. My mother would work a full twelve- to fourteen-hour day at the hospital, then come home and often put five or six dishes on the table for us to eat. She was a great cook who imparted her love of food to all three of her children. And like my own cuisine, my mother's cooking came from all over the planet. She would labor with the same intensity over crisp Southern fried chicken as she would over a New England lobster dinner or Malaysian *laksa*—a spicy coconut broth made with shrimp paste, lemongrass, and ginger, filled with noodles.

We were also lucky enough to take family vacations back to China, where the food tasted familiar because

we regularly experienced its flavors in Michigan. My parents loved foreign travel. As a toddler, I journeyed to Malaysia and Tokyo. At the age of seven, I was pulled out of school—along with my brother and sister—for a few months of roaming the world. Everywhere we went, we had to try the local ingredients and explore the scope of that country's cuisine. In Iran, I remember drinking mouth-puckering sour yogurt, so cold it was crunchy with ice particles. In China, which we visited pre-Nixon (earning FBI files as a result) my uncles and aunts—my father's brothers and their wives—treated us to elaborate banquets. In Belgium, my sister and I snuck off to get cones of *frites* between meals of mussels and stewed rabbit. There were dinners of reindeer in Copenhagen, and a boat trip in Sweden that had us facing daily smorgasbords filled with Scandinavian delicacies. The fact that all this tasting took place during my formative years was a vital building block for the success I've found as a chef.

My first solo voyage took place when I was sent to high school in Concord, Massachusetts. Now, boarding-school food is nothing to write home about, but trips into Boston and visits to the homes of friends who came from far and wide allowed me to indulge my appetite and curiosity even further. The first time I had

chilled sake was with a classmate from Japan (no, the school didn't allow this; we were nowhere near our parents and having a good time). My first fresh sugar-snap peas were eaten while staying at a classmate's home on Long Island. We ate them raw during an afternoon picnic, with cold fried chicken; they were chilled, crunchy, and sweet, and when we popped them on our tongues, a little salt would travel up our noses as we caught whiffs of the neighboring beach. Just after graduation, a high school friend, who had grown up in France and whose mother was a food writer for the *New York Times*, introduced me to fried zucchini blossoms and roasted squab.

When I'm standing at the stove, it is these bites that make the kitchen feel like home to me. Traveling the world, going to boarding school in New England, attending college in New York City, and, during that time, taking semesters abroad gave me a sense that my life had no borders. In the kitchen, I apply that mind-set to my cuisine.

In the 1980s, while I was in high school and college, American chefs became increasingly curious, and the term *fusion* made its appearance on the U.S. food scene. To me, the word described an emboldening of the American palate that was catalyzed by a collective embracing of other cuisines. Because of my multi-cultural upbringing, as far as I was concerned, *fusion* meant that my very identity finally had a name.

Eventually, perhaps due to some less-skilled chefs being overly creative, the word *fusion* came to have negative connotations; it began to signify a diluting of clarity within flavor profiles. Now we need another word to describe what is, in essence, *all* cuisine. There are no true borders in food. Each cuisine has been affected by another, be it Vietnamese with its French and Chinese influences; French Alsatian with its German influences; or South African with its Dutch and Indonesian influences. And food, like language, is constantly evolving. It is a living entity that grows and changes at each individual stovetop, at the hands of cooks across the globe.

Although I often think of myself as a fusion chef in the original sense of the word, in some ways that's an oversimplification. While I celebrate Asian flavors and my identity, too often the rest is overlooked. Countless times, I have been asked to sit on panels as an expert on Chinese cuisine, assumed to speak that language, or even advised to write a cookbook on Asian street food. I admit, this has happily been the impetus for me to learn more about my father's culture, which I've achieved through the usual routes of Google, cookbooks, and friends; however, my grounding is French. Not only is it my most proficient second language—I've spent two years, collectively, in Paris, Burgundy, and Normandy—but, more important, it's also the food I know best.

I hold a BA in French from Columbia, and I've trained in the kitchens of Bouley, Chanterelle, and various restaurants in France. The French technique is the base upon which I've built my cuisine. It's a solid foundation that has allowed me to develop a highly personal way of cooking that is as much of a hybrid as my upbringing. The most accurate term for my culinary style would be *Contemporary American*—a broad category that celebrates the diversity of this country. Ours is a vast nation, and likewise its cooking influences

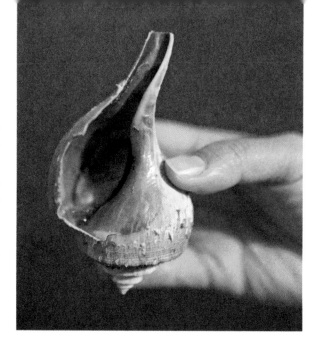

cover a huge range. American cuisine needn't be pigeonholed into its subcategory of Germanic-based dishes—that is, hot dogs, hamburgers, and apple pie.

People say that American food has become grossly homogenous and are quick to point out that large fast-food chains and processed-food giants feed most of the population. I would argue that we are constantly surrounded by a variety of alternatives and that, with a little ingenuity and elbow grease, we can all eat well, and diversely. I have a small house in a quiet fishing town on Long Island, just off of Moriches Bay. I'm an avid fisherwoman, with a small, old-fashioned skiff I borrow from my neighbors. Whenever weather permits I go off looking for clams and hoping for striped bass, bluefish, fluke, or flounder. Sometimes, though, I happen upon the unexpected and find a wealth of mussels growing underneath the dock I launch from, or, while digging for hard-shell clams with my toes, I haul up a conch from on top of the sand. (They hang out there, in shallow water.)

The first time I found a conch was also the first time I cooked one, although I'd eaten the mollusk many times before in ceviches, long braises, and fritters. I'd already dragged in an abundance of both hard-shell and steamer clams, and instead of throwing the lone conch back, I brought it home and did a little impromptu Internet research. My maiden conch chowder—a bastardized version of Manhattan clam

chowder—was whipped up that night. It simmered alongside my pots of New England clam chowder and steamers.

I could have just thrown the conch back and not taken the leap to explore a new ingredient for my repertoire; instead, I created something that yielded two quarts and, subsequently, fed me for four separate meals. It was economical, ecologically sound, local, educational, and, yes, delicious.

There are times when I visit a greenmarket and overhear a shopper buying a bunch of turnips or beets ask the farmers to discard the tops. All I can think is, what a shame; that was an entire separate meal's worth of vegetables. That's a free side dish with purchase, and it leaves no carbon footprint! Just as heartbreaking is when someone throws out the liver of a chicken; it's like throwing out a potential appetizer or lunch for the following day. You have to ask yourself: Is it sustainable to eat only the *prime* cuts of local, well-raised animals?

People often shy away from new taste experiences; they assume they could never like what is being offered to them—novel spice profiles, different cuts of meat they weren't brought up with, or entire animals they have never seen at the table. I find this frustrating because I believe it is rooted in cultural bias. The mind is born without prejudice or preconceived notions, but it is trained to "dislike" certain foods. These seemingly small biases have serious repercussions. We ultimately control what is grown or produced; if we believe we won't enjoy something and deem it unappealing, we won't cultivate it. On the other hand, more adventurous palates can lead to biodiversity, a key to the survival of this planet.

There is, thankfully, evidence that things are improving. While many of the products I use can be esoteric or hard to find, foodways continue to evolve. Ingredients like mesclun, kimchi, and jicama were exotic when I first started cooking; now they can be found in most grocery stores across the States.

I have always tried to keep my dishes and menus original in an attempt to engage—and, sometimes, challenge—people's tastebuds. I'm lucky enough to have built my career in New York City, where I am surrounded by bright and inspiring palates. It is a city full of energy, with access to fabulous products and a diverse clientele, a metropolis that has championed *annisa*, my small fine-dining restaurant in the West Village, and the sadly short-lived bar Q, my attempt at Asian raw bar and barbecue.

It is also a city that feeds me well. Besides being only blocks away from many other talented, innovative chefs, I love my neighborhood falafel joint, the women who set up tables for tacos outside the church on Sunday mornings, and my favorite stall in Chinatown for dumplings or turnip cakes. I've been eating and cooking here for twenty-five years and now consider myself a New Yorker. I've built a home for myself, and my cuisine, in the West Village. I am grateful to have been able to carve out my own niche in one of the world's biggest urban epicenters. And that is what I think the American palate aspires to do—create its own unique, complex identity.

A tightly crowded city is a breeding ground for cultural differences—new strains develop and evolve at a rapid rate. Studying and developing these mutations on the culinary front is one of the mainstays of my cuisine; I'm always striving to achieve balance without borders. This book is an assimilation of all those elements that contribute to my perspective on the wonderful, ever-shifting cultural chaos around me: my years of cooking, traveling, and eating.

I wrestled with the desire to write a chef's cookbook, filled with intricate recipes that are challenging to replicate at home, where we're not graced with massive amounts of space, an employed prep crew at our beck and call, or a staff of dishwashers to clean up our messes. Those books are beautiful; I own many of them—I turn to them often for inspiration or to satisfy a curiosity about a place too far to travel to at that moment. This book has elements of a chef's cookbook, but, for me, food isn't really about aspiration; it's about eating, and sharing time at the table with others. So this book is also one that you can go to a daily basis, if you'd like. It is full of stories, ideas, and techniques that can be used and passed along, and contains many recipes that can be executed to varying degrees of complexity. There are some dishes that can be simplified to suit a weeknight dinner, and others that, with a few suggested twists, are appropriate for a festive event or holiday meal—and, of course, there are many that are fit for any occasion.

Don't be daunted by the unfamiliar ingredients—*ankimo* (monkfish liver) or lobster tomalley come to mind. They are just untried delicacies and among the easier foods to work with; they usually infuse a dish with a distinct, strong burst of flavor without demanding a lot of manipulation. When you see one in a recipe, keep reading. I hope that you'll learn something new and be motivated to try a dish whose biggest challenge lies in tasting a substance you haven't seen before.

Fancy-sounding French items—like pot-au-feu (page 190) or beef bourguignon—are most often born from peasant food; they're economical and teach you how to use every part of your produce. One of the reasons braises are such an integral part of that cuisine is that they were employed, originally, to elevate the lesser—often chewier—cuts of meat that needed to be cooked down to become tender. Beef bourguignon isn't much more than a stew. Pot-au-feu translates, literally, to "pot on the fire," referring to the pot of water in which the protein is cooked; it's a process that yields a brothy richness you love to dip your bread into: It's essentially a special pot roast. These dishes might require you to leave them on the stove a little longer, but the steps and techniques involved are entirely within the range of any home cook.

I like to change these basics by bringing in complementary elements from different cultures or locales, or throwing in an unexpected ingredient from the haute-cuisine pantry. My take on Vietnamese pho (page 44) is an excellent example. That hearty noodle soup is made, traditionally, with oxtails, that part of the animal you'd easily discard if you could afford to. Combined with cinnamon and star anise, among other aromatics, those oxtails make a deeply flavorful, fragrant, and protein-rich broth in which noodles, a cheap staple in Vietnam, can bathe. When I wanted to find a way to use the remains of a duck I'd cooked, I decided to use the carcass and leftover meat for my own pho. I created a duck stock, and, to mix some "high" (gourmet) with the "low" (street food), I garnished my bowl with some foie gras, an unnecessary but tasty measure.

Another dish you will find within these pages is Chilled Sweet Pea Soup with Smoked Sturgeon and Caviar (page 39). I've altered this recipe numerous ways to suit time and place. The combination is an *annisa* creation, one that has been served in the dining room to many customers at the height of spring. When I am at my house on Long Island, the peas in my vegetable garden don't always have a good year, so I might make the soup from local asparagus. I may have been lucky enough to catch a bluefish or find some local oysters and will smoke those instead of sturgeon for my garnish. Sometimes I'm enjoying the good company of guests, or the season's first really hot days, and would rather buy some smoked salmon at the local fine-foods shop. As for the caviar, well, that is irreplaceable, true; still, the soup tastes delicious without it—just add a hint of lemon zest and bit of sea salt.

I have included my suggestions for tweaking dishes, but your environs will lead you there and elsewhere. I hope this book provides the same freedom and sense of place for you, the reader, that I have found at the stove.

Food has defined me ever since I can remember. I was first what I ate, and became what I cook. Let me help you take your own journey to that place.

Dig in.

THE BASICS

Blanching and shocking: These are culinary terms that refer, respectively, to cooking an ingredient (usually a vegetable) in an ample amount of heavily salted boiling water for a couple of minutes, and then transferring it—to stop the cooking process—to an ice water bath (this is best achieved with a wire strainer, or a large perforated scoop). The blanching yields a bright green color in vegetables; the shocking in ice water locks it in. The boiling water should be as salty as seawater—a quick taste test before adding your ingredient is advised.

Clarified butter: To clarify butter, warm it over low heat until completely melted. With a small ladle or spoon, skim off and discard the white milky bits that come to the top. Very slowly and carefully, pour the clear yellow liquid (the clarified butter) through a fine-mesh sieve, leaving the milky sediment behind. Discard the sediment.

Cooking times: When I was in culinary school in France, my classmates and I would constantly ask how long items should cook. My instructors would invariably answer, "When the ingredient starts singing '*Cuit, cuit, cuit!*'"—or "Cooked, cooked, cooked!" In other words, you cannot cook by the clock; you must use your senses to ascertain whether the item is ready or not. Cooking times can vary greatly depending on the calibration of your oven, the BTUs (British thermal units, a measure of the power of your heating element) of your range, the size and/or thickness of your pan, and so on. In this book, when I cannot provide a cooking time, I will try to provide a clear description of what the end result should be.

Frying: I deep-fry in soy oil because it is lighter than other oils and it's inexpensive, so I can change it often. That unappealing greasy fried flavor comes from oil that has been reused one time too many. I usually don't reuse oil more than once, if at all, and only when working with the same kind of ingredient—you wouldn't, for example, want to fry something sweet in an oil that you've previously used for frying fish. You want to fry most things between 350° and 375°F to achieve a greaseless, crisp crust. My preferred gadget for this task is an electric tabletop deep-fryer (Waring makes a good one). Some vegetable chips (beet and eggplant, for example) and onions that are naturally higher in sugar content are better off fried at a lower temperature to achieve crispness before they start to burn.

At home, to waste less oil, I usually shallow-fry. This entails adding a relatively small amount of oil to a pan. I use a thermometer to gauge the oil's temperature. You can purchase a fat thermometer in most grocery stores. If you choose not to use a thermometer, heat your oil over medium to medium-high heat, and when a small leaf or thin shaving of vegetable sizzles immediately when you drop it in, and the oil is not smoking, the oil is ready. Choose a pan that is deep enough that your oil comes only halfway to the top—otherwise the oil might spill over (and possibly ignite) when you add whatever you're frying.

Hot water bath: A hot water bath (or bain-marie) helps maintain even cooking temperatures and is particularly beneficial for dishes that require consistent lower heat. Many ovens, especially those fueled by gas, go through a range of temperatures. For instance, you may have your oven set at 350°F, but it will cycle between 325° and 375°F, maintaining an average heat of 350°F. For items like custards, you need to make sure that the higher end of that temperature range doesn't overcook part of the mixture or else you might end up with a soufflé (of sorts). The best way to prevent such disasters is to surround the cooking vessel with water, which changes temperature at a much slower rate than air. To make a hot water bath, place the larger bath vessel in the oven with the smaller cooking vessel or vessels (such as ramekins) inside. (Don't try to transport a water bath from your counter to the oven; you risk splashing water into whatever you're cooking.) Using a tea kettle, pour hot tap water around the latter to fill the former. If you're cooking something particularly delicate, you can also line the bottom of the bath vessel with a kitchen cloth to buffer any heat transference to the baking dish's bottom. The liquid should come three-quarters up the sides of the smaller cooking vessels. Cover the whole with aluminum foil and you're ready to go.

Oil: Soy oil, which is what you're getting when you purchase "vegetable oil," is an inexpensive, light, trans-fat-free, neutral oil and my implied choice (unless otherwise stipulated) for recipes that call for neutral-flavored oil. You may substitute other flavorless oils such as canola or grapeseed. Many people cook with olive oil as their base, which is fine if you're only cooking Mediterranean dishes. The olive flavor doesn't go with everything, so it is important to think about which oil makes the most sense for each preparation.

Salt: I use kosher salt for all my recipes because it's a pure product and inexpensive. Sea salt will work too, but fine sea salt will be a bit saltier than the kosher, so adjust accordingly and slightly reduce the amount. I do not suggest using iodized salt. For a finishing salt, I like the Hawaiian pink coarse variety for its sweetness, color, and crunch. I also use Maldon occasionally for British-inspired dishes. Coarse sea salt and fleur de sel are perfectly acceptable substitutions, or you can forgo the crunch and just use kosher salt.

Smoking: There are two main types of smoking—hot and cold. The only difference between the two is the addition of ample ice to prevent the ingredient from cooking by keeping it cold (hence the name).

Different types of wood lend different nuances of flavor. My local hardware store has alder wood, mesquite, applewood, and hickory. I tend to use hickory for most foods and, rarely, alder wood for lighter,

more delicately flavored ingredients. I used applewood, which has a nice sweet smell, at *annisa* for my smoked lamb chop dish, but I've noticed that hickory has a purer and even sweeter flavor. I've found mesquite to be too strong, with a resinous element, although it may have its applications (gamy meats or liver, or vegetables such as peppers). Don't take my word for it: Experiment, taste, and discover which wood suits you best.

You have other smoking options besides wood. The classic Chinese method uses black tea, rice, and sugar (brown sugar will give your food a darker look). Chamomile will add floral notes. Herbs are also a good choice. This is a subject ripe for exploration.

- To hot-smoke: Cook slow, at low heat. Barbecue was originally designed for tougher cuts of meat and cooking them slowly over a long period of time helps break down the collagens, tenderizing the flesh. However, with fish, or with smaller cuts of tender meat, you can smoke and cook for a shorter time at a higher heat.

- To cold-smoke: Place the item to be cold-smoked in a container that's surrounded by plenty of ice, or elevate the item on a grill set above a baking dish that has been filled with lots of ice. Make sure the baking dish is large enough that your ingredient rests within the perimeter of the vessel. Follow your stovetop smoker manufacturer's directions, or if using an outdoor grill, make a small fire that's contained to one side of the cooker, as far away from the food you are smoking as possible. When the fire has turned to glowing embers, top with the soaked wood chips, tea-and-sugar mix, dried herbs, or whatever you are using to generate smoke. Place the container of ice with your ingredient at the other side of the grill, far from the embers, and cover the grill, opening the vents just a little. When cold-smoking, the temperature should always remain around 150°F—you rely on indirect heat to smoke the meat. The amount of time required to smoke something depends on that ingredient's size and composition. Longer smoking, obviously, will intensify the smoky flavor.

CHAPTER TWO

APPETIZERS

INSPIRATION: MY OWN BACKYARD

Jennifer Scism, my ex-girlfriend and the former co-owner of *annisa*, planted the garden at my beach house, which we once shared. The official recipe tester for this cookbook, she was and remains a better gardener than I could ever be. She cared for that land so much.

Sadly, it hasn't made much progress lately because for the last two years I was opening a restaurant during planting time. Plus, we've had some bad rainy seasons and the increasing deer population ate a good deal of the yield. Now, I have a fence.

Jen filled four raised beds with organic vegetation. There are four different fruit trees: sour cherry (if I were out there year-round, I could make pie), Asian pear (the only other consistent fruit-bearer), plum (it produced its first fruit ever this year), and pear. I have rhubarb, strawberries, a blueberry bush, and—thanks to the formidable Dorothy Kalins, my neighbor—blackberries. There's a Concord grapevine, too. There's also my herb garden, plus a separate mint plot (mint spreads with zeal, so it needs to be contained).

It's always exciting to find that first little green tomato, and I never tire of seeing the flowers bloom on my zucchini plant. I can't wait to take the blossoms, stuff them with some Manchego cheese, and fry them. As a rule, I try to grow things I'm going to use—Thai bird chiles, jalapeño peppers, red cherry peppers, cucumber, and eggplant. And then there are my peas.

I plant peas in the garden of my house on Long Island every spring. The yield is very low, they take up a good amount of room in the soil, and if you're only able to do your picking on weekends, you rarely get them at their peak. Most often, you're harvesting them a bit too late (they're too big and starchy), or too early (they're very small). I've never been able to make a complete side of peas, a soup, or even a sauce.

I put up with all of these snafus because if you pick and cook these peas right away, they are so much sweeter than anything you can buy, even at the greenmarket. The trick is to use them in recipes that call for very few, such as risotto with peas and Parmesan.

My favorite way to enjoy them requires no cooking at all. I just bring a few ripe pods with me while I'm fishing in Moriches Bay, and I catch the salt air on my tongue as each orb of green sweetness bursts in my mouth. Generally, I like to pit the pea's natural sugary flavor against a salty presence. It doesn't have to be Parmesan, per se—you could easily choose a saline element with a different profile, like a cured pork product. I love the juxtaposition of peas and bacon in spaghetti carbonara, for example. And my mom used to make a Chinese pea-and-pork meal that she served over rice. Don't forget split pea soup. When I prepare it, I incorporate another staple of my youth, HoneyBaked Ham.

You can also draw out the pea's earthy, green-tasting notes. Mint is the reliable choice here, and a well-known one; in Britain, minted peas are standard fare. The herb's bright, clean pungency is an ideal mate for that part of the pea that reminds you where it came from—it almost tastes like the soil, but in a good way.

When I want mint, I can walk outside to my garden and snip as much as I need. That, especially for anyone who loves to cook, is one of life's greatest (and least expensive) luxuries.

I. CANAPÉS

CURRY PUFFS

SERVES 4

6 tablespoons butter

1 pound ground chicken

Salt and black pepper

1 large onion, finely chopped

3 tablespoons curry powder

¼ cup all-purpose flour

1 bay leaf

1¼ cups chicken stock (page 231)

¼ cup dried currants

2 (17¼-ounce) packages puff pastry
    (four 9-inch square sheets)

Egg wash (1 large egg, beaten
    together with 2 tablespoons water
    and a pinch of salt)

My mother's curry was Malaysian. Her sisters, who live in Kuala Lumpur, would drive to Malacca for the sole purpose of visiting a spice shop where their preferred powder was ground; once a year, they would mail some to us. At home in Michigan, my mother used the spice blend to prepare a broth in which she cooked chicken, potatoes, and lots of onions. She finished the curry with coconut milk and would serve it, over rice, for dinner. I made this all the time when I was learning how to cook, but not since; I was too busy learning other things. Whenever I have a curry that's reminiscent of my mother's in any way, it's always comforting—even a Japanese version, although it's made completely differently, with a roux of flour and butter.

Technically, a canapé is an appetizer served on some form of prepared, thinly sliced bread—toasted or sautéed. But the term is also loosely applied to the general category of passed hors d'oeuvres. When I began working at Bouley, that's all I did—I was assigned to the canapé station. To turn my mother's curry into one of these in a literal manner would be difficult. Instead, I try to re-create the experience of tasting that dish by incorporating its flavors into a dough-based morsel that can be eaten in two or three bites. It's not as complicated as it might sound; curry puffs are actually a typical Malaysian snack, so I have a precedent, and one that's quite similar to what I've developed. The difference is that the original include potatoes as well as chicken thigh meat inside, while mine has only the ground poultry and a few currants.

In a preferably nonstick saucepan, melt 2 tablespoons of the butter over high heat. Add the chicken and season with 1 teaspoon salt and a few grinds of pepper. Sauté, crumbling with a wooden spoon, until cooked through. Remove the chicken from the pan and set aside. Return the pan to the heat, add the remaining butter and the onion and cook over medium heat until the onion is soft and translucent. Add the curry powder and stir, then add the flour and cook, stirring constantly, for 3 minutes. Add the bay leaf, then add the stock in a slow stream, stirring constantly with a whisk. Return the chicken and any accumulated juices to the pan, along with the currants, and simmer until thickened, about 8 minutes. Season to taste with salt and pepper and set the mixture aside to cool completely.

Lay the pastry sheets out on a lightly floured surface and roll them out into 10-inch squares. Cut into 2-inch squares. Brush the edges with the egg wash and place 1 teaspoon of the chicken mixture in the center of each. Fold in half to form a triangle, then press, removing as much air as possible to form a small sealed package. If desired, press with a fork to crimp the edges. Brush the tops with egg wash. (At this point, the triangles can be put in an airtight container and frozen for up to 1 month. Although you shouldn't thaw the triangles before baking, remember that it may take a few minutes longer for them to cook through if they've been frozen.)

Preheat the oven to 400°F. Put the triangles on baking sheets and bake until golden brown and cooked through, about 12 minutes. Serve hot or at room temperature.

BABY TOMATOES
WITH SHISO AND WASABI

The idea for this hors d'oeuvre came about thanks to my days of tireless work with tomatoes at Bouley. It was at that time that the chef, David Bouley, invented tomato water. I was in the garde-manger station (or the cold station) and responsible for making tomato concassé (the term usually refers to rough-chopped small cubes, but at Bouley it referenced something precisely and finely diced). It was horrible. Everyone on the line seemed to need some, and at some point, they all started yelling at me for more at the same time. That was when, finally, I cried.

As the prepped tomatoes would sit, waiting to be used, water would leach out of them. One day, Chef took a spoonful, and tasted. It wasn't until after I'd left the restaurant that he began serving his discovery; once he did, it became something of a sensation and started to show up on other menus. He would hang chopped yellow tomatoes in an apron over-night and collect the resulting juice. The liquid would be clarified by being heated and strained. What remained of the hung, water-leached tomato was a pulpy center that was discarded at Bouley, if I remember correctly; I don't like to let anything go to waste, so I found a way to make use of that vegetal flesh.

Years later, at *annisa*, I served an appetizer that paired a tartare of tomato with its water plus some tonburi (the dried seeds of the Japanese broom cypress, *Kochia scopari*). Here, I've transformed that into a canapé;

SERVES 4

1 large yellow beefsteak tomato, peeled (see Notes), seeded, and finely diced

½ teaspoon salt

2 tablespoons soy sauce, or to taste

1 tablespoon neutral-flavored vegetable oil

3 to 4 leaves fresh shiso (see Notes), cut into small squares

1 heaping tablespoon thinly sliced (on a bias) scallion greens

¼ teaspoon prepared wasabi

A few grinds of black pepper

1 pint mixed heirloom cherry tomatoes

I peel, seed, and finely dice a larger beefsteak tomato and drain it. Next, the raw "meat" gets flavored with soy, bright, herbaceous, palate-cleansing shiso, sweetly pungent scallion greens, and some spicy, sharp wasabi. This mixture goes into hollowed-out baby tomatoes, which are then re-capped with their own tops. The juice collected from the beefsteak is given the Bouley treatment, and both components are served together on a Chinese soup spoon. It's a biteful of concentrated tomato flavor; packed with umami, it is comparable to vegetarian sashimi. And its preparation won't make you cry.

Combine the yellow tomato with the salt and put in a fine-mesh sieve set over a bowl. Let sit several hours or up to overnight to drain. Combine the drained pulp with the soy sauce, oil, shiso, scallion, wasabi, and pepper. Reserve the accumulated liquid in the bowl to make reduced tomato water (for serving with the stuffed baby tomatoes) or drink.

Cut off and reserve the top third from the stem end of each cherry tomato. Hollow out the tomatoes and cut a very thin slice off the bottoms to make them stable enough to stand. Stuff the yellow tomato mixture into the cherry tomatoes, mounding it slightly, then replace the tops.

If desired, put the reserved tomato liquid in a saucepan, leaving any sediment behind. Very gently heat until yellow matter forms at the surface, separating the solids from the liquids. Skim off the solids and pour the liquid through a fine-mesh sieve, then chill. Serve the stuffed tomatoes in Chinese soup spoons with a little of the tomato water.

NOTES: Bring a small pan of water to a boil, and fill a bowl with ice water. Cut an X at the base of each tomato, and remove their stems. Drop each tomato into the hot water for 30 seconds, remove it, and immediately drop it into the ice bath to stop the cooking. The skin should peel right off.

Shiso is an Asian herb that imparts a clean, floral taste and helps bring out the sweetness of whatever it is paired with. It is available at Japanese and Korean markets. Substitute mint for a different, yet still delicious, result.

You can always save the tomato water for another use (or drink it), if you don't have Chinese soup spoons to pass around. On their own, the baby tomatoes are easy to pick up and pop into your mouth.

UNAGI AND SALTED-EGG
FRITTERS

I grew up eating salted eggs. My mother would make them by submerging large white eggs, whole and raw, in a simple heavy brine made from 2 cups of salt dissolved in a gallon of water. She'd leave them to sit in that bath, on the counter, by the windowsill, for one month. Then we would eat them. We'd crack them over once-steamed ground pork that had been seasoned with ginger and dried shiitake mushrooms, and then let the whole delicious mess steam again quickly. We'd also hard-boil them; they could then be chopped over rice porridge for Sunday breakfast, or, my favorite, left intact, cooled, and cut in half with a knife, so you could scoop out the interior with a small spoon. Now, at *annisa*, I serve the eggs as bar snacks.

Another typical bar bite, the fritter, inspired the following recipe, which pits the egg's salinity against the sweetness of unagi kabayaki, Japanese barbecued eel. It's a global free-for-all: The Chinese first developed this way of treating the egg as a preservation measure, but you'll find salted eggs all over Southeast Asia—in the Phillipines, Malaysia, Singapore, and elsewhere. The fried ball is ubiquitous—France has its beignets, New England its clam fritters. Enveloped in a classic thick batter and accented with cooked scallions, the eel and egg become a well-rounded treat dipped in sweet and salty soy glaze. Look for prepared unagi in the frozen section of most Asian grocery stores, or ask your local sushi restaurant for a package.

In a large bowl, beat the eggs and milk together, then add the flour, baking powder, and salt. Mix well. Fold in the scallions, unagi, and salted eggs (if using). (This batter can be made a day in advance and refrigerated.)

Put the soy sauce, sugar, corn syrup, and ginger in a saucepan and bring to a boil. Remove and discard the ginger. Add a few grinds of pepper. Taste and adjust seasonings. Set the dipping sauce aside.

In a heavy pot, heat at least 2 inches of oil to 350°F. Working in batches, drop in rounded teaspoonfuls of the unagi mixture and fry, turning frequently, until golden and crisp and cooked through, about 4 to 5 minutes. Drain on paper towels and serve with the dipping sauce.

NOTE: Salted eggs are available in Chinese and Southeast Asian grocery stores (see Resources, page 233).

SERVES 4
2 large eggs
¾ cup whole milk
6 ounces all-purpose flour
¾ tablespoon baking powder
½ teaspoon salt
½ cup thinly sliced (on a bias) scallions
1¾ cups unagi kabayaki (Japanese barbecued eel), finely diced
⅓ cup hard-cooked and finely diced salted chicken or duck egg (optional; see Note)
½ cup soy sauce
¼ cup sugar
½ cup light corn syrup
3 slices fresh ginger
Black pepper
Neutral-flavored vegetable oil for deep-frying

Although the egg is what sets these fritters apart, they'd still taste great without the salted product, because, on some level, the soy sauce already plays that saline role. You could also substitute chopped clams, for a New England take on the Japanese preparation.

RILLETTES OF DUCK
WITH RAISINS AND MUSTARD-SEED CAVIAR

SERVES 4

1 (6-pound) duck, quartered (leave all fat and skin), or 6 pounds duck wings, backs, necks, hearts, gizzards, and skin

Plenty of salt and black pepper

3 tablespoons neutral-flavored vegetable oil

1 onion, chopped

4 cloves garlic, smashed

1 sprig fresh thyme

1 bay leaf

3 cups white wine

Warmed clarified butter (optional)

FOR THE MUSTARD-SEED GARNISH:

¼ cup yellow mustard seeds

3 tablespoons raisins

1 tablespoon sugar

White wine vinegar

Salt and pepper, to taste

TO SERVE:

Toast or crackers

Fresh chives, cut into 1-inch lengths

I contracted Francophilia at a very early age. It was between high school and college that the obsession really took hold. I had moved to New York in the summer of 1984 with no plans but to live in my sister's abandoned apartment on the Upper West Side (she was off climbing mountains in Africa, I think) and to anticipate my first semester at Columbia. I remember feeling terribly lost until Philip, an acquaintance from boarding school, phoned me. He had grown up in Paris, and his mother, Susan, was a food writer for the *New York Times* and, when she lived in France, the *Herald Tribune*. She was a wonderful character. Her apartment was hot pink with a zebra-skin rug. Thanks to her work for the *Times*, she would get invitations to the best spots in town—Philip and I would profit from these invitations: We crashed the opening night of the downtown "it" club of the moment, Area, and had dinners with the owners of various restaurants. I especially remember one supper at Shun Lee, a posh Chinese place, hosted by its proprietor, Michael Tong, and attended by Philippe Petrossian of the caviar empire and Paula Wolfert, famed cookbook author.

Best of all, though, was Susan's tiny Manhattan kitchen; magic was performed there. Philip would sometimes cook and introduce me to new ingredients, and Susan would make rillettes, treats we indulged in copiously from the seemingly bottomless Mason jar she stored them in.

Here is a recipe I learned in cooking school that reminds me of those early days raiding Susan's fridge. I've added raisins and cooked mustard seeds to lend, respectively, some sweetness and spiciness to balance the fat of the duck. The vinegar brings acidity, which will also help to cut through the richness while softening the mustard seeds and glazing them so that they have a bit of the appearance and texture of caviar.

Make the duck: Heat a heavy pot over high heat. Season the duck pieces generously on both sides with salt and pepper. Add the oil, and, when smoking, add the duck pieces, skin side down, and lower the heat to medium-high. Brown the duck, then add the onion and lower the heat to medium. Cook, stirring, until the onion is translucent. Add the garlic and stir again. Add the thyme, bay leaf, and wine and cover. Simmer over low heat for 3 to 3½ hours, until the meat is falling off the bone, making sure there is still a

small amount of liquid at the bottom of the pot so it doesn't burn, adding ½ cup of water, if necessary, at a time. Uncover and cook until most of the remaining liquid is evaporated.

While the duck is still warm, remove the meat and skin from the bones; chop the skin into small bits. Combine the meat and skin in a bowl. Pour the clear fat from the liquid in the pot through a fine-mesh strainer over the meat and skin, discarding any remaining liquid. Stir the mixture intermittently while it cools to form shreds of meat. When the mixture is cool and the fat is incorporated into the shreds of meat, taste and adjust the seasonings, adding more salt and pepper if necessary. Pack into clean jars or a terrine mold and, if you wish to keep the rilletes for more than a week, top with a layer of melted duck fat or clarified butter. Refrigerate.

Make the mustard-seed garnish: Put the mustard seeds, raisins, and sugar in a small saucepan with enough vinegar to just cover them. Bring to a boil, then simmer until the liquid is almost gone and the mixture is glazed. Season to taste with salt and pepper.

Serve rillettes on toast at room temperature, topped with a small dollop of the mustard seed mixture and a piece of chive.

Rillettes can be made with many different meats. The most traditional are goose and pork, and the raisin–mustard seed garnish would work well with those, too. With leaner animals such as rabbit or guinea fowl, you will need to add another fat—traditionally pork, as it's most abundant, or, when making a fish rillette, butter. The flavor profiles will change slightly, depending on which protein you choose, but a rillette will, or should, always be a fatty spread of shredded meat.

TERRINE OF FOIE GRAS
WITH PLUM WINE

I love animals (not just as food!), so to make sure their lives weren't taken in vain, I use every part and ensure nothing goes to waste. I also try to buy from sources that both embrace ethical slaughtering and run a sustainable operation, which generally results in better-tasting meat.

Foie gras, or the fattened livers of ducks or geese, is at the epicenter of food controversy. Some say the practice, which takes young birds and places tubes down their throats in order to pour copious grain into their gullets, is inhumane—legislation is in place to make it illegal in California in the future, and it was illegal in the city of Chicago for two years. Others say that it mimics the natural fattening creatures undergo premigration. I have no idea if the process is painful; I don't think that anyone could be sure of that either way. I've been told by Michael Ginor, the owner of Hudson Valley Foie Gras, one of the three or four artisanal farms in this country that produce this delicacy, that a duck's gullet is made to withstand rough grains. Ducks breathe through small openings at the tips of their tongues, so they are not being choked when fed. The process is quick, and the amount of grain is calibrated to ensure it doesn't injure the fowls' stomachs, or "crops." At Hudson Valley, where all my foie comes from, Temple Grandin inspects the farm periodically, to make sure the ducks are treated well.

I think there are much better ways to go about improving the world than to protest these small farms that practice an art that dates back to 2500 BCE. Aren't there bigger flocks to fry? There are large corporations producing tasteless chickens and thin-shelled eggs from animals cooped up on top of each other all their lives in tiny, overcrowded, dirty cages; we could start by outlawing those companies instead of shutting down farms like Michael's.

Foie gras is a delicacy whose deliciousness words cannot describe. It is a luxury item, meant to be cherished and, because of its intense richness, enjoyed sparingly. This terrine is a classic, such as we learned to prepare at cooking school in France, only the traditional Sauternes has been replaced by a plum wine, and I've supplied Japanese pickles for some crunchy sharpness. The base recipe is easy to build upon: Use any sweet wine and balance the fattiness with pickles from the same country—or a nearby relative—as the wine. And savor it. One day it may be contraband.

Separate the lobes of the foie, removing any extra fat and membrane.

SERVES 4

1 large lobe grade-A foie gras (see Resources, page 233)

Salt and black pepper

1 (750 ml) bottle plum wine or any sweet wine such as Sauternes (these come in smaller bottles, so you may need to buy two—375 ml each—if substituting)

TO SERVE:

Brioche toasts

Pickled burdock root (see Resources, page 233), cut into 1-inch lengths

Pickled daikon (see Resources, page 233), finely diced

Julienned scallion greens

Foie gras, for all its preciousness, is one of the easiest meats to handle. There is no silverskin to remove, no difficult butchering, just a vein down the center of each lobe that pulls out easily when the liver is softened at room temperature. The acid and sugar from the sweet wine in which it is doused infuses the organ and helps balance and bring out the inherent foie flavors. In France, this wine would be a Bordeaux-born Sauternes made from grapes that are left on the vine to literally rot. Botrytis cinera, a.k.a. noble rot, is brought on by high humidity from the surrounding rivers plus daytimes spent drying in the sun. The desirable fungal growth feeds on the water from the grapes; as the botrytis saps the grapes of their liquid, it dries them and concentrates their flavors by leaving the fruit's sugars behind. The juice produced from these dehydrated grapes makes a viscous, sweet, and slightly funky wine much celebrated the world over. The foie, marinated in a bit of the wine and cured in salt and pepper overnight, is then placed in a terrine—the name of the earthenware mold and anything cooked within. All that is left is to cook it—the only trick here is to not overcook, which renders too much fat; you want to keep that fat inside so your terrine is unctuous, buttery, and rich.

Allow the foie to come to room temperature, then remove the veins: With the tip of a thin pairing knife, pierce the center of each of the lobes, twisting the knife sideways as you enter the center, catching the main vein. Pull it out—it should come with its various ducts. Pull also at any hanging bits of fat and vein from the tip of each lobe—more should come with it. Season the lobes liberally with salt and pepper, then sprinkle both sides with ¼ cup of the wine. Let marinate in the refrigerator overnight.

The next day, let the foie sit out to come to room temperature. Preheat the oven to 275°F. Oil a French terrine mold (11 inches long, 2½ inches wide, and 2½ inches deep) and line it with plastic wrap, leaving enough wrap hanging over the edge to cover the top once it is filled.

Place the largest lobe of foie on the bottom, smooth side down, and press to fill the bottom. Place any smaller pieces that may have broken off on top, then top with the smaller lobe. Press to fill the mold, then fold the plastic wrap over the top and press again. Cover and set in a hot water bath. (Line a roasting pan with a hand towel, center the terrine mold in it, and fill the pan with hot water. This technique buffers the heat between the terrine mold and the metal and ensures even cooking; see The Basics, page 16.) Bake for 1 hour, or until the foie is soft, slightly melted, and heated through. Remove from the water bath and remove the lid. Weight with a heavy piece of wood or a brick that fits the area of exposed foie and refrigerate for at least 3 days.

Place the remaining wine in a saucepan and cook over high heat until reduced and syrupy. Let cool.

To serve: Unmold the terrine by placing the mold in a pan of hot water to melt the edges and by lifting out the foie with the plastic wrap. Unwrap and cut into ½-inch-thick slices with a knife that has been run under hot water. Serve with brioche toast, a drizzle of the reduced plum wine, and a scattering of the pickles and scallion.

II. SOUP

VEGETARIAN MUSHROOM SOUP
WITH SHAOXING WINE

SERVES 4

3 dried shiitake mushrooms

4 dried porcini mushrooms

1 tablespoon neutral-flavored
vegetable oil

½ small onion, thinly sliced

1 clove garlic, finely chopped

¼ cup Shaoxing wine or dry sherry

1 piece kombu, rinsed (optional)

8 ounces mixed fresh mushrooms,
such as oyster, cremini, maitake, and
hon-shimeji, cleaned and sliced

¼ cup mushroom soy sauce (see
Resources, page 233) or regular
soy sauce

¾ cup peeled and diced acorn squash

Salt and black pepper

Lemon juice (optional)

4 pinches chopped scallion greens

I am an omnivore with her feet planted firmly on the carnivorous side of the farm fence. No disrespect to the vegetarians—I like them; grass-fed flesh really is delicious—but I don't believe vegetable stock can ever achieve the depth of flavor that a long-simmered meat version provides. Sometimes, as this mushroom soup proves, when necessity is forced to accept her responsibility as the mother of invention, a vegetable stock can achieve near-meaty greatness.

I first created this dish using chicken stock, varieties of both wild and cultivated mushrooms, acorn squash, and acorn jelly, a Korean delicacy made from the ground nuts of an oak tree. The jelly is slightly bitter and faintly starchy; its primary contribution is bouncy texture. As satisfying as that cooking liquid may be, we often get requests for vegetarian tasting menus. I don't mind the challenge. The truth is, I love all ingredients and believe each deserves to be celebrated and given a spotlight, and this can be done with or without meat.

The following recipe was adapted from the original for the sake of an animal-eschewing diner, and I've included it because I would be just as happy to eat it as I would the carnivorous template. To give the stock body, I use umami-rich kombu—a sea kelp characterized by a distinct taste profile that's simultaneously earthy and oceanic—and mushroom soy, a Chinese sauce flavored with shiitake mushrooms. Both additions are strong in glutamate, which is what gives food a certain meaty quality. The onion and garlic further bolster the broth's depth and complexity. The Shaoxing, a Chinese aged rice wine, adds a touch of acidity and a round, musty funk that draws out the essence of the fungi. The wine is nutty and raisiny, much like a dry sherry, which, when paired with mushrooms, forms a classic Spanish combination that was one of the early inspirations for this soup. Onto that, I layered the Asian flavors of soy and scallion. The acorn squash grounds the dish in American soil, where this cross-cultural creation belongs.

Put the shiitake mushrooms in a small bowl; cover with hot water and set aside. Put the porcini mushrooms in a separate bowl; cover with hot water and set aside. Heat the oil in a medium saucepan over medium-low heat. Add the onion and sauté until translucent, about 5 minutes.

Add the garlic and sauté until fragrant, about 1 minute. Add the wine and cook until it is reduced by half. If you're planning to use mushroom soy sauce, add 5 cups water. If you're planning to use regular soy sauce, add 4⅔ cups water plus ⅓ cup soaking water from the porcini mushrooms. Drain the porcini mushrooms and add them to the pan. Add the kombu (if using). Bring to a full boil, then lower the heat to low and remove and reserve the kombu. Drain the shiitake mushrooms and cut off and discard the stems. Slice the caps and add them to the pan. Add the fresh mushrooms and soy sauce. Cut the kombu into bite-size pieces and return it to the pan. Add the squash and simmer until softened, about 3 minutes. Season to taste with salt and pepper and, if desired, a touch of lemon juice. To serve: Divide among 4 warmed soup bowls and garnish each with a pinch of scallion greens.

KIMCHI GAZPACHO WITH SHRIMP

"Everything exquisitely delicious is on the verge of putrefaction." I'm not sure who immortalized this aphorism, but it's the first thing I think of when anyone mentions fermentation. It is like a purgatorial stage for food—it's a breaking-down process, but it's also a form of preservation. Fermentation keeps an ingredient in limbo—somewhere between partially decomposed and rotten. Indeed, many of the things we love the most are fermented—wine, chocolate, pickles.

Kimchi, a pickled vegetable that no Korean meal is served without, is so beloved by the citizens of that country that the government has proclaimed it a national treasure. It was first created to preserve the harvest for the long, cold north Asian winters. Conserved with brine, then packed in large earthenware jars and buried underground where temperatures were stable and cold (not freezing), this pickle would sustain the Koreans through the frigid months. Variations depend on region and on seasonality. The vegetables are soaked in salted water, which helps prevent the wrong bacteria from getting in, but there is no vinegar—itself a fermented substance—involved. The fermentation creates the acidic flavor.

I came up with the concept for this dish when I first visited Korea, just before I opened Mirezi, a pan-Asian spot on lower Fifth Avenue in New York

SERVES 4

3 cups peeled (see page 24), seeded, and roughly chopped ripe tomatoes

½ cup peeled and roughly chopped seedless or Kirby cucumbers

1 large clove garlic, center sprout removed

1 cup kimchi with juice, finely diced, or less to taste

3 tablespoons rice vinegar, or to taste

½ teaspoon salt

Black pepper to taste

TO SERVE:

1 cup cooked shrimp or shucked raw littleneck or Manila clams

Julienned scallion greens

City owned by Cheil Jedang, a subsidiary of Samsung that deals in food-stuffs and pharmaceuticals. The company had sent me to Seoul to meet the head honchos, to go to cooking school, and to sample the food. One of the many things I ate (we went to an average of seven restaurants per day) was a water kimchi, a chilled, soupy concoction made from young summer radishes served in their brine. This was dished up with a variety of other *panchan*, the assorted small salads and kimchi served at the beginning of a Korean meal. With its garlicky, oniony, vegetal flavors, it reminded me of a gazpacho. I thought the chile heat of the most common *baechu* kimchi, or napa cabbage kimchi, would go well with the traditional Spanish base of tomato and cucumber, and so this hybrid was born. As *baechu* kimchi is made with fermented baby shrimp, or *krill*, it seemed only right to pair my soup with chilled cooked shrimp, a twist that at the same time, draws comparisons to shrimp cocktail, a favorite American dish also served with a spicy tomato-based sauce.

Put the tomatoes, cucumber, and garlic in a blender and process until smooth. In a separate bowl, add the blended ingredients to the kimchi with its juice, the vinegar, salt, and pepper. Cover and refrigerate until chilled.

Ladle into chilled serving bowls, garnish with the shrimp and scallion greens, and serve. The soup is best served the same day it's made, as the kimchi will eventually cause the tomatoes to ferment.

If you're not in the mood for shrimp, you can use something strong-flavored like clams—littlenecks or Manilas. I tried the gazpacho with oysters and they got lost. Since the soup is chilled, I recommend using raw clams; texturally, they're better this way too.

CHILLED AVOCADO SOUP WITH KOMBU

You can take pretty much any vegetable, puree it, and make soup. If you want to reinvent a familiar staple, just change your notes. In my vichyssoise, for example, I use lobster stock instead of the more predictable chicken. For this avocado soup, it's dashi, which is a foundation of Japanese cuisine. The broth, flavored with kombu (sea kelp), is the basis of noodle soups like ramen, soba, and udon, among other things. Kombu, they say, is one of the greatest sources of glutamates, the amino acids responsible for creating umami, "the fifth taste." It's surprising that a green could have such intense meatiness. Actually, this dense vegetable is one of few that can stand alone as a source of flavor. Although it may sound obscure, nowadays you'll find it in any health food store and at Whole Foods. It's sold and used in dried form. Dashi is one of the simplest and quickest stocks to prepare, but if you're at all intimidated by kombu and bonito flakes, feel free to use the packets of instant dashi. I borrow those on occasion, when I'm preparing a small portion, but I prefer making the slight extra effort to do it myself: If you're already cooking, you might as well boil a quick pot of dashi.

In this dish, the dashi provides a savory, smoky depth, while the avocado brings its smooth, mild sweetness. Each gives a different aspect of richness—the former offers the taste sensation; the latter, the textural quality. Together, they combine to create a harmonious experience of fattiness.

Make the dashi: Rinse the kombu in cold water. In a medium saucepan, combine the kombu with 1 quart of cold water. Bring to a boil. Turn off the heat and add the bonito flakes. Let steep for 15 minutes, then remove and reserve the kombu. Pour the dashi through a fine-mesh sieve lined with rinsed and squeezed cheesecloth into a bowl; cover and refrigerate until chilled.

Make the sweetened kombu: In a saucepan, combine the reserved kombu, ¼ cup of the dashi, the soy sauce, mirin, and sugar and bring to a boil. Lower the heat and slowly simmer, stirring occasionally, until the liquid has thickened to the consistency of light syrup. Let cool to room temperature. Cut the kombu into small squares and set aside.

Make the soup: Puree the avocados, remaining chilled dashi, the mirin, yuzu juice, and soy sauce in a blender. Add black pepper to taste.

SERVES 4

FOR THE DASHI:

1 (3-inch) square dried kombu

1 cup loosely packed bonito flakes (see Note)

FOR THE SWEETENED KOMBU:

¼ cup dashi

2 tablespoons soy sauce

2 tablespoons mirin

1 ounce sugar (scant 3 tablespoons)

FOR THE SOUP:

2½ large ripe Hass avocados, peeled and pitted

4 tablespoons mirin

1 tablespoon yuzu juice or regular lemon juice

2 tablespoons soy sauce

Black pepper

TO SERVE:

½ large ripe Hass avocado, diced

1 tablespoon thinly sliced (on a bias) scallion greens, plus 4 pinches julienned scallion

½ teaspoon soy sauce

½ teaspoon yuzu juice or regular lemon juice

Black pepper to taste

This appetizer would also make a good passed hors d'oeuvre or amuse bouche; you can serve it as a shooter, in a shot glass.

To serve: In a bowl, combine the diced avocado with the bias-sliced scallion, soy sauce, yuzu juice, and pepper. Mound the diced-avocado mixture in the center of each serving bowl, pour the soup around it, and top with the sweetened kombu squares and julienned scallion greens.

NOTE: Bonito flakes are shavings from dried smoked skipjack tuna or bonito fish; they're available at Asian food stores (see Resources, page 233).

CHILLED OYSTERS IN VICHYSSOISE
WITH SHISO AND APPLE

SERVES 4

2 tablespoons butter

3 cups washed and roughly chopped leek whites

1½ cups Idaho potatoes, peeled and roughly chopped

3 cups lobster stock or chicken stock (page 231)

⅓ cup heavy cream

1 tablespoon salt (or more if you use chicken stock)

Black pepper to taste

1 teaspoon lemon juice

TO SERVE:

20 oysters, shucked, ½ cup of their liquor (liquid) reserved

(CONTINUED)

Vichyssoise—a chilled potato and leek soup—is a classic French dish and surprisingly easy to make. It's also seasonally versatile (potatoes are readily available year-round, and leeks are never hard to find). We made it at the very first cooking school I attended, when I was in Paris for a summer during college. Years later, I put this version on the menu at annisa when we opened. It borrows the vichyssoise as a canvas for a combination that you might find in Nordic countries or Eastern Europe—the saline, seawater overtones of fish, the tart, sweet brightness of pomaceous fruit, and the pungent, astringent, mustardy punch of horseradish. Here, those components are represented, respectively, by oyster, red-skinned apple, and wasabi. Potato, leek, apple, and horseradish (or its Japanese counterpart) all make sense together: Think of a potato pancake made with onions and topped with applesauce, for example, and then imagine adding some sharp heat. The oyster gives the earthiness of that familiar grouping an unexpected depth and briny richness. That impact is amplified by incorporating the bivalves' liquid into the soup, which simultaneously lets you put an often wasted, flavor-packed ingredient to good use. Splurging for lobster stock instead of the more traditional chicken further enhances the oyster's effects and turns the relatively humble potage into something more luxurious. If you'd rather stick with a chicken foundation, the outcome will still be delicious. In the months when oysters aren't at the market, you can substitute another salty chilled fish or seafood like smoked salmon or raw clams.

In a large saucepan, melt the butter and add the leeks and potatoes. Cook over medium-low heat until the leeks are wilted and translucent, about 5 minutes. Add the stock and bring to a boil. Lower the heat to a simmer and cook until the potatoes and leeks are tender, about 10 minutes. Puree in a blender or with a hand blender until smooth. Add the cream, salt, pepper, and lemon juice. Taste and adjust the seasonings. Refrigerate until chilled.

To serve: Stir the oyster liquor into the soup and divide among 4 soup plates. Float 5 oysters in each bowl. In a small bowl, toss the apple with the remaining lemon juice and set aside. Garnish the soup with the shiso and a few very small crumbles of the wasabi and top each oyster with a bit of the apple.

TO SERVE (CONT'D):
2 tablespoons finely diced red apple with peel
2 teaspoons lemon juice
3 shiso leaves, cut into small squares, or 4 large fresh mint leaves, or 1 tablespoon chopped fresh chives plus 1 teaspoon chopped fresh tarragon
½ teaspoon prepared wasabi

Pureed soups are all pretty much the same. Once you've learned the formula, you can improvise freely and come up with any number of mixtures. Basically, you are sweating something—potatoes and leeks, for example—with foundations like onion, garlic, carrots, celery, or tomato paste, and then adding your liquid in the form of a stock, which can be made from vegetables, poultry, fish, seafood, or meat. After the initial pulverizing has taken place, cream—or even crème fraîche or yogurt—can be blended in.

CHICKEN AND GARDEN VEGETABLE SOUP
WITH CHILE, LIME, AND CILANTRO

SERVES 4

3 tablespoons olive oil

1 large onion, diced

5 large cloves garlic, chopped

3 chiles (1 jalapeño, 1 hot cherry, 1 Thai
   bird, or other chiles), finely chopped,
   or more or less to taste

1 tablespoon ground cumin

1 (3½-pound) chicken

2 bay leaves

2 beefsteak tomatoes, roughly
   chopped

1 daikon, peeled and cubed

2 large zucchini, cubed

1 small butternut squash, peeled and
   cubed

Salt and black pepper to taste

Lime juice to taste

TO SERVE:

Chopped scallions

Chopped fresh cilantro

Jennifer, my ex-partner in life (we were together for nine years) and, up until recently, my partner in crime at *annisa*, prepared a version of this soup for me when I was sick. Made with hearty vegetables from my Long Island garden and large chunks of chicken, plus chiles and plenty of garlic to ward off viruses, and vitamin C–packed lime juice to bolster the immune system, this was a healthy, nutritious meal on its own. I continue to make this soup in large batches on Long Island, or for staff meals at *annisa*, always freezing extra quarts for those nights when the flu has beaten me down, or when I just need to feel nourished.

It builds on a familiar restorative, "Jewish penicillin," that classic chicken soup served with matzoh balls. The lime and chiles brighten and sharpen the flavors and help to clear the sinuses and clean the back of your throat. All the vegetables are important, but I love the juxtaposition of the sweet and earthy yet watery daikon, which really picks up the flavor of the stock, against the similarly sweet and earthy pumpkin, which is denser and starchier. The zucchini adds a little green and offsets the heavier pumpkin, making the whole soup seem like a more balanced meal.

Heat a large stockpot over medium heat. Add the oil and swirl the pot to coat the bottom, then add the onion and cook over medium heat for about 5 minutes, until the onion is translucent but not browned. Add the garlic and chiles and cook for another minute. Add the cumin and stir. Add the chicken, cover with cold water, and bring to a boil over high heat. Skim off the foam and scum that rise to the top, then lower the heat to a simmer. Add the bay leaves and tomatoes. Cook, skimming occasionally, until the chicken meat is just falling from the bone, about 1 hour. Remove the chicken to a bowl and let cool. Add the daikon to the soup and bring back to a simmer. Cook for 2 minutes, then add the zucchini and butternut squash and simmer until the vegetables are just cooked through, about 3 minutes. Pick the meat from the chicken and cut it into bite-size pieces, return it to the pot, and season with salt, pepper, and lime juice.

To serve: Ladle into warmed soup bowls and garnish with a pinch each of scallions and cilantro.

CHILLED SWEET PEA SOUP
WITH SMOKED STURGEON AND CAVIAR

Here is a dish that is a prime example of the multicultural influences in urban American cooking. I can name four cuisines from which these combinations derive. The Japanese influence is obvious in the wasabi and shiso (remember those wasabi-flavored crunchy peas?). The Eastern European sway is evident in the combination of smoked fish and horseradish, even if the latter happens to be Japanese. The same argument can be made for the English combination of peas with (Japanese) mint. Then there are the peas with the smoky stuff, which in the American South would be bacon. At *annisa*, we make the dish even more American by using local peashoots whenever possible and sturgeon and its roe from the Pacific Northwest. Enjoy it in the spring when peas are at their peak of sweetness and when the tendrils are young and tender, hand-selected from your garden or local greenmarket.

(Of course, if you want to skip the curing and smoking steps, just use presmoked sturgeon or any other smoked white-fleshed fish.)

Cure and smoke the sturgeon: Mix the salt and sugar together and sprinkle the mixture evenly over both sides of the sturgeon fillet. Sprinkle both sides with the lemon juice and pepper. Cover and refrigerate overnight. Hot-smoke the sturgeon, either in an electric smoker, in a wok, or on an outdoor grill: If using an electric smoker, follow the manufacturer's directions to hot-smoke with hardwood for about 30 minutes, until smoky and just cooked through. If using a wok, place the hardwood chips in a small pile at the bottom of the wok. Elevate the fish a few inches above with a wire rack, and cover. Place over high heat until the chips begin to smoke, then lower the heat to medium and hot-smoke for about 30 minutes, until the fish is smoky and just cooked through. If the fish requires extra cooking time, place on a baking sheet in a 375°F oven until a toothpick can be inserted into the thickest part of the fish easily. If using an outdoor grill, make a small fire and when embers are ashed and just glowing red, cover with soaked hardwood chips. Place the fish on the grill grate away from the fire, cover, and hot-smoke for about 30 minutes, until smoky and just cooked through. Let cool to room temperature.

SERVES 4

FOR THE STURGEON:

1 tablespoon salt

1 teaspoon sugar

5 ounces sturgeon fillet

A few drops of lemon juice

Several grinds of black pepper

1½ cups hardwood chips, soaked in water for 20 minutes and then drained

FOR THE SALAD:

1 tablespoon melted butter, not too hot

1 teaspoon chopped fresh chives

1 large pinch grated lemon zest

Lemon juice to taste

2 tablespoons whipped crème fraîche

Salt and black pepper to taste

FOR THE SOUP:

2 cups shelled fresh sweet peas (sweet, nonstarchy ones), blanched and shocked, or frozen peas, thawed

About 1½ cups lobster stock (page 231)

Salt and black pepper to taste

TO SERVE:

2 teaspoons American sturgeon caviar (optional)

4 very small pinches prepared wasabi, or to taste

(CONTINUED)

TO SERVE (CONT'D):

2 leaves chopped fresh shiso (or
  4 leaves fresh mint)

6 sugarsnap peas, halved lengthwise,
  blanched and shocked

Pea shoots

Lemon juice

Salt and black pepper to taste

Make the salad: Shred the smoked fish, discarding any bones. Add the butter, chives, lemon zest, and lemon juice and stir. Fold in the whipped crème fraîche. Taste and adjust the seasonings with salt, pepper, and lemon juice.

Make the soup: Put the peas in a blender and add enough stock to cover them. Blend until smooth, adding more stock if necessary to keep the blades running, then pour through a fine-mesh sieve, pressing through as much pulp as possible. Season with pepper and salt, if necessary (the lobster stock will already be salty).

To serve: Divide the soup among 4 chilled soup plates. Place a small dollop of the sturgeon salad in the center of each and top each with one-quarter of the caviar (if using). Sprinkle the soup with the wasabi and shiso and arrange three sugarsnap pea halves around, cut side up. In a separate bowl, season the pea shoots with lemon juice, salt, and pepper and garnish the top of the caviar with it.

SALAD OF
HON-SHIMEJI AND KOREAN BUCKWHEAT NOODLES IN BROTH

I created this for *Iron Chef America* to showcase one of the five different kinds of mushrooms (the secret ingredient) they gave us to work with. This particular strain, the hon-shimeji (shimeji is the group of mushrooms of which hon-shimeji is a type) is a cultivated variety; it's a small, brown-capped, long-stemmed fungus that grows in clusters. Not one of the stronger-flavored mushrooms, its strength lies in its texture—the stems are a little chewier than most. I played up that attribute by shredding the stems and intermingling them with naengmyun, Korean buckwheat noodles, which have a similar consistency. Coincidentally, while preparing this dish, I relied on a technique I learned in Korea. There, when you're making *japchae*, a stir-fry of *dangmyeon*, cellophane yam noodles (not to be confused with the Chinese cellophane noodles that are made out of mung bean), zucchini, carrots, scallions, and peppers dressed with a sauce of soy, garlic, and sugar, you cut the vegetables to the same thickness of the noodles so that everything tangles uniformly.

While the technical approach may have been inspired by Korean cuisine, the concept is more Japanese in spirit. I was thinking about soba and how those buckwheat noodles are typical breakfast food in Japan. They're served simply, with a dipping sauce made from dashi (a stock infused with kombu, or sea kelp) and soy sauce, and garnished with scallions. This salad takes those basic elements, combines them, and features an addition, the hon-shimeji—their stems trimmed to the length of the noodles, their caps a worthy topping, especially when given a quick tempura treatment. The flavor of those mushrooms prevails in each bowlful, because I use the dashi-based liquid in which they were blanched to bolster my sauce.

SERVES 4

FOR THE MUSHROOMS AND BROTH:

4 ounces hon-shimeji mushrooms or beech mushrooms, some small and some larger

1 quart dashi (see page 231)

Pinch of salt

2 tablespoons mushroom soy sauce or regular soy sauce

2 tablespoons lemon juice

FOR THE NOODLES:

8 ounces fresh naengmyun (Korean buckwheat noodles) or Japanese soba noodles

1 teaspoon neutral-flavored vegetable oil

2 cups buckwheat sprouts, daikon sprouts, or bean sprouts

2 tablespoons julienned scallion greens

2 tablespoons mushroom soy sauce, or to taste

2 teaspoons lemon juice, or to taste

Black pepper to taste

FOR THE TEMPURA (OPTIONAL):

½ cup all-purpose flour

3 tablespoons cornstarch

Pinch of baking soda

(CONTINUED)

Cook the mushrooms and make the broth: Cut the stems from the larger mushrooms (if making tempura, reserve the caps for later) and leave the smaller mushrooms whole. Bring the dashi to a boil in a medium saucepan. Add the salt and the smaller whole mushrooms. Bring to a simmer and cook for 3 minutes, or until tender. Remove with a strainer and set aside. Repeat with the large mushroom stems (and caps, if not making tempura), setting the stems aside in a separate bowl. When the stems are cool enough to handle, shred them and set aside. Stir the mushroom soy sauce and lemon juice into the broth and refrigerate until chilled.

Make the noodles: Bring 3 quarts of water to a boil in a large pot. Add the noodles and boil for 2 to 3 minutes, until just tender. Drain in a colander and immediately rinse in cold water three times, until the water runs clear. Combine the noodles (if they're stuck together, rinse with cold water and drain again) with the shredded mushroom stems, oil, sprouts, and scallions. Add the mushroom soy sauce, lemon juice, and pepper and toss to coat.

Just before serving, make the tempura, if desired: In a medium bowl, combine the flour, cornstarch, baking soda, salt, and pepper. In a separate bowl, combine the egg yolk and seltzer. Add the wet ingredients to the dry ingredients and stir together using chopsticks, just until barely combined; the batter will be lumpy. In a heavy pot, heat 1 inch of oil to 350°F. Dip the reserved mushroom caps in the batter and fry until golden and crisp, about 1 to 2 minutes. Drain on a paper towel. Keep warm.

To serve: Twirl a tangle of the noodle mixture into a nest using a fork and place one in each serving bowl. Top with a quail egg yolk (if using). Ladle ½ to ¾ cup broth around the noodles and top with a few blanched whole mushrooms and a few tempura mushroom caps.

FOR THE TEMPURA (CONT'D):

½ teaspoon salt

Black pepper, to taste

1 large egg yolk

½ cup iced seltzer water (not tap water)

Neutral-flavored vegetable oil for deep-frying

TO SERVE:

4 quail egg yolks (optional)

In its most basic form, this dish is a great foundation for any meal. It's well balanced; the mushrooms are an excellent source of protein, and the buckwheat noodles are a gluten- and wheat-free way to get slow-releasing carbs. You could add a quail or chicken egg yolk to make it richer, or serve it warm with a poached egg and some sliced chicken on top. For a quick meal, just take your dashi, boil the mushrooms in it, and toss in your flavorings, noodles, and an egg. If you're dressing it up, do tempura those mushroom caps, which will give you a great contrast of temperatures— a burst of hot on the chilled noodles— and a touch of crunchiness.

DUCK PHO

SERVES 4 AS AN APPETIZER

1 tablespoon neutral-flavored
    vegetable oil

1 onion, thinly sliced lengthwise

Raw carcass and legs of 1 duck
    (see Note)

3 cloves garlic, smashed

1 slice fresh ginger

3 pieces star anise

5 whole cloves

1 cinnamon stick

1 dried shiitake mushroom

3 sprigs fresh cilantro

¼ cup fish sauce, or to taste

Salt and black pepper

TO SERVE:

1 package rice noodles

4 (1-ounce) pieces foie gras
    (optional)

A few thin slices red onion

A few leaves fresh Thai basil or mint

Vietnamese chile-garlic sauce (tuong
    ot toi Vietnam)

Hoisin sauce

1 lime, quartered

1 cup bean sprouts

I'd eaten pho, the traditional Vietnamese rice noodle soup, as a snack long before I ever visited its country of origin. In college, I'd get my pho in New York City's Chinatown for $3.50 a bowl, a price that fit right into my budget back then.

The classic beef version was on the menu at Can, a French Vietnamese restaurant in SoHo where I had my very first executive chef job. We made it the long, slow way, blanching oxtails, blackening onions, and toasting dried squid, then putting it all in a pot with spices and simmering it for hours, skimming constantly. Our broth was crystal clear, like a consommé, with a deep, complex, and meaty flavor highlighted by cinnamon, star anise, and clove. We semi-froze beef eye round and cut it paper thin on a slicing machine, then poured the hot broth over the slices until the meat cooked.

At Maxim's, we would make a quick version of the soup at the end of service, or in the afternoon, if we were hungry, out of shredded chicken and chicken stock. At Mirezi, my third chef job, it was on the menu and prepared with a spicy, rich oxtail broth, barbecued slices of beef, and loads of lemongrass and fish sauce. We topped it with crushed peanuts.

Letting nothing go to waste, I once tried using duck carcass and legs in a reinterpretation of pho. It was delicious, and I've since added it to my repertoire. Instead of the standard beef liquid, I make a duck broth with the bird's bones to flavor it; I cook the legs in that liquid too. The carcass gets pulled out once the soup is done, but the leg meat will go into each bowlful of pho. At the last minute, I quickly sear some foie gras and use that to garnish the dish—it takes a little of the humility (and healthfulness) out of what's essentially peasant food, adds an unexpected richness of flavor, and drives home the duck theme.

> *The foie gras is optional. You could substitute or supplement it with other duck parts—grilled hearts, for example. Or, you could choose another garnish altogether. Peanuts or cashews work well.*

Heat the oil in a stockpot over low heat and add the onion. Cook, stirring, until golden brown. Add the duck carcass and legs, garlic, ginger, star anise, cloves, cinnamon, mushroom, cilantro, and enough cold water to cover. Bring to a boil. Skim off the foam and scum that rise to the top, then lower the heat to a simmer. Simmer until well flavored, 1 to 2 hours, adding more cold water if necessary to keep the ingredients covered and skimming when necessary. Remove the duck legs and set them aside, then pour the broth through a fine-mesh sieve and discard the other solids. Season the broth to taste with the fish sauce and add 1 teaspoon each of salt and pepper. Shred the duck leg meat and season with ¼ teaspoon each of salt and pepper. Set aside.

Just before serving, reheat the broth. Cook the noodles in a large pot of boiling salted water until tender, then drain. Divide among 4 soup bowls and top with the broth. In a smoking-hot dry pan, sear the foie gras, then add one piece to each bowl. Divide the duck leg meat, red onion, Thai basil, and bean sprouts among the bowls. Serve with the chile-garlic sauce, hoisin sauce, and lime wedges on the side.

NOTE: From a whole duck, cut off the legs, breast meat, and fat. Use the carcass and the legs with the skin removed for this soup. Refrigerate or freeze the boneless breasts for another use. The fat can be rendered (melted over low heat and then strained) and kept for another use.

III. RAW

BAY SCALLOP SASHIMI
WITH MEYER LEMON AND
BOTTARGA DI MUGGINE

One thing that makes me look forward to winter is that brief window of opportunity when Peconic Bay scallops are in season. They're so sweet. When we get them at my fish store in East Moriches they're just shucked and couldn't be fresher. I don't want to do anything to tamper with their natural flavor; I want to celebrate that sweetness for the fleeting moment it's here. Sometimes I remove the connector muscle that most people throw away when cooking this shellfish and I eat it straight (I wash it first if it's sandy). It's that good and should only be enjoyed raw.

At some point, we got a pound of these bivalves. I treated the connector muscle to a quick sprinkle of lemon juice, olive oil, and mint and ate them as is. Dorothy Kalins, my neighbor, gave me a head of escarole—a French variety—from her garden, hearty and prime for braising. First I coated a pan with olive oil and laid slices of garlic, red pepper flakes, and lemons down into that. Once they'd begun to brown, I added the escarole, some butter, and sugar, then covered the pan. I let everything cook down until the vegetable's leaves turned glossy. Separately, I quickly sautéed the scallop meat and then served it with the finished escarole plus some bottarga, a dried cured roe that has the same impact as caviar. That remains one of my most memorable Long Island meals.

With this sashimi combination, I've transformed the highlights of that dinner into a light appetizer. Bottarga is great on anything raw; its salinity brings out a fish's sweetness without compromising any of its seawater notes.

SERVES 4

8 ounces bay scallops, cleaned

1 tablespoon Meyer lemon juice or regular lemon juice

Pinch of grated Meyer lemon zest or regular lemon zest

2 tablespoons extra-virgin olive oil

1 teaspoon chopped fresh chives

Salt and black pepper to taste

20 thin slices *bottarga di muggine* (see Resources, page 233)

I prefer the muggine *or gray mullet bottarga. You will also find a tuna option, but I find it stronger and not as luxurious; it's less of a delicacy and better for things like pasta sauce.*

In a bowl, combine the scallops, lemon juice, lemon zest, oil, chives, and salt and pepper. Taste and adjust the seasonings. Divide among 4 serving plates and top with the bottarga.

CEVICHE OF SEA SCALLOPS

WITH CELERY AND GREEN APPLE

SERVES 4

FOR THE CELERY-JUICE GELÉE:

1 cup celery juice (see Note)

½ teaspoon unflavored gelatin,
   softened in 1 teaspoon lukewarm
   water

¼ teaspoon salt

Black pepper

FOR THE SALAD:

1 teaspoon lemon juice

1 teaspoon grainy mustard

2 teaspoons neutral-flavored
   vegetable oil

1 teaspoon extra-virgin olive oil

⅛ teaspoon salt, or more to taste

A few grinds of black pepper, or more
   to taste

⅓ cup julienned peeled celery root

1 tablespoon julienned green apple

1 tablespoon julienned scallion

TO SERVE:

4 jumbo diver scallops, sashimi quality

Salt and black pepper

2 tablespoons lemon juice

1 tablespoon extra-virgin olive oil

4 celery leaves

I got into this industry in 1988, during one of the longest heat waves in the last few decades. It was 115 degrees in the kitchen, and that was in the cold station where I worked. We put in gruelingly long days—twelve to fourteen hours, six days per week, with no breaks, no sitting down. For the first two weeks, every night I would get sick from heat exhaustion, and my calves would ache so badly that I developed a serious muscle knot that became red and inflamed. My mother, who was a doctor, and perhaps over-cautious, thought I had a blood clot and told me to go directly to the emergency room, as it could dislodge and go to my heart or lungs and kill me. I never went. Who had time? I was in my early twenties and had found my calling. This is why I sometimes liken cooking to an obsessive-compulsive disorder.

I believe part of what kept me there were the ingredients. There were pear-shaped baby tomatoes that were just picked that morning. And the best were the scallops, which were so fresh that when you sliced them the edges would move, crinkling and cresting like turbulent water where two tides meet. I had never loved scallops until then. For some time thereafter, I thought that I only really liked raw ones. In retrospect, it was the fresh-ness, not the cooking method or lack thereof, that drew me to them. Here is a recipe that relies on that freshness of the scallops for its success. It's not a true ceviche, which would require a long soak in the acid of the citrus to cook it; rather, it's more like a quick bath, all a great scallop really needs. The garnishes employ two types of celery: celery root and regular stalk cel-ery, two separate species with similar, cleansing flavors. The green apple adds brightness and sugar, and the mustard, a sharp counterpoint, helps bring out the sweetness of the seafood (not that a great scallop needs it). Serve this in fall or winter when these ingredients are best.

Make the celery-juice gelée: Heat ¼ cup of the celery juice in a small saucepan, then remove from the heat and stir in the gelatin mixture. When the gelatin is dissolved, add the remaining juice, stirring. Season to taste with salt and pepper. Transfer to a container and refrigerate until set.

Make the salad: In a small bowl, whisk the lemon juice and mustard together, then drizzle in the oils, whisking to emulsify. Add the salt and pepper. In a medium bowl, combine the celery root, apple, and scallion. Add the vinaigrette and toss to coat. Taste and adjust the seasoning.

To serve: Cut each scallop horizontally into 3 rounds just before serving. Season with salt and pepper and toss in a small bowl with the lemon juice and oil. Let stand for 2 to 3 minutes. Place 3 tablespoons of the gelée in the center of each of 4 plates. Fan the scallop disks on top, then place a mound of the salad in the center of the scallops. Garnish with the celery leaves and serve.

NOTE: If you have a juicer, 1 large head of celery will make 1 cup juice. Or you can ask your local source for fresh juice to do it for you.

CEVICHE OF TILEFISH
WITH FIG, ANCHOVY, AND PISTACHIO

There used to be a sushi bar next to *annisa*, **and every morning its owner** went out on a party boat, rod in hand, and came back with a car trunk full of fish. There are limits placed on specific species. Porgies, of which he often caught a plethora, were restricted to thirty per person. The regulations change annually, and those applied to recreational operators differ from those created for commercial fishermen. I have no idea whether or not my neighbor adhered to the rules, but he certainly knew how to keep his food costs low, and I definitely benefitted from his bounty.

He probably went to Sheepshead Bay, off the bottom of Brooklyn. In the fall, he'd often return with porgy and serve it uncooked, thinly sliced, a couple of hours after he pulled it out of the ocean waters. Once, he brought me a piece of a tilefish he had just hooked. Known as *amadai* in Japanese, it's a lesser-known fish, which is one of the reasons I champion it. Lots of people fear tilefish, because they can grow to huge sizes and then have high mercury contents. Smaller ones (the two-pounders), however, are available and worth trying; they're beautiful fresh and, as my neighbor showed me, an excellent choice for sashimi.

Like him, I did a raw preparation. The tilefish itself is drizzled with olive oil and a fig balsamic glaze. Although you might not see fruit incorporated

SERVES 4

½ small clove garlic, finely chopped

½ small anchovy fillet, finely chopped

1 tablespoon red wine vinegar, plus
  more for the fig

5 tablespoons extra-virgin olive oil

Salt and black pepper

1 dried fig, diced

10 ounces tilefish fillet, skin removed,
  sliced

¾ cup fig balsamic vinegar or regular
  balsamic vinegar, reduced to a glaze
  (see Notes)

½ teaspoon Hawaiian pink coarse salt
  or any coarse salt

1 large cured anchovy fillet, cut into
  very thin strips

20 shelled pistachios, toasted in
  oil (see Notes), or shelled roasted
  pistachios

1 teaspoon coriander seeds, toasted
  and cracked

1 cup loose frisée

1 tablespoon fresh mint cut into
  chiffonnade

this way in Japanese cuisine, it's common practice when making a ceviche in Central and South America. The figs and the nuts both draw out the fish's sweetness. The anchovy echoes the *amadai*'s marine flavors and simultaneously brings some saltiness. Finally, there is the garnish, a frisée salad tossed in a vinaigrette made with olive oil, red wine vinegar, garlic, and anchovy. The latter always pairs well with a bitter component like these greens—they take the sting out of one another.

Whisk the garlic, anchovy, and red wine vinegar in a bowl and slowly add 3 tablespoons of the oil, whisking to emulsify. Whisk in ⅛ teaspoon of salt and a few grinds pepper.

In a small bowl, toss the fig with red wine vinegar to cover and a pinch each of salt and pepper and set aside to soak.

Lay the fish out on 4 chilled serving plates and drizzle with the remaining oil, then drizzle each with 1 tablespoon of the balsamic glaze. In a small sieve or colander placed over a bowl, drain the red wine vinegar from the fig. Sprinkle the fish with the Hawaiian salt and arrange the anchovy, pistachios, fig, and coriander over the top evenly. In a separate bowl, combine the frisée and mint, then season with salt and pepper to taste. Dress the salad with the vinaigrette and divide among the plates, putting the salad in the center of each. Serve immediately.

NOTES: To reduce the vinegar, put it in a small saucepan and cook over high heat until it has reduced to become thick and syrupy.

  To toast the pistachios, cook them over medium heat with 2 teaspoons olive oil in a small sauté pan until golden. Add salt to taste.

If it seems odd to pair the tilefish with anchovies, think about all those times you eat raw fish with caviar on it. As long as you apply the salted fillets with restraint, you won't overpower the amadai. *It should be noted that no matter how measured the use of anchovies, you do need to like them to enjoy this dish.*

SASHIMI FLUKE
WITH PLUMS AND PICKLED RED ONION

Throughout Japan, people have a fanatical reverence for ingredients. Embedded in that country's food culture is a deep appreciation for products at the peak of their season, treated simply, allowed to shine in their purest forms. It's as though the Japanese strive to find the ingredient ideal—it becomes a Zen experience from which the diner greatly benefits. From dining at sushi bars (mostly in New York), I've learned to love different parts of various creatures, such as fluke, a.k.a. summer flounder. The Japanese eat almost every section: the roe, the liver, and the fin meat, which is the richest part of the flesh, as well as the bones, which make a nice crunchy snack. In Japan, *hirame*, as fluke is known there, is expensive; but fish, regardless of price, is given its due respect and nothing goes to waste.

Methods for killing and storing fish are no less attentively studied. The Japanese have found that the best way to kill fish for sashimi is the *ike jime* approach: First the live fish is bled; then a long needle is inserted into its spinal cord, removing the fish's impulses to go into rigor mortis, thereby producing better-textured flesh and maximizing the natural glutamates, or umami, the fifth taste that some describe as meaty. I have yet to employ this practice, as local fluke regulations keep getting more restrictive; it's harder than ever for me to catch a legal one off Long Island, where this fish lives in the summer months. The following preparation makes use of much of what is edible and delicious on the fluke. I paired it with plums, another seasonal summer ingredient.

Make the plum ice and plum sauce: Bring a saucepan of water to a boil. Score an X in the top of the plum and plunge the plum into the boiling water for 60 seconds, then remove to a bowl of ice water. Peel and pit the plum, roughly chop it, and put it in a blender with ⅓ cup of water, 1 tablespoon of the sugar, and the salt. Blend until smooth. Set aside 3 tablespoons for the plum sauce. Put the remaining plum juice in a container and freeze until firm. Crumble and keep in the freezer until ready to use.

In a bowl, whisk the umeboshi paste with the 3 tablespoons reserved plum juice until smooth. Whisk in the remaining sugar, the chile, and mirin. Set aside.

SERVES 4

FOR THE PLUM ICE AND PLUM SAUCE:

1 large black plum

1 tablespoon plus ½ teaspoon sugar

Pinch of salt

2 tablespoons umeboshi paste (Japanese salted plum paste)

⅛ teaspoon finely chopped Thai bird chile

1 teaspoon mirin

FOR THE *ENGAWA* CEVICHE:

¼ cup fluke fin muscles (*engawa;* see Notes), cut into bite-size pieces, or thinly sliced strips of fluke fillet

1 tablespoon lemon juice

1 teaspoon rice vinegar

2 teaspoons white soy sauce or regular soy sauce

⅛ teaspoon black pepper

Pinch of salt

FOR THE PICKLED RED ONION:

3 lengthwise slices red onion

Rice vinegar

FOR THE BONE CHIPS (OPTIONAL):

Fluke fin bones and *engawa* bones, cut into ⅓-inch-thick strips (see Notes)

Cornstarch

Neutral-flavored vegetable oil for frying

Salt

TO SERVE:

8 ounces fluke fillet, sliced into ⅛-inch-thick sashimi-size strips

(CONTINUED)

Make the *engawa* ceviche: Combine the fluke fin muscles, lemon juice, vinegar, soy sauce, pepper, and salt in a small bowl. Let sit for at least 5 minutes, until the flesh starts to turn white.

Make the pickled red onion: Cut the onion slices into thin slivers and cover with rice vinegar in a small bowl.

Make the bone chips, if desired: Dredge the bones in cornstarch. Heat 1 inch of oil in a sauté pan to 300°F. Add the bones and lower the heat. Fry until crisp and golden brown. Drain on a paper towel and season with salt.

To serve: Arrange the fluke slices in the center of each of 4 chilled serving plates. Frame with the plum sauce and decorate with the sliced plum, ceviche, pickled onion, and scallion. Finish with the plum ice, bone chips (if using), and Hawaiian salt and serve immediately.

NOTES: *Engawa,* or fish fin, as it's defined in English, is actually the fin muscle—that fringelike strip responsible for moving the fins on the outer portion of the fish. It's the fattiest part of the creature and is separated into small sections that make it reminiscent of a grapefruit. Ask your fishmonger to separate and save it when you order your fluke.

For the bone chips, follow the natural direction of the bones to cut; they will be about 2 inches long if using a 1½-pound fish. Order your fish in advance and ask your fishmonger to save the bones. Small fish work best.

Umeboshi can be found at Whole Foods, and in Asian and health food stores. You can puree or mash it to get the paste, or buy it already in paste form. Thai bird chiles can be replaced with any fiery chile, such as habanero. If all you can find are jalapeños, you'll need a few more of them than what is called for here. I use white soy in this recipe for color. Using a light soy will taste just as good, but will add the brown color I was avoiding. White soy can be purchased at Japanese grocery stores.

TO SERVE (CONT'D):
½ white- or red-fleshed plum, thinly
  sliced
1 teaspoon julienned scallion
Hawaiian pink coarse salt or any
  coarse salt to taste

Fish bones are often overlooked. People think of them as dangerous things you can choke on. But small, brittle bones such as those from fluke or eel are delicious (and safe) deep-fried. They become crisp, like a thick potato chip. (I use a few bones at a time here, in bite-size bits, but often the entire set is fried and you break off pieces to eat.) Other bones can yield delicious stocks and soups. Softer fish, such as tuna or salmon, have bones that can be scraped and the flesh used for tartare or rillettes. At bar Q, we used bones from large tuna to make "ribs," as the Japanese sometimes do. We also borrowed their idea and used the marrow, the white, translucent, gelatinous orbs that are found in each vertebra and taste like the sea—we served it as a shooter with ponzu; now, at annisa, *it garnishes tuna tartare. It's an interesting novelty.*

SASHIMI TUNA
WITH SPICY COD ROE AND MEYER LEMON

SERVES 4

FOR THE *MENTAIKO* MAYONNAISE:

1 large egg yolk

½ teaspoon Dijon mustard

¾ cup neutral-flavored oil

5 small sacs (about ½ cup) *mentaiko* (spicy cod roe; see Note)

1 tablespoon Meyer lemon juice, or to taste, or ¼ teaspoon yuzu juice plus 1½ teaspoons regular lemon juice, or 2 teaspoons regular lemon juice

Dashi as needed

¼ teaspoon salt

A few grinds black pepper

FOR THE PONZU:

½ cup dashi (page 231)

2 tablespoons plus 2 teaspoons soy sauce

2 tablespoons Meyer lemon juice (or 1½ tablespoons lemon juice)

TO SERVE:

10 ounces sashimi-quality tuna, thinly sliced

½ teaspoon grated Meyer lemon zest or regular lemon zest

2 tablespoons julienned or thinly sliced (on a bias) scallion greens

¼ packed daikon sprouts (*kaiware;* optional)

2 pink radishes, thinly sliced into rounds

2 leaves fresh shiso or mint cut into ¼-inch squares

Salt and black pepper

Shichimi togarashi (Japanese "seven-spice" powder; optional)

Although devised for Mirezi in 1995, this is a dish that doesn't feel dated. I still serve it once in a while, and it seems more recognizable now than it did then. It's kind of an amalgam of all my favorite flavors—there's mentaiko, yuzu, and shiso. What can I say? I love Japanese ingredients. *Mentaiko* is the marinated roe of pollock fish; it's both salty and full-bodied. Citrusy yuzu juice cuts through the pungency of those fish eggs and the creaminess of the mayo. A radish salad brings a refreshing astringent bitterness and some crunch; adding some green, herby shiso has a balancing and brightening effect. With its blend of red pepper, green seaweed flakes, black and white sesame seeds, brown hemp seeds, orange peel, and sansho pepper, *sichimi togarashi*, or Japanese "seven-spice" mix, makes a pretty final touch, if you would like to try it .

Make the *mentaiko* mayonnaise: Put the egg yolk and mustard in a bowl and slowly whisk in the oil in a small stream to emulsify. Remove the *mentaiko* from the sacs and add it to the egg mixture. Add the lemon juice. Whisk in a little dashi if necessary to thin it to piping consistency. Whisk in the salt and pepper and pour the mayonnaise into a pastry bag fitted with a fine tip for piping or into a squeeze bottle.

Make the ponzu: Combine the dashi, soy sauce, and lemon juice in a small bowl.

To serve: Lay the sliced fish out on 4 chilled serving plates. Squeeze a thin line of the mayonnaise alongside the fish, about 1 to 1½ tablespoons per plate. In a small bowl, combine the lemon zest, scallions, daikon sprouts, radishes, and shiso and toss with 5 tablespoons of the ponzu; season with salt and pepper to taste. Place a small pinch of the mixture next to the tuna. Sprinkle all with the *shichimi togarashi* (if using) and salt and serve immediately.

NOTE: If you can't source *mentaiko*, then *tarama*, or Turkish-style salted roe, is fine to use instead. If using, combine ½ cup *tarama* and ½ teaspoon ground cayenne. Or combine as much of the mayonnaise as needed with ½ pound *taramasalata* to achieve a puddinglike consistency.

STEAK TARTARE
WITH SHISO, TONBURI, AND GOCHUJANG

Mike Bloomberg came to *annisa* **years ago, before he was the mayor of** New York City, and he ordered the menu's steak tartare; it wasn't much different from this one. He tasted it and said, "This isn't steak tartare." He was expecting the classic French bistro offering—raw beef mixed with raw egg and seasoned with condiments such as capers, onions, and mustard. That is what most people have in mind when they think of steak tartare, and it's delicious. France does not have a monopoly on the dish, though; it's a global concept. In Korea, I had tried *yuk hwe*, that country's version, served with a flight of garnishes that you mixed in yourself, according to your taste. There were slices of bumpy-skinned, round Korean pear, which is crunchier and less fruity than our own, and a minty perilla leaf (known as shiso in Japan) in which you would package your tartare up, before eating it.

That experience led me to this recipe. The *gochujang* is a Korean fermented hot chile paste that provides both piquancy and heat. I borrow the shiso idea, but I mix the fresh herb into the tartare, and I incorporate tonburi, or "land caviar," which has a gray-green color reminiscent of the real (from the sea) thing and darkens (so it resembles the blacker eggs) once exposed to the sugar and soy mixture that seasons the beef.

Make the daikon salad: Combine the daikon, vinegar, sugar, and salt in a small bowl.

Make the *gochujang* **sauce:** Combine the *gochujang*, sugar, and 1 tablespoon warm water in a small bowl.

Make the steak tartare: In a large bowl, mix the beef with the shiso, scallion, soy sauce, sugar, and oil and season to taste with salt and pepper.

To serve: Beat the egg yolk with salt to taste to make a sauce. Put mounds of the tartare on chilled plates, garnish with the daikon salad, tonburi, scallion, Asian pear, and the *gochujang* and egg-yolk sauces.

SERVES 4

FOR THE DAIKON SALAD:
½ cup julienned daikon
1 teaspoon rice vinegar
½ teaspoon sugar
¼ teaspoon salt

FOR THE *GOCHUJANG* SAUCE:
2 tablespoons *gochujang* (Korean chile paste)
1 tablespoon sugar

FOR THE STEAK TARTARE:
10 ounces filet of beef, trimmed and finely julienned
3 fresh shiso leaves, or 3 mint and 2 basil leaves, cut into small squares
2 tablespoons thinly sliced (on a bias) scallion greens
2 tablespoons soy sauce
1½ tablespoons sugar
1 tablespoon neutral-flavored vegetable oil
Salt and black pepper

TO SERVE:
2 large egg yolks
Salt
Tonburi (broom cypress seeds or "land caviar"; optional)
4 pinches julienned scallion greens
12 half-moon slices Asian pear

> *Whenever I make steak tartare, I use filet of beef hand cut into strips. The texture is better—the flavor of the beef comes through more strongly and you get a cleaner, less mushy outcome. I also prefer grass-fed beef here. If I'm cooking meats, I like my beef grain-finished because it has that good layer of fat. For a raw dish, you don't want that fat. Grass-fed is leaner and imparts that beautiful soil-rich flavor you want when you're enjoying tartare.*

HAMACHI CARPACCIO
WITH CAVIAR AND BEETS

SERVES 4

FOR THE CARPACCIO:

8 ounces hamachi, in 4 cubes, red part
 removed

Neutral-flavored vegetable oil

FOR THE BEET SALAD:

1 large beet, roasted, peeled, and
 finely diced (about ½ cup)

1 teaspoon grainy mustard

1 teaspoon lemon juice

1 tablespoon neutral-flavored
 vegetable oil

Pinch of grated horseradish, or to taste

1 teaspoon chopped fresh dill

1 teaspoon chopped fresh chives

⅛ teaspoon salt

A few grinds of fresh pepper

TO SERVE:

2 pink radishes, thinly sliced on a
 mandoline or by hand

Lemon juice

Salt

1 teaspoon Hawaiian pink coarse salt
 or any coarse salt

4 teaspoons American sturgeon caviar
 (optional)

4 sprigs fresh dill

1 baby candy-cane beet, thinly sliced
 on a mandoline or by hand

*You can also prepare this carpaccio
with tuna or salmon. If you're not a beet
lover, another root vegetable will do.*

A true global amalgam, this appetizer applies an Italian preparation and European flavors to a Japanese fish garnished with American caviar. Hamachi is part of the jack family, which means it's a yellowtail and not, as some assume, a tuna. (Kanpachi is simply the baby version.) The white-fleshed fish has a high fat content and is oily in a meaty, firm-textured way, like a buttery swordfish, which means it can stand up to bold flavors. Here, you pound the fish flat between oil and parchment paper and you put it on a serving plate. A salad of roasted beets brings saturated colors—red, magenta, gold—and sweet earthiness, while a sharp mustard- and horse-radish-flavored dressing based on a vinaigrette lends acidity to cut the hamachi's richness. This combination is inspired by the Nordic pairing of smoked trout with horseradish sauce and by the Eastern European custom of mixing that same spicy root with beets. The black caviar—often used to top smoked salmon—offers a briny saltiness. Chives are added for a mild oniony note and color. Paper-thin discs of raw, baby pink-and-white candy cane beet make a pretty final touch.

Make the carpaccio: Oil a sheet of parchment paper and place the cubes of hamachi at least 10 inches apart, 5 inches from any edge. Use multiple sheets of parchment if necessary. Oil another sheet of parchment and place it on top of the hamachi. Using the smooth side of a meat hammer, pound out to ¼-inch thick, moving the square edges around to form rounds (or try pounding a square—this is just for aesthetic purposes). Put the hamachi, still in the parchment, in the refrigerator until ready to use.

Make the beet salad: Combine the beet, mustard, lemon juice, oil, horseradish, dill, chives, and salt and pepper.

To serve: Toss the radishes with lemon juice and salt to taste. Cut the parchment "sandwiches" to separate the 4 pieces of hamachi. Peel the parchment from one side of one piece of hamachi and place, fish side down, on a chilled serving plate; peel off the top layer of parchment. Sprinkle the fish evenly with the Hawaiian salt, then place a mound of the beet salad in the center. Top with 1 teaspoon of the caviar (if using) and a dill sprig, then place a few of the seasoned radishes and candy-cane beets around on top of the fish. Repeat with the remaining fish and garnishes and serve immediately.

TARTARE OF MAINE SWEET SHRIMP

SERVES 4

FOR THE VERJUS GELÉE:

¼ cup verjus, green grapes saved (see sidebar) and cut in half

½ teaspoon unflavored gelatin, softened in ½ teaspoon water

FOR THE SHRIMP TARTARE:

1 pound peeled Maine sweet shrimp, heads reserved (save the roe for garnishing your plates)

½ teaspoon lemon juice, or to taste

1 teaspoon chopped fresh chives

Salt and black pepper

Neutral-flavored vegetable oil for deep-frying

Wondra flour, seasoned with salt and pepper

These sweet shrimp do require a good amount of labor. In my opinion, it's worth the effort. If you want to cut out a step, skip the gelée making and just splash the verjus over the tartare. Verjus is the pressed juice of unripened grapes. For this recipe, look for a brand of verjus with grapes left in the bottle.

Maine sweet shrimp have a famously short season that begins in February and lasts for around six weeks. You really shouldn't miss it—not only are they delicious, but at just a few dollars per pound retail, they're also a steal. If you don't live in the Northeast, you're probably out of luck, although *amaebi* from your local sushi bar or Japanese market make a nice substitute. Both types of shrimp are small—they run about forty to fifty pieces per pound—but they make up for their size in sweetness. In Maine, people eat them boiled with butter. I prefer them raw, peeled and dipped in soy sauce with a little wasabi and shiso, or slightly more dressed up, as they are in the following recipe. After giving them a spritz of lemon, a sprinkle of salt and pepper, and a hint of green chives, I leave them alone. Verjus gelée makes a refreshing and elegant condiment—the juice made from unripe grapes is tamely acidic, and not too sugary; it supports the shrimp without outshining the main ingredient.

The heads should not be tossed; they're actually the best part of the shellfish and where you find the most concentrated (though sweet) flavor. These are irresistible dredged in flour or cornstarch and deep-fried. The perfect crunchy contrast to the soft, raw meat, they can be eaten whole—their thin shells become crisp in the hot oil. They also make a great foundation for sauce or stock, simmered with a bit of tomato, shallot, garlic, wine or Cognac, water, and tarragon.

Make the verjus gelée: Heat the verjus in a small saucepan until almost to a boil. Remove from the heat and whisk in the softened gelatin. Pour into a container and refrigerate until set, then stir with a fork.

Make the shrimp tartare and fried heads: Toss the shrimp tails with the lemon juice, chives, and salt and pepper to taste. Peel the top shell off the heads, leaving the legs and noses intact. In a heavy pot, heat oil to 350°F. Dredge the shrimp heads in the seasoned flour and fry until golden and crisp. Drain on a paper towel.

To serve: Place the shrimp-tail mixture in the center of each of 4 chilled serving plates and top with a few heads. Ring with the gelée and garnish the plate with a few of the grape halves and the reserved shrimp roe.

IV. SALAD

SALAD OF FETA AND GRAPES
WITH DILL AND PINE NUTS

SERVES 4 AS AN APPETIZER

FOR THE PROSECCO CUBES:

¾ cup prosecco

1 tablespoon sugar

2 teaspoons unflavored gelatin
   softened in 1 tablespoon water

FOR THE SALAD:

1 head frisée, core removed, leaves
   separated, washed, and spun dry

¼ cup loosely packed fresh dill sprigs

2 tablespoons lemon juice

7 tablespoons extra-virgin olive oil

⅛ teaspoon salt

A few grinds black pepper

4 (3½-inch-square) slices (¼-inch
   thick) Feta cheese

1 bunch (about ¾ pound) Kyoho
   grapes, cut in half and seeded

1 heaping tablespoon pine nuts,
   toasted

I have a lot of regulars at *annisa*, **and they usually do tasting menus.** Because some of them eat at the restaurant more than once a week and I can't give these loyal diners the same set of dishes over and over again, I usually cook a meal especially for them, or I'll add some intermediary courses they've never seen before.

One evening, when one of my best customers, Adam Rapoport, a magazine editor who lived above the restaurant and frequently ate at the bar, came in, I wanted to send him an off-the-menu extra. That was the initial incentive for this salad. I looked around the kitchen to see what we had and remembered the prosecco jelly that was intended for a dessert and hadn't worked out the way I'd planned. And there were the Kyoho grapes I had found at the Korean food market on Thirty-second Street. I had first tried these in Japan, where they originated. One of the best things I'd had in that country was the fruit, and this was no exception. The Kyohos tasted like Concord grapes, but you could eat them whole (you don't have to peel them like you do the Concord)—they're big and purple, with a classic grape texture (unlike the Concord) and a wonderful floral, sweet, round flavor. In that moment when I was trying to come up with a standout appetizer for Adam, the Kyohos suddenly gave the failed prosecco creation a purpose. I put some Feta cheese down on a plate, added the jelly, and placed the beautiful grapes in the center. I topped the pile with some fresh dill, sprinkled some toasted pine nuts I had on hand for that same unsuccessful dessert, and called it a day. It was a perfect marriage of salty and sweet. The jelly offers something effervescent and mildly acidic, while the fronds bring a green, herbal component and the the pignoli contribute crunchy nuttiness. He really liked it and didn't believe that I just happened to have prosecco jelly on hand.

Make the prosecco cubes: Combine ¼ cup of the prosecco and the sugar in a small saucepan and bring almost to a boil. Remove from the heat, add the softened gelatin, and whisk until the gelatin is completely dissolved. Stir in the remaining prosecco, pour into a container, and refrigerate until set, about 1½ hours or overnight. Finely dice and set aside.

Make the salad: In a large bowl, toss the frisée with the dill, lemon juice, oil, salt, and pepper. Divide the prosecco cubes among 4 chilled serving plates. Top with the Feta, then with the grapes, ending with the salad. Garnish the plate with the pine nuts and serve.

What makes this salad special is nicer grapes. For a long time, we couldn't enjoy great grapes in this country—I remember when I was a kid, in the '60s, we had to boycott the fruit because the California-based growers were mistreating their workers. Now, fortunately, conditions have improved, and we have access to multiple strains. The Kyoho, which is also planted in South America and exported to the United States, comes around in the spring. I love Muscats in summertime and, recently, people have begun offering a varietal called the Thomcat, a Thompson-Muscat hybrid. Either of these would be good in this dish, but if you can't find any of these fancier grapes, don't worry: It will still be solid with whatever your market is selling. For visual effect, you can put a few of the tiny Champagne grapes in there too.

SALAD OF LOBSTER AND AVOCADO
WITH MINT AND CORAL SAUCE

The old-fashioned combination of crab, grapefruit, and avocado is a regular on French menus. I wasn't really thinking about that when I came up with this salad; I was focused on the equally timeless (and French) partnering of lobster and avocado. I see the strong resemblance to the classic triad now. Consciously or not, I replaced that trio's original crustacean with lobster and included the citrus in gelée form. It's an excellent opportunity to make use of leftover lobster and the roe, which people will often avoid out of ignorance. This "coral" (so called because it turns red when you cook it) is a prized delicacy; it's the most concentrated expression of the shellfish's flavor—rich, meaty, and sweet. Folded into the mayonnaise that usually binds this salad together, the roe conveys an unexpected unctuousness and depth. It's decadent, in a good way. The fragrant, refreshing green mint helps cut that richness and adds an interesting complexity. And to bring in additional texture and some extra saltiness, I crumble crisp potato gaufrettes (French waffle-cut potato chips) over the top. It's a strong contrast to the creaminess of the avocado and a fun surprise. You could also just use thick purchased potato chips.

The grapefruit's flavor isn't altered by the gelée preparation; the gelatin acts as an interesting textural enhancer. If you're in a hurry, you can skip the extra step and just use fresh segments.

SERVES 4

FOR THE CORAL MAYONNAISE:
- 1 large egg yolk, at room temperature
- 1 teaspoon Dijon mustard
- ¾ cup neutral-flavored vegetable oil
- 2 heaping tablespoons lobster roe, cooked and finely chopped (optional)
- ½ teaspoon salt
- Black pepper to taste
- ½ teaspoon lemon juice, or to taste

FOR THE GRAPEFRUIT GELÉE:
- ½ cup ruby grapefruit juice
- 1 teaspoon unflavored gelatin, softened in 2 teaspoons water
- Pinch of salt

FOR THE POMMES GAUFRETTES:
- 1 Idaho potato, peeled
- 4 cups neutral-flavored vegetable oil
- Salt

TO SERVE:
- 1 tablespoon sliced fresh mint
- 4 sections grapefruit, cut into triangles

- 1 ripe Haas avocado, pitted, peeled, quartered, and thinly sliced
- Lemon juice
- Salt
- 2 (1-pound) lobsters, cooked, shelled, and chopped (leave claws whole)
- 1 tablespoon julienned scallion greens
- 1 tablespoon finely crumbled pommes gaufrettes (or substitute waffle potato chips, or the ridged variety)

Make the coral mayonnaise: Put the egg yolks in a large bowl, add the mustard, and slowly and steadily whisk in the oil to make a loose mayonnaise. Add roe, salt, pepper, and lemon juice.

Make the grapefruit gelée: Bring the grapefruit juice to a boil in a small saucepan, then remove from the heat. Add the softened gelatin and whisk until it is completely melted. Add the salt, transfer to a container, and refrigerate until set.

Make the pommes gaufrettes: Using a mandoline, make thin waffle-cut slices of the potato. Heat the oil to 350°F, then deep-fry the potato until crisp and golden, then drain on a paper towel and season with salt.

To serve: Place a spoonful of the coral mayonnaise in the center of a chilled serving plate and shape it into a flat circle; decorate with a little mint. Ring with some of the grapefruit gelée and top the gelée with a few pieces of grapefruit. Season the avocado with lemon juice and salt. Layer alternating pieces of lobster and avocado to form a stack that finishes with a claw on top. Sprinkle the stack with mint and scallion and, finally, with a little of the crumbled pommes gaufrettes. Repeat with the remaining ingredients. Serve immediately.

MAINE CRABMEAT AND POMELO SALAD
WITH ANKIMO AND WHITE SOY

I feel guilty. A lot of my favorite recipes are the hardest to pull off. But there are always simpler versions to be found and they're usually just as likable. Seen as a pair, this dish and the one preceding it prove my point. If the last salad was a straightforward reinterpretation of a classic, this is its more complex counterpart. It relies on the same thematic trio—crab, grapefruit, and avocado—but now the crab is the only recognizable ingredient.

Pomelo provides the fat-cutting citrus. It looks like a big green grapefruit, but it's more delicate and less acidic. It's also more fun texturally; it breaks apart easily—its subsections, oblong sacs, are clearly delineated and can be shredded with little effort. In Thailand, you find salads composed of these micro-segments, and that's what I had in mind when I chose this fruit.

As for the ankimo, the disk-shaped monkfish liver, it's a highly prized item in Japan, its fishiness deliciously mitigated by a natural sweetness. I've made it into terrines, as Japanese chefs frequently do. Some people call it "foie gras of the sea," which was the primary impetus for this particular usage. Lobster plus foie gras (the real thing) is a traditional pairing in French cuisine. That crustacean goes quite well with fat, whether it's mayonnaise, butter, or goose liver. The gentle brininess of the shellfish is bolstered—bettered, even—by the extra richness. Crab, cheaper than lobster (if more work) seems like the right partner for the organ of a monkfish, formerly known as "poor man's lobster." And, in turn, the ankimo was the perfect substitute for the original salad's smooth avocado. I use white soy sauce for its saltiness and its color (or lack thereof)—it doesn't affect the pomelo's pink hue or the crab's whiteness.

Make the monkfish liver: Sprinkle the monkfish liver with the salt, pepper to taste, and sake. Wrap into a sausage shape with plastic wrap, tying both ends tightly to form a tight, firm package. Wrap in aluminum foil, twisting the ends, then steam for 15 to 20 minutes. Let cool, then put in the refrigerator to chill.

Make the crab salad: Combine the pomelo, crabmeat, scallions, shiso, lemon juice, soy sauce, sugar, salt, and pepper.

SERVES 4

½ **pound monkfish liver (ankimo),** cleaned (have your fishmonger order this and remove membranes and veins)

1 **teaspoon salt**

Black pepper

Splash of sake

FOR THE CRAB SALAD:

½ **cup peeled, sectioned, and** shredded pomelo

¾ **pound picked-over Maine** crabmeat, all leg-meat pack (lump crabmeat works fine as well)

2 **tablespoons thinly sliced (on a bias)** scallions

1 **bunch fresh shiso, cut into** chiffonade, or 2 tablespoons mint, cut into chiffonade

2 **teaspoons lemon juice**

1 **tablespoon white soy sauce or** regular soy sauce

¼ **teaspoon sugar**

¼ **teaspoon salt**

Black pepper to taste

TO SERVE:

Pinch of shredded nori (optional)

Julienned scallion

To serve: Cut the liver into 12 rounds and arrange 3 per plate. Top with the crab salad. Garnish with the nori (if using) and scallion.

> *Both the ankimo and the pomelo are wintertime phenomena, which is exactly when you should enjoy this dish. If you want to adapt it to another season, you could substitute uni (sea urchin) or avocado for the monkfish liver (no need to steam them), and grapefruit for the pomelo.*

GRILLED QUAIL
WITH FRISÉE AND A FRIED QUAIL EGG

SERVES 4 AS A LARGE APPETIZER
OR LUNCH ENTRÉE

4 boned quail

Salt and black pepper

2 cloves garlic, roughly chopped

4 sprigs fresh thyme

1 teaspoon whole black peppercorns

2 bay leaves

1½ cups hardwood chips

1 tablespoon plus ¼ cup rendered
    duck fat, or olive oil

4 quail eggs

1 small shallot, minced

3 tablespoons red wine vinegar

8 ounces frisée, washed and spun dry

1 tablespoon mixed chopped fresh
    chives, tarragon, thyme leaves, and
    parsley

One of the most popular items on any typical bistro menu is the salad of frisée and lardons (diced bacon that is blanched and fried—like a pork crouton). When I lived in Paris during college, I would prepare this for myself all the time, because it was so easy and cheap—I'd buy an egg to fry (one is often placed atop the greens), a bag of prewashed lettuce, and another of precut lardons. If you want to build on that basic premise, you could replace the cubes of pork with cold-smoked, grilled quail. It's easy to do if you have an outdoor grill, but not difficult even without one. You get the smokiness provided by the bacon, but in a different, gamy form. I keep the optional egg on top, but I use a quail's to be consistent and enhance the effect of the bird meat. Then I drizzle on a vinaigrette made with shallots, red wine vinegar, and, in keeping with the fowl theme, duck fat (the secret to making anything taste good). It's a one-pan wonder.

Sprinkle the quail on both sides with 2 tablespoons salt and toss with the garlic, thyme sprigs, peppercorns, and bay leaves. Cover and refrigerate overnight to cure. Soak 1½ cups hardwood chips (hickory or applewood is nice) overnight in water; drain.

Cold-smoke the quail on a stovetop smoker following the manufacturer's instructions, or cold-smoke on an outdoor grill: Make a small charcoal fire on one side of the grill. When the fire is reduced to hot embers, place the soaked wood chips over the top in a small metal tray (a toaster oven's tray would work). Scrape excess curing mixture off the quail and place them on a rack over a baking dish filled with salted ice, then place it on the far side of the grill away from the fire. Cover the grill and smoke for 30 minutes. The grill should stay cool, 150°F or lower. This can be done up to a few days in advance.

Reheat (or heat, if you've used a stovetop smoker) the grill and cook the quail to desired doneness, then let rest on a warm plate.

Heat a nonstick frying pan over medium-high heat and add the 1 tablespoon of duck fat. Fry the quail eggs, sunny-side up, season with a pinch of salt and pepper, and remove to a warm plate. Add the shallot to the pan and stir, then add the vinegar and bring to a boil. Remove from the heat and add the remaining duck fat. Put the frisée and mixed herbs in a large bowl, pour the duck-fat mixture over them, season with salt (about ¼ teaspoon) and pepper, and toss to combine. Divide among 4 plates and top each with a grilled quail and an egg. Serve immediately.

If you find quail too strong in taste or daunting as an ingredient, you can use duck. You don't even need to smoke it. You could be really lazy and buy a confit (rendered from the leg meat); D'Artagnan sells it premade, as well as for boned quail. If you choose duck, you might also go with its egg for your fried garnish. You can always go back to basics and produce the original. If you do, when it comes to the lardons, I recommend a thick cut of unsliced bacon to give you the chewy, substantial meatiness this classic requires.

ROASTED KABOCHA AND MAITAKE
WITH BITTER CHOCOLATE

Mexico and Japan couldn't be farther away in distance and in culture, but in the contemporary American kitchen their ingredients find common ground. Here, sweet and earthy Japanese pumpkin and wild mushrooms are paired with a rich and bitter chocolate sauce based on mole, a famous Mexican stew. I don't want to mislead anyone. This dish was certainly inspired, in part, by that wonderful sauce, but mine is so far from the authentic thing that to call it a mole would be insulting to the real article or anyone who has taken the time and gathered all of the ingredients necessary to make one.

As for kabocha squash, it won me over when I tasted it in Japanese stews, with its skin on and designs carved into the bite-size chunks. The pumpkin tends to pick up the flavors of its braising liquid, and the skin is tender enough to eat. I would have used its own seeds for garnish in this preparation, but their shells are a bit tough, and my prep cooks would have killed me. Besides, *pepitas* (the Spanish word for a prolific variety of pumpkin seeds) are a popular ingredient in Mexican cuisine and get the job done just as well.

Preheat the oven to 350°F. Brush the inside of the spaghetti squash with 1 tablespoon of the oil and sprinkle with ½ teaspoon of the salt and a few grinds of pepper. Put in a roasting pan or on a baking sheet sheet and roast for about 30 minutes, until soft. Meanwhile, cut the kabocha into wedges radiating from the center stem of both halves. Place in a bowl with the remaining oil and salt and a generous amount of pepper and toss to coat. Arrange in one layer on a roasting pan or on a baking sheet and bake for about 25 minutes, until soft and slightly caramelized on the edges. Set the spaghetti and kabocha squashes aside to cool. When cool, scrape out the flesh of the spaghetti squash with a fork to remove strands; discard the tough outer shell. There should be about 1 cup.

Make the sauce: In a small saucepan, melt 1 tablespoon of the butter, add the shallot and garlic, and cook over low heat until soft and translucent, but not browned. Add the cumin, cinnamon, sesame seeds, and star anise and stir. Add the mushroom juice and brown sugar and cook until the

SERVES 8 AS AN APPETIZER OR 4 AS AN ENTRÉE

½ **small spaghetti squash, halved, seeds scooped out**

3 **tablespoons neutral-flavored vegetable oil**

1½ **teaspoons salt**

Black pepper

1 **small kabocha squash, rinsed, stem removed, halved horizontally, seeds scooped out (see Notes)**

FOR THE SAUCE:

4 **tablespoons butter**

1 **large shallot, minced**

1 **clove garlic, minced**

1 **teaspoon ground cumin**

1 **teaspoon ground cinnamon**

¼ **cup sesame seeds**

1 **piece star anise**

¾ **cup mushroom juice (see Notes) or vegetable or chicken stock (page 231)**

1½ **tablespoons light brown sugar, or more to taste**

⅓ **cup finely chopped extra-bitter chocolate (2½ ounces)**

Pinch each of salt and pepper

(CONTINUED)

TO SERVE:

24 large, bite-size clusters fresh
    maitake mushroom or fresh shiitake
    or oyster mushrooms (about
    ⅔ pound)
2 tablespoons butter
½ cup julienned scallion greens
    (about ½ bunch)
1½ teaspoons salt
A few grinds of pepper
1 teaspoon lemon juice
1 tablespoon neutral-flavored
    vegetable oil
½ teaspoon sugar
3 tablespoons roasted hulled
    pumpkin seeds (pepitas)
Ground pequin chiles or red pepper
    flakes

liquid is reduced by half. Over medium-high heat, whisk in the chocolate and the remaining butter until fully incorporated and smooth. Season to taste with salt and pepper, adding more brown sugar if necessary. Remove and discard the star anise and set the sauce aside in a warm place; gently reheat before serving to preserve the consistency of the chocolate.

To serve: Sauté the mushrooms in the butter over high heat until golden brown and crisp. Reheat the kabocha in a 400°F oven. Combine the spaghetti squash with the scallion and season with the salt and pepper, lemon juice, oil, and sugar. Place 3 warm kabocha pieces in the center of each plate. Ring with the sauce and arrange 3 pieces of mushroom around on top of the sauce. Scatter a few pumpkin seeds in between. Top the kabocha with a little of the spaghetti-squash mixture and sprinkle with some ground chiles. Serve.

NOTES: You can substitute buttercup squash or any other sweet, dense winter squash or pumpkin. For kabocha, leave the edible skin on; other types of squash may require peeling.

To make mushroom juice, simmer 12 ounces button or cremini mushrooms in 2 cups water for 30 minutes, then pour through a fine-mesh sieve set over a bowl. Reserve the mushrooms for another use.

> Maitake, or hen of the woods, are fragrant mushrooms that typically grow at the base of oak trees. These appear in my yard every year, but I rarely catch them at their edible stage—once they get older, they become too tough to eat. Even so, their perfume is heady and makes me salivate. Apparently, the Chinese and Japanese employ them for medicinal purposes; they have balancing properties.

CRISP SILKEN TOFU
WITH BLACK BEANS AND GINGER

Those familiar with *agedashi tofu*, the popular Japanese dish of deep-fried silken tofu, will recognize the crisp exterior and soft interior of these "steaks"; dredging them in cornstarch before placing them in the hot oil is the easy trick. The sauce is a departure from what you would find in Japan; it's inspired by both Chinese and Vietnamese cuisines. From the former, I borrow fermented black beans (the ones used in classic black bean sauces), and from the latter, butter.

I came up with this sauce at Can, the French-Vietnamese place in SoHo where I had my first executive-chef job. The restaurant was based on one in Paris called Restaurant A, where half of the dishes were French and the other half Vietnamese. In order to prepare for the second side of the menu, I read cookbooks on that food and learned that unlike many East or Southeast Asian cuisines, due to the French colonial influence, this one uses butter. In one book there was a recipe for a fish *en papillote* (in paper) with a sauce of black beans, Thai basil, oyster sauce, ginger, and butter.

Can didn't last, but the sauce did. It goes beautifully with this tofu, and also with other things like poached oysters or grilled wild king salmon. To accompany those proteins, serve some sautéed dark, leafy Asian greens.

Make the tofu: Heat 1 to 2 inches of oil in a shallow pot or saucepan to 350°F. Dredge the tofu in the cornstarch on all sides and shallow-fry until crisp, turning once. Drain on a paper towel.

Make the yow choy: Sauté the greens in a saucepan with a little water and the butter and salt until wilted and just tender, then drain on a clean paper towel.

Make the sauce: In a sauté pan, combine 2 tablespoons water, the oyster sauce, sugar, ginger, garlic, and black beans over high heat. When boiling, whisk in the butter, little by little, to emulsify. Season with pepper to taste.

To serve: Surround the yow choy with the sauce, topped with the fried tofu and garnished with the mint.

SERVES 4 AS AN APPETIZER OR 2 AS AN ENTRÉE

FOR THE TOFU:
Neutral-flavored vegetable oil
2 (14-ounce) packages silken tofu, cut into 4 rectangles
Cornstarch for dredging

FOR THE YOW CHOY:
1 bunch yow choy or other Asian greens such as bok choy
2 tablespoons butter
Salt

FOR THE SAUCE:
2 tablespoons oyster sauce
1½ teaspoons sugar
Pinch of julienned fresh ginger
Pinch of chopped garlic
1 tablespoon Chinese fermented black beans
5 tablespoons butter, cut into pieces
Black pepper

TO SERVE:
4 fresh mint leaves, sliced

Vegetarians might have some concern about the inclusion of oyster sauce. According to Chinese-cookbook author Ken Hom, there's no oyster in most of the sauces on the market today (only the really expensive ones).

ZUCCHINI BLOSSOMS
STUFFED WITH MANCHEGO CHEESE

SERVES 4

FOR THE STUFFING:

1 cup diced day-old bread

½ cup grated young Manchego
   cheese or Gruyère

1 large egg yolk

3 tablespoons milk

½ clove garlic, finely chopped

2 teaspoons chopped fresh chives

½ teaspoon salt

Black pepper to taste

FOR THE SAUCE:

⅓ cup drained jarred piquillo peppers
   or roasted red bell pepper plus a
   pinch of cayenne

½ clove garlic

1 tablespoon sherry vinegar

2 tablespoons olive oil

½ teaspoon salt

Black pepper to taste

FOR THE ZUCCHINI BLOSSOMS:

8 large zucchini blossoms with baby
   zucchini attached, or 8 "male"
   blossoms plus 20 slices zucchini
   rounds cut ¼-inch thick

1 cup all-purpose flour

1 tablespoon salt, plus more to taste

10 grinds black pepper

1 large egg white, beaten together
   with 3 tablespoons water

¼ cup olive oil

TO SERVE:

1 tablespoon dried currants

Too much zucchini is a recurring summertime problem. This breed of squash is so prolific that just one plant can yield more fruit than any single household can use. The overspill results in those bags of green baseball bats that get passed from neighbor to neighbor, and in zucchini bread, which to me doesn't really taste like zucchini (but is delicious nonetheless). I once grew enough from two or three plants to supply my restaurant with more than ample filling for these blossoms. With the rest of that summer squash, we cooked stuffed zucchini with ground lamb and bechamel, stewed zucchini with pork and cilantro, zucchini gratins…the list goes on. If it could be made with zucchini, it was—all for staff meals. One way to get around the excessive proliferation is to pick the zucchini young while they still have flowers attached and can't reproduce. (Don't pick all of them—you want to leave some males and females to grow to size and keep the population going.) Here is a Spanish-inspired recipe that calls for young Manchego cheese, which melts in a lovely, oozy way inside the blossom's crisp and sweet vegetal crust. Piquillo peppers—small red cone-shaped peppers grilled and sold in a jar or a can—are sweet and faintly spicy, a nice foil for the zucchini-cheese mixture.

Make the stuffing: Combine all the ingredients in a large bowl. Taste and adjust the seasonings.

Make the sauce: Put all the ingredients in a blender, or use a hand blender to pulverize until smooth. Taste and adjust the seasonings.

Make the zucchini blossoms: Remove the stamens from the inside of the blossoms. Pinch off the baby zucchini and set aside. Stuff the blossoms with the stuffing mixture and set aside. Season the flour with the salt and pepper. Dip the base of each blossom into the egg-white mixture, keeping the yellow tips of the petals dry, then dip in the seasoned flour to coat.

Heat a skillet over high heat, then add the oil. Swirl the oil, then add the blossoms with the baby zucchini (or zucchini rounds). Season the zucchini with salt. Fry, turning and lightly browning each side, then drain on a paper towel.

To serve: Divide the sauce among 4 plates and top with the baby zucchini or rounds, followed by the blossoms. Garnish with the currants and serve.

SPICY GRILLED EGGPLANT
WITH YOGURT AND LENTILS

SERVES 4

FOR THE EGGPLANT:

¼ cup neutral-flavored vegetable oil

1 tablespoon curry powder (vindaloo or madras)

1 tablespoon garam masala

2 baby eggplant, halved lengthwise, scored, salted, left to sit for 20 minutes, and blotted dry

FOR THE YOGURT SAUCE:

1 cup full-fat Greek yogurt

2 teaspoons grated lemon zest

2 teaspoons lemon juice

1 teaspoon salt

A few grinds of black pepper

FOR THE LENTIL SALAD:

½ cup French green lentils, cooked in 2¼ cups water until soft but still holding their shape (about 20 minutes), then drained

2 to 3 tablespoons sliced shallots, fried in oil until golden brown and drained on a paper towel (makes about 1 tablespoon fried)

(CONTINUED)

I made a version of this on *Top Chef Masters*, **and it bombed. There were a** number of reasons for that; I was exhausted and could only find the wrong kind of lentils, but also, and more important, it was a vegan challenge, which meant yogurt wasn't allowed. And then, to throw us another curve ball (as if we needed that), they banned soy sauce. Take away meat or wheat and I can always find a solution in Asian cuisine—but they removed soy. That day, this was crippling for me. I came up with a cashew-based sauce that had the yogurt's creaminess and cooling effect, but it didn't matter. The dish wasn't right. Sometimes you just know.

When we prepare it the "right" way—with yogurt and the proper lentils (the French green ones—they hold up in cooking, while the plain green ones often fall apart), it's a crowd-pleaser. I always try to have something on the menu that can be served as a vegetarian entrée. My rule is that it has to appeal to an omnivore as an appetizer, and this item does. It gets its personality and structure from South Asia and features some of India's most pungent aromatics—garam masala and curry powder. It's a simple grilled piece of eggplant with a prominent spice component and, to off-set the density of the vegetable and the intensity of the seasonings, yogurt mixed with lemon. The lentils have substantial earthiness and provide great nutritional value; I put some of the garam into the beans to make sure the spices pervade every layer. Finally, I add some fried shallots to the lentils as well; a secret weapon, they're able to contribute sweetness and savory richness all at once.

Make the eggplant: In a bowl, combine the oil, curry powder, and garam masala and toss with the eggplant.

Make the yogurt sauce: In a small bowl, combine the yogurt, lemon zest, lemon juice, salt, and pepper.

Make the lentil salad: In a large bowl, combine all the ingredients.

To serve: Season the eggplant with salt just before serving and grill (or broil) on both sides until soft and wilted (but not charred black). Serve with the yogurt sauce and lentil salad.

FOR THE LENTIL SALAD (CONT'D):

1 teaspoon chopped fresh chives

3 tablespoons neutral-flavored vegetable oil

1 tablespoon lemon juice

1 teaspoon garam masala

Pinch of curry powder (vindaloo or madras)

¼ teaspoon salt

A few grinds of black pepper

TO GRILL AND SERVE:

1 teaspoon salt

> *The matter of cooking eggplant is one that food people don't agree on. Not everybody enjoys it my way. I like it grilled, soft, and saturated with lots of oil. When it's steamed and cold, however, I prefer the nightshade less mushy. As for salting, I do think it makes a difference; it diminishes the ingredient's natural bitterness, which I don't like, and removes water so you get a denser, more flavorful vegetable. There are different kinds of eggplant, and my choice is the little Japanese type—it has small seeds and isn't acrid. The petite Italian sort is a good substitute, or you can always use the regular, larger one.*

SEARED FOIE GRAS
WITH FOIE GRAS SOUP DUMPLINGS

SERVES 12

FOR THE JELLIED "SOUP" FILLING:

1 pig foot, split

5 cups chicken stock (page 231)

1 cup veal stock (page 232) or more
 chicken stock

1 cinnamon stick

3 pieces star anise

1 dried shiitake mushroom

2 slices fresh ginger

1 teaspoon whole black peppercorns

Soy sauce to taste

FOR THE FOIE-GRAS MOUSSE:

1 lobe grade-B foie gras, cleaned and
 deveined (see page 233)

Salt and black pepper

FOR THE VINEGAR REDUCTION:

2 cups balsamic vinegar

1 cup Chinese black vinegar or more
 balsamic vinegar

5 (¼-inch-thick) slices fresh ginger

½ teaspoon whole black peppercorns

FOR THE DUMPLINGS:

1 large egg

1 tablespoon cornstarch

1 package white gyoza wrappers

48 (⅓-inch-square) pieces jicama
 (about ¾ cup)

12 ounces grade-A foie gras, deveined
 and sliced into 12 pieces

Salt and black pepper

Wondra flour

TO SERVE:

12 pinches of julienned scallion greens

People tend to associate me with this dish; it's certainly the best-known item on the menu at *annisa* and one I invented right before we opened the restaurant. Although the foie gras in the title might indicate otherwise, this appetizer is based on the humble soup dumplings of Shanghai that my father grew up eating there. These *xiao long bao* are identified by their molten centers—when you bite in, hot liquid explodes into your mouth. Usually, it's a really rich pork broth. I started there with pig feet, whose natural gelatin makes the broth set into a solid so it can be used to fill the dumplings before they are steamed, and in addition to cinnamon and star anise, I brought in veal and chicken stocks for a multilayered concentration of flavor.

Why foie gras? It goes wonderfully with the stock's aromatics; it also makes for a playful pairing—you have an inexpensive, everyday food and a luxurious, haute-cuisine ingredient. The foie enhances the soup's savory notes with its unctuous, gamy overtones. The duck liver's intensity can border on decadence without some balancing acidity. Traditionally, the dumplings are served with a dipping sauce of ginger-infused black vinegar. Often referred to as "Chinese balsamic," this is a sweet, dark, rice wine–based vinegar that acts as a perfect foil for the foie. For my sauce, I mix some actual balsamic in with the black vinegar to mellow the latter out, toss some ginger in with it, and reduce everything until it gets viscous. I drizzle the syrup on the plate, and rest the steamed pockets in the center. Because this is a special dish and not the sort of thing you make every day, I recommend you put some extra seared foie gras on top for utter lusciousness.

Make the jellied "soup" filling: Put the pig foot and stocks in a pot and bring to a boil. Skim off any foam and scum, add the remaining ingredients, and simmer, skimming occasionally, until the pig foot is soft, about 3 hours. Pour through a fine-mesh sieve to remove the solids. Taste the broth and adjust the seasonings; you may have to add a little water to dilute the soy. Place in an ice bath to cool to room temperature, then transfer to a sealed container and refrigerate until set, overnight.

Make the foie-gras mousse: Season the foie liberally with salt and pepper and let sit overnight. Preheat the oven to 275°F. Pack the foie gras into a terrine mold, put the lid on, and place in a hot water bath (see page 16). Bake for about 45 minutes, until the foie just starts to melt and is warm in

If you don't want to make the foie-gras mousse, you can substitute 7 ounces purchased duck liver mousse. You can buy round dumpling wrappers at most supermarkets. Make sure you buy white ones (not yellow) and that the only ingredients are the ones my mother used when she made hers from scratch: She would add hot water to flour, knead and roll. It's time-consuming, but worth it.

the center. Put in a food processor and puree until smooth. Push the foie gras through a tamis (a drum sieve) or a fine-mesh sieve with a rubber spatula and repack it into the terrine mold. Cover and refrigerate.

Make the vinegar reduction: Combine the vinegars, ginger, and peppercorns in a saucepan over medium heat and cook until syrupy and reduced to ⅓ cup, making sure it doesn't burn; when the bubbles become very small, it's ready. Pour through a fine-mesh sieve, discard the solids, and refrigerate.

Make the dumplings: In a small bowl, beat the egg with the cornstarch and 3 tablespoons of water. Brush each wrapper with egg wash and place a small square of foie-gras mousse in the center, along with a few pieces of jicama and 1 tablespoon of the jellied "soup." Fold in half and crease the top to form half moons. (You can make the dumplings to this point and freeze them in an airtight container for a month; there's no need to thaw them before steaming.)

Steam the dumplings in a bamboo or stainless-steel steamer lined with perforated parchment paper or lettuce until puffed; fresh dumplings for about 5 minutes, the frozen about 8 minutes.

Meanwhile, season the foie gras with salt and pepper, dust lightly with the Wondra, and sear in a small, heavy sauté pan over high heat, turning once, until nicely browned and just soft all the way through. The pan should be heated for 1 minute on high and should be close to smoking before adding the foie gras.

To serve: Decorate 4 serving plates with the vinegar reduction and organize 3 dumplings on top on each plate. Top each dumpling with a third of the seared foie gras and place a pinch of the scallion in the center. Serve with chopsticks and a Chinese soup spoon.

CHILLED CORN-AND-CRAB
CHAWAN MUSHI

The pairing of corn and crab is a popular one in both Eastern and Western cuisines. Chawan mushi is like a flan but less rich, or maybe a different kind of rich. While flan has cream and a higher proportion of egg to liquid (there's an extra yolk per cup), chawan mushi is flavored with dashi and some mirin, a sweet cooking wine of sorts. Where the flan has a higher fat content, its Eastern counterpart has plenty of umami. Their textures are also different. While flan is set, chawan mushi isn't quite solid, and once shattered, it becomes almost souplike. Both provide a certain velvety, creamy mouthfeel, but flan is smoother, drier; the Japanese custard traditionally also features bite-size pieces of ingredients such as gingko nuts and chicken. One dish tends to be uniform throughout, while the other provides multiple sensations.

A dining experience in the 1990s at a sushi bar in New York City really made me take notice of this special custard. Blue Ribbon Sushi on Sullivan Street in SoHo had just opened and I decided to try it. I ordered the chawan mushi. No bite I took was the same—each contained an unrepeated mix of components. My version is a bit simpler. Kernels of corn and lumps of crabmeat become interspersed in the unctuous custard. I hope it will open your eyes to something new that you'll want to try again and again.

Make the chawan mushi: In a bowl, combine the dashi, corn puree, and eggs and add the soy sauce, mirin, salt, and pepper; taste the batter and adjust the seasonings. To steam, fill a saucepan with water, leaving enough room to place a rack above the water. Divide the batter among 6 (4-ounce) ramekins and cover each with plastic wrap. Bring the water to a boil, then place the ramekins on the rack. Cover the pot and bring the water to a boil. Steam just until set, about 16 minutes. Remove the ramekins and refrigerate until chilled.

Make the corn-and-crab salad: Combine the corn, shiso, oil, crabmeat, lemon juice, and lemon zest and season with salt and pepper.

To serve: Top the chawan mushi with the salad and garnish each with a pinch of scallion and 3 pieces sea urchin (if using). Serve immediately.

SERVES 6 AS AN APPETIZER

FOR THE CHAWAN MUSHI:

1 cup dashi (page 231)

2 cups fresh corn kernels, pureed and pressed through a fine-mesh sieve to make just under 1 cup puree

2 large eggs, beaten

2 tablespoons soy sauce, or to taste

3 tablespoons mirin, or to taste

¼ teaspoon salt

A few grinds of black pepper

FOR THE CORN-AND-CRAB SALAD:

⅓ cup fresh corn kernels, blanched

2 fresh shiso leaves, cut into small squares, or ¼ teaspoon chopped fresh tarragon leaves

1 tablespoon neutral-flavored vegetable oil

6 ounces jumbo lump crabmeat

¾ teaspoon lemon juice, or to taste

Pinch of grated lemon zest

½ teaspoon salt, or to taste

A few grinds of black pepper

TO SERVE:

1 tablespoon julienned scallion greens

12 pieces sea urchin (optional)

The Chinese also have a savory custard that I once tried in San Francisco. It was served in a shallower vessel than those that hold flan or chawan mushi. Coincidentally, this too contained crabmeat.

ESCARGOTS IN POTATO CUPS

WITH BLACK TRUFFLES AND TOASTED PISTACHIOS

SERVES 4

FOR THE TRUFFLE SAUCE (OPTIONAL):

⅓ cup Madeira wine

4 cups veal stock (page 232), or
  2 cups demi-glace (see Note)

1 black truffle, chopped, plus any
  juices it comes with

1 tablespoon black-truffle butter
  (see Note)

Salt and black pepper

FOR THE GARLIC CHIVE SAUCE:

½ cup blanched, shocked, and
  squeezed dry garlic chive stems,
  woody ends removed, or a mixture
  of 2 parts chives, 2 parts parsley, and
  1 part tarragon and thyme leaves

About ½ cup neutral-flavored
  vegetable oil

½ teaspoon salt

A few grinds of black pepper

TO SERVE:

20 escargots, rinsed, blanched for
  1 minute in boiling salted water

20 baby potatoes such as German
  butterball, about 1 inch in diameter,
  two ends sliced off, one end
  hollowed out to form a cup,
  blanched in boiling, heavily salted
  water until tender

¼ cup black-truffle butter, softened
(CONTINUED)

Snails are prized as food around the world. All over Europe, from Greek *kholi* to Spanish *caracoles* to the well-known French escargots, they are an ordinary protein source. In Africa, some of the largest edible snails are grown. The ancient Romans considered them food fit for the upper classes, and snail shells have even been found on archaeological digs in Texas, proof that the consumption of snails dates to prehistoric times. So how did the diminutive gastropod become so widely shunned in the United States? The majority of our ancestors come from snail-eating countries, and those people grew up just like we did, finding the slimy creatures in gardens. The excuse that Americans are too used to packaged, processed foods won't wash either—snails come in cans.

Regardless of the provenance of this cultural prejudice, snails are delicious. Mild tasting and earthy, they pick up the flavors of whatever they are cooked with. The spiral-shelled creatures are best known for being doused in butter, garlic, and herbs—à la French brasserie fare. This is not the only way to appreciate them; if anything, that preparation seems like a form of overkill that can easily overpower the feature ingredient. Here, to showcase the snails themselves, I've paired them with a chorus of other earthy flavors—heady black truffles full of umami, sweet and toasty pistachios, nutty potatoes, and green herbs. These make fine canapés as well as appetizers. Just don't tell the fearful what they are. I'm sure they'll like them if they don't know.

Make the truffle sauce, if desired: Put the wine in a small saucepan over medium-high heat and cook until it is reduced to a syrupy consistency. Add the stock, lower the heat to medium, and simmer, skimming occasionally, until slightly thickened and well flavored. Add the truffle and its juices and simmer for 5 minutes. Whisk in the truffle butter and season to taste with salt and pepper.

Make the garlic chive sauce: Put the garlic chives in a blender with just enough oil to cover them and blend until smooth. Pour through a fine-mesh sieve and add the salt and pepper.

TO SERVE (CONT'D):

Scant ¼ cup toasted shelled
  pistachios, finely chopped

20 garlic chive stems, blanched and
  shocked, or raw fresh chives, cut
  into 1-inch lengths

To serve: Preheat the oven to 400°F. Place an escargot into each potato cup and pack the remaining space with the truffle butter. Put on a baking sheet and bake until hot and bubbling, about 10 minutes. Top with the pistachios. Decorate warmed serving plates, then top with the escargot-filled potatoes. Garnish each with a garlic chive. Serve.

NOTE: Demi-glace is reduced veal stock and, along with truffle butter, can be found in specialty food shops or online. See Resources, p. 233.

> *If you must do it, the snail can be replaced with a mushroom cooked in chicken stock or sautéed—don't choose anything too strong, such as shiitakes or porcinis; they will compete with the truffles. Opt for something mild and straightforward, like an oyster mushroom or cremini. If you have access to interesting wild mushrooms, hen of the woods would add great texture as well.*

FRIED OYSTERS
WITH BUCKWHEAT AND CAVIAR

SERVES 4

FOR THE DRESSING:

2 tablespoons oyster liquor (liquid
  from shucked oysters)

6 tablespoons dashi (page 231),
  3 tablespoons soy sauce, or to taste

2 tablespoons lemon juice, or to taste

A few grinds of black pepper

FOR THE NOODLE SALAD:

12 ounces dried *naengmyun* noodles
  (Korean buckwheat noodles) or
  Japanese soba

(CONTINUED)

I'm a big soba fan. Earlier, I used the Japanese buckwheat noodles as a jumping-off point for a salad (page 41). Here, they provide the base for another appetizer. I had a particular soba experience in mind: a dish I enjoyed in Japan, where the garnishes are often incorporated into the noodles before they're served. In this memorable instance, the soba was combined with unctuous, velvety uni (sea urchin) and pleasantly slimy and somewhat sticky *yamaimo* (white-fleshed mountain yam). It was a surprising contrast of textures and flavors. The mild nuttiness of the dense pasta collided with the sweet brininess of the creamy uni, while the starchy potato offered a light, fresh, crunchy, slippery slime and an earthy (as opposed to the sea urchin's marine example) sweetness.

Instead of uni and *yamaimo*, I mix fried oysters and caviar into my noodles, and I use *naengmyun*, Korea's chewier answer to soba. It's a different medley of sensations but equally well calibrated. This time, the noodles' cool slipperiness is matched by the oyster, which provides a brackish saltiness. I fry the shellfish to give the dish some crisp crunchiness, which ricochets off the gentle, bursting pops of caviar eggs. The latter, a wonderful complement to oysters, offer an alternative layer of marine salinity. The dressing is a light, ponzu-style sauce that balances the sharp tartness of lemon with soy, the reserved bivalves' juice, and, for depth, dashi broth. You want to control the acidity—too little and the finished product reads flat; too much and the citrus becomes the overpowering star that obscures everything else. You could do a short-cut version of this dish using soba, which are often easier to source than the *naengmyun*; cook them and get them cold, and then toss those with caviar, scallions, and a store-bought ponzu.

Make the dressing: Combine all the ingredients in a small bowl.

Make the noodle salad: In a large pot, bring 3 quarts of water to a boil. Add the noodles and boil for 2 to 3 minutes, until tender. Drain the noodles and immediately rinse in cold water 3 times, or until the water runs clear. In a large bowl, toss the noodles with the remaining ingredients and the dressing. Set aside.

Make the fried oysters: Heat 1 inch of oil in a sauté pan to 350°F. In a shallow bowl, combine the flours, salt, and pepper. Dredge the oysters in the flour mixture. Fry until golden on both sides, turning once halfway through the cooking. Remove to a warmed plate lined with paper towels.

To serve: Divide the noodle salad among 4 plates, top with the oysters, and garnish with the nori (if using). Serve immediately.

FOR THE NOODLE SALAD (CONT'D):

4 tablespoons American sturgeon caviar (paddlefish or hackleback can be substituted)

1 teaspoon grated lemon zest

2 tablespoons thinly sliced (on a bias) scallion greens

½ cup buckwheat sprouts or daikon sprouts (optional)

¼ cup julienned watermelon radish or pink radish

FOR THE FRIED OYSTERS:

Neutral-flavored vegetable oil

⅓ cup buckwheat flour (optional)

⅓ cup Wondra flour

1 teaspoon salt

Several grinds of black pepper

20 oysters, shucked

TO SERVE:

4 pinches shredded nori (optional)

Caviar is a luxury, true. But there are affordable alternatives, and now that we have more U.S.-born varieties of the eggs to choose from, the price range has expanded in a buyer-friendly direction. I like to buy American caviar because I know I'm not getting anything illegal; when it comes to foreign imports, I'm never sure if the regulations are actually being followed. Domestic caviar is also cheaper, and for this preparation you don't need to have the ultra-plus. It's a garnish. If you do feel like splurging on a pricier strain, remember that a little will go a long way. If you'd rather ditch the caviar altogether, there's the perfectly serviceable salmon roe—you can find it in your grocery store, and it will impart wonderful flavor. You can even try trout roe or whitefish caviar. I grew up eating that out of a jar and loved it. My mother used to mix it up with cream cheese.

SOFTSHELL CRAB
WITH A SWEET CORN CUSTARD, CHINESE SAUSAGE, AND GARLIC CHIVES

SERVES 4

FOR THE CUSTARD:

1 large egg

1 large egg yolk

2 cups fresh corn kernels, pureed and pressed through a fine-mesh sieve to make just under 1 cup puree

½ cup heavy cream

1½ teaspoons salt

Black pepper to taste

Sugar as needed, to taste

FOR THE GARLIC CHIVE SAUCE:

1 bunch garlic chive buds, top 1 inch cut off and reserved for garnish and any dry bottoms removed and discarded, or 2 ounces sugarsnap peas

1 teaspoon salt

A few grinds of pepper

½ cup (1 stick) butter, softened

¼ cup lobster stock or chicken stock (page 231)

FOR THE CRABS:

4 medium, or "prime," softshell crabs, cleaned (cut off faces, pull off tails, and remove lungs)

Salt and black pepper

2 tablespoons Wondra flour

3 tablespoons neutral-flavored vegetable oil

(CONTINUED)

It's not unusual to see crab, corn, and bacon brought together in modern American cuisine. That combination certainly helped shape this dish, but so did a Chinese preparation. I was thinking, specifically, of those crab sauces that contain sweet corn and egg. I've never worked in a Chinese restaurant, so I'm not entirely sure how it's done, but my sous chef, who is from Taiwain, thinks it's made with a can of creamed corn. I imagine you would stir your eggs into the corn so that the proteins form solid strands as they cook. The sauce, to which fermented black beans can be added, is usually served over seafood or tofu. I took the ingredients of that sauce (minus the black beans) and repurposed them in a more Western way. The egg and corn become the two main components of a flan, and the crab, here a seasonal softshell, is lightly coated in flour and simply pan-fried for crispness.

With the bacon, I went in the opposite direction and looked East. Chinese sausage is a dried pork product that is cured with salt, sugar, and soy sauce. It's a lot sweeter (and drier) than loose-meat sweet Italian sausage (which, actually, isn't very sweet at all). If you have a hard time finding the *lap cheong* (its Cantonese name), you can use maple-glazed bacon, but any Chinatown grocer should have it, and some Whole Foods carry it. I grew up eating the narrow Chinese tubes (they're thicker than generic beef jerky, but thinner than most Italian links) cut up into fried or sticky rice, or packed into turnip cakes. Its sugar brings out the natural sweetness in the corn, the crab, and the chive blossom. The latter, another Asian item, has the taste of garlic without its concentrated pungency, and when cooked it releases its own natural sugars. It also has a mild grassiness that brightens the other flavors on the plate and delivers something clean and fresh. I use the chive stems to make a compound butter that, once heated and infused with a bit of lobster stock, becomes a bright-green flavor-packed sauce. The blossoms, along with a few kernels of corn, get a quick boil before becoming garnishes.

Make the custard: Preheat the oven to 300°F. Butter 4 (4-ounce) round molds or custard cups or spray them with nonstick cooking spray. In a bowl, beat the egg and egg yolk and stir in the remaining ingredients. Allow all the air bubbles to settle, then divide the custard among the

TO SERVE (CONT'D):

⅓ cup fresh corn kernels

1 Chinese sausage (*lap cheong*), cut into ¼-inch-thick rounds and cooked (see Note)

1 tablespoon lemon juice

Unless I'm dealing with a Japanese chawan mushi (page 81), I tend to approach savory custards from the flan side, and this corn rendition is no different. Although people often worry that there's a lot of technical skill required, it's a surprisingly easy operation. This recipe is a great base that you can build on. It's a cup of anything that has been pureed and, when necessary, strained, to which you add half a cup of heavy cream and whisk in one egg plus another yolk, which will set the flan. Placing the custard in a water bath promotes even, gentle cooking. Covering the pan with foil does the same, and simultaneously keeps the top from forming a crust or hard scum.

---

molds. Place the molds in a hot water bath (see page 16), cover the pan with aluminum foil, and bake until just set, about 40 minutes.

Make the garlic chive sauce: Finely chop the chive stems. Put them in a food processor with the salt, pepper, and butter and puree until smooth. Right before serving, after making the crabs, heat the stock in a small sauté pan over high heat and bring to a boil. Whisk in 4 tablespoons of the chive butter to emulsify.

Make the crabs: Preheat the oven to 400°F. Heat a large sauté pan over high heat. Season the crabs on both sides with salt and pepper, then dust lightly with the flour. Add the oil to the pan and when it is just beginning to smoke, add the crabs, top side down. Lower the heat to medium-high and cook until browned and crisp, 2 to 3 minutes, then turn and brown on the other side.

To serve: Return the custards to the water bath and put in the oven to reheat.

Put the corn kernels and reserved chive tops in a saucepan with a little salted water and bring to a boil; drain. Unmold the custards onto the centers of round serving plates. Spoon a little sauce around each. Place a few rounds of the Chinese sausage around and top the sauce with the corn and chive tops. Top the custards with the crabs, drizzle with the lemon juice, and serve.

NOTE: Cook the *lap cheong* over low heat in a dry sauté pan until slightly browned and crisp (the sugars in the sausage tend to burn so they require low heat).

I choose Wondra flour for dredging the softshell crab because it doesn't clump and is finer than all-purpose flour. It yields a more uniform layer for a cleaner fry. In most high-end professional kitchens, Wondra is used to coat fish before cooking because it prevents sticking and results in a nice thin shell. With something as delicate as this crab, it's particularly effective—you get just the right crisp without a weighty batter. If it's not readily available, regular flour is a reliable substitute.

GRILLED OCTOPUS
WITH GARLIC CHIVES AND FINGERLING POTATO SALAD

I've tried all the tricks that anyone has ever suggested to make octopus tender. There's the one about cooking the tentacles with a wine cork; another insists there has to be a little vinegar in the water. Traditionally, recipes call for long periods of pounding against a hard, rough stone, as it's done in Greece. The cork, in my experiment at least, didn't do anything. Neither did the vinegar, except to impart a little of that flavor. And the pounding—unless I did it incorrectly—resulted in ripped and ugly bits of cephalopod meat. I've found that the best way, if you're going to grill it Mediterranean style, is just to braise the octopus first for three to four hours. After the tentacles have spent quality time in that pot, you can easily slip off their gelatinous outer part to reveal white, smooth, horn-shaped pieces ready to be marinated and grilled. The meat is so succulent; as soon as you taste it, you realize why the braising was worth it. Once the octopus has achieved its perfect texture and picked up some smoky char from the grill, it doesn't need much improvement.

As a final touch, and to honor every usable part of the main ingredient, I take a cue from my favorite sushi restaurant in New York City, Jewel Bako. One night, when I was having dinner at the counter, the chef made a salad for me out of the tiny suction cups. I loved it because it was something I had never seen before; it made me think about the qualities of these little parts of the animal and why they are so special. They're not as soft as the braised tentacle flesh, and they're less chewy than a sashimi slice. In addition, they present a striking visual contrast with their diminutive size, unique shape, and deep purple color. You can easily remove them after you've performed the initial blanching of the octopus, and before you begin braising. It's a small gesture, but it provides an element of surprise.

Bring a large pot of salted water to a boil. With tongs, dip the octopus into the boiling water, count to three, and remove. When the water reboils, repeat two more times. Remove about 28 of the suction cups of varying sizes and set aside in the refrigerator. Return the octopus to the water and bring to a simmer. Cook, replenishing the water if necessary to keep the octopus covered, for 3½ hours, or until tender. Remove from the water and let cool slightly. Remove and discard the outer layer of

SERVES 4

Salt

1 small octopus, cleaned

2 lengthwise slices red onion

Rice wine vinegar

FOR THE POTATO SALAD:

1 cup fingerling potatoes cut on a mandoline into rounds

1 clove garlic, smashed to a paste

2 tablespoons lemon juice

2 teaspoons mustard

6 tablespoons extra-virgin olive oil

Salt and black pepper to taste

TO GRILL AND SERVE:

Salt and black pepper

About 28 garlic chive buds, hard bottoms removed, or green garlic or garlic scapes (optional)

1 tablespoon olive oil

1 small purple potato, finely diced, cooked, and cooled (optional)

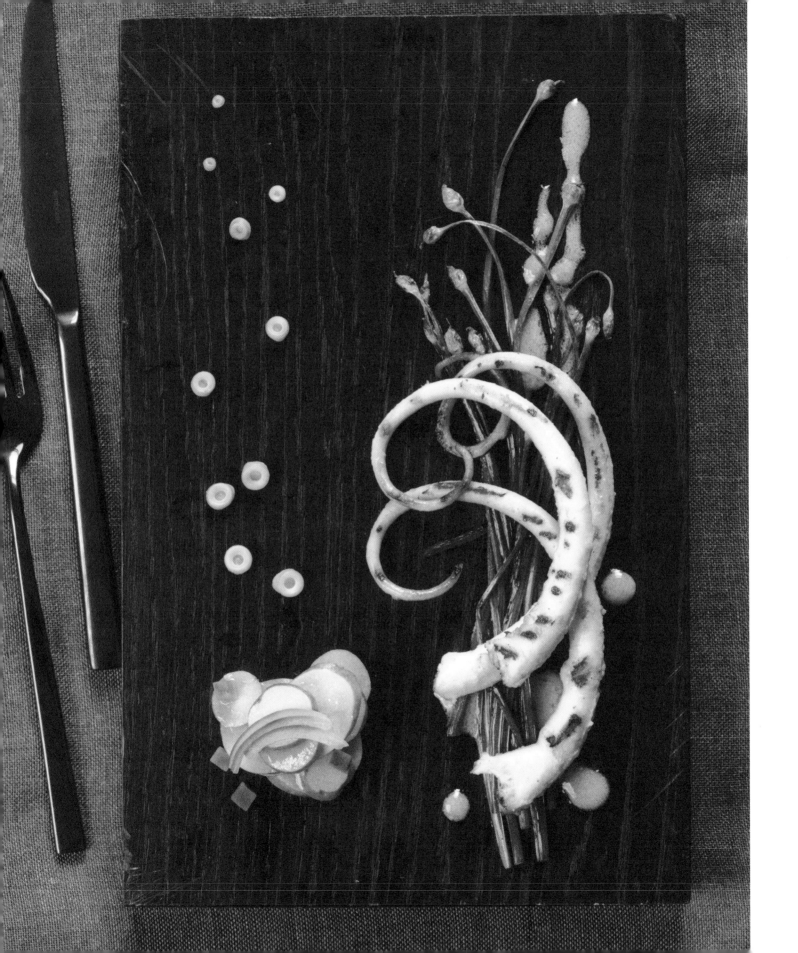

the tentacles—this part should easily slough off with your hands, leaving round white tubes that taper at the ends.

Put the onion in a small bowl with enough vinegar to cover and let steep until the onion is bright pink, about 30 minutes; drain.

Make the potato salad: Cook the potatoes in salted water over medium to medium-high heat until fork tender. Drain and set aside. Put the garlic, lemon juice, and mustard in a bowl and whisk in the oil in a thin stream to emulsify. Season to taste with salt and pepper. Use a quarter of this to marinate the tentacles. Mix half of the remaining vinaigrette with the fingerling potatoes, and season to taste with salt and pepper.

To grill and serve: Season the marinated octopus with salt and pepper and grill until marked and heated through. (You could also use a broiler if you don't have access to a grill—the goal is to get a quick char on the octopus, which has already been cooked.) Combine the garlic chive buds with the oil and season with salt and pepper. Grill. Divide the potato salad among 4 serving plates. Garnish with the red onion and the diced purple potato (if using). Use the remaining vinaigrette to garnish the plate, then lay the garlic chive buds and grilled octopus on top. Decorate with the suction cups, and serve.

I also love eating octopus thinly sliced in sashimi form. If you want to enjoy it that way, try the Japanese method of cleaning the seafood with daikon and coarse salt and treat it to a quick cook (blanch it briefly three times).

BARBECUED SQUID
WITH EDAMAME AND BOILED PEANUTS

SERVES 4

FOR THE SQUID BODIES:

¼ cup light brown sugar

¾ cup granulated sugar

½ cup fish sauce

5 cloves garlic

2 stalks lemongrass, dry leaves
   removed, roughly chopped

4 (5- to 6-inch) squid bodies,
   cleaned, outside scored (reserve the
   tentacles)

FOR THE VINAIGRETTE:

1 tablespoon fish sauce

2 tablespoons lime juice

1 tablespoon sugar

1 small clove garlic, smashed to a
   paste

1 small Thai bird chile, habanero, or
   jalapeño, finely chopped, or more or
   less to taste

2 tablespoons peanut oil

FOR THE FRIED SQUID TENTACLES
(OPTIONAL; SEE NOTES):

Tentacles reserved from 4 squid

About ¼ cup milk

½ cup all-purpose flour

1 teaspoon salt, plus more for
   seasoning fried tentacles

Several grinds of black pepper

Neutral-flavored vegetable oil

FOR THE SALAD:

1 cup shelled edamame

(CONTINUED)

This appetizer is not unlike the pork ribs stuffed with kohlrabi discussed on page 163. The idea that calamari and spare ribs could have much in common might seem odd, but each dish showcases the same combination of flavors, to a different end result.

The squid features a Vietnamese take on barbecue; it is marinated in a combination of light brown and white sugars, fish sauce, garlic, and lemongrass. What differentiates the preparation from its Southeast Asian counterparts is the choice of herbs deployed for the accompanying salad—Thai basil and mint. Instead of the traditional crushed roasted peanuts, I use whole, boiled peanuts, which, although they're associated with the American South, I've never actually tried in that region. I like them because they're less nutty than conventional store-bought peanuts and have a legume-y quality. You might call them the edamame of the South. The young green soybeans, compared to the boiled peanuts, are more vegetal, with quieter nutlike undertones. They're both included in this dish because of their complementary natures and sizes—together, they form the culinary equivalent of a pun.

Marinate the squid bodies: Put the brown and granulated sugars, fish sauce, garlic, and lemongrass in a small food processor or hand blender attachment and puree. Let sit for 30 minutes, then pour through a fine-mesh sieve to remove large bits of lemongrass. Pour over the squid and let marinate for at least 1 hour at room temperature or overnight refrigerated.

Make the vinaigrette: Combine all the ingredients together in a small bowl.

Make the fried squid tentacles, if desired: Put the tentacles in a large bowl with enough milk to cover. In a separate bowl, combine the flour, 1 teaspoon of salt, and pepper. Heat 1 inch of oil in a small saucepan to 350°F. Remove the tentacles from the milk and dredge them in the flour mixture, shaking off any excess. Fry until golden brown and crisp, turning once halfway through the cooking, if necessary, and drain on a paper towel. Season with salt.

FOR THE SALAD (CONT'D):

1 cup boiled, shelled fresh peanuts
   (see Notes)

½ teaspoon finely diced red onion

4 large leaves fresh Thai basil, cut
   into thin strips

4 large leaves fresh mint, cut into thin
   strips

1 teaspoon salt

Several grinds of black pepper

TO GRILL AND SERVE:

Salt

Several grinds of black pepper

2 tablespoons neutral-flavored
   vegetable oil

2 tablespoons hoisin mixed with
   1 tablespoon water (optional)

¼ teaspoon sriracha (optional)

24 baby frilly red mustard leaves
   (optional)

Make the salad: Combine the edamame, peanuts, onion, basil, and mint in a bowl and season with the salt and pepper. Add the vinaigrette and toss to combine.

To grill and serve: Divide the salad among 4 serving plates.

Brush off any excess marinade from the squid bodies, season lightly with salt and pepper, and drizzle with the oil. Grill for about 1 minute per side, just until they curl into cylinders. Cut into ⅓-inch-thick round pinwheels and place on top of the salad. Frame with the hoisin sauce and decorate with a few dots of sriracha (if using). Top with the mustard greens (if using), tossed in any vinaigrette left in the bottom of the salad bowl, and garnish each serving with a fried tentacle.

NOTES: Boil fresh peanuts in salted water for 3 hours, then shell. Or use more edamame with a sprinkling of crushed roasted salted peanuts.

   If you don't wish to fry the tentacles, simply marinate and grill them along with the squid bodies.

It has been said before, but bears repeating: Squid must be cooked really fast over high heat—it immediately begins to curl—or slowly, for a long braise. You don't have to grill it here if you don't have access to a grill; you could sauté the seafood. Just make sure you use a hot, hot pan, such as a wok.

UNAGI
WITH CELERY ROOT AND WASABI

Unagi, or freshwater eel, with anything sweet and starchy is delicious. Celery root has both of those traits, so it's the perfect match. I like to present it in remoulade form, which is a classic way to treat the root vegetable. I learned to make it in France, where they invented the preparation; comparable to cole slaw, it's a salad mixed with mayonnaise and a lot of mustard.

To play off the eel, a staple of Japanese cuisine, I add that country's mustard, *karashi*, and some horseradish-like *wasabi* to this remoulade; those condiments' spiciness cuts through the sweet, wondrously gelatinous eel and offers a balancing contrast.

In Japan, unagi is considered a summertime delicacy, and out on Long Island we have summer eeling too. I caught one once in Manhattan. It was off Pier 40 on the Hudson River, and while I would never eat a catch from those waters, this particular fish does make a good striper bait. Dealing with a just-caught example isn't for the faint of heart. You have to skin it live, which is challenging. This requires impaling the creature with a meat hook to the head, and, although the thing is still moving, making an incision around the neck, then peeling its skin off like a sock, or, as my cooking school teacher described it, a condom.

Surprisingly, the Japanese think eel is an aphrodisiac—because of its shape, perhaps. All I know is that I can't get enough of the rich, sweet serpentine fish. It is best to make it fresh yourself, as with most things. But here in the United States, it's easiest to find it already barbecued and frozen, which is all you need for this straightforward, low-maintenance recipe.

Make the unagi sauce: Place all the ingredients in a saucepan and simmer over medium heat until syrupy and reduced to about ½ cup. Remove and discard the ginger and let cool.

Make the celery-root "remoulade": Combine the mayonnaise, mustard powder mixture, mustard seeds, lemon juice, and lemon zest in a bowl. Add the celery root and scallion, season with salt and pepper, and toss to combine.

To serve: Preheat the oven or a toaster oven to 350°F. Cut the unagi into 4 equal pieces, put them on a baking sheet, brush with a little of the unagi sauce, and place in the oven to just heat through. Divide the "remoulade" among 4 serving plates and top with the unagi. Ring with

SERVES 4

FOR THE UNAGI SAUCE:
3 tablespoons dashi (page 231; optional)
1 tablespoon mirin
¼ cup soy sauce
2 tablespoons sugar
¼ cup light corn syrup
2 slices fresh ginger
Black pepper to taste

FOR THE CELERY-ROOT "REMOULADE":
¼ cup mayonnaise
1 tablespoon dry mustard powder mixed with 1 tablespoon water
1 teaspoon brown mustard seeds
1 teaspoon lemon juice
Pinch of grated lemon zest
1 small celery root, peeled and julienned (about 2 packed cups)
2 tablespoons thinly sliced (on a bias) scallion greens
¾ teaspoon salt
Black pepper

TO SERVE:
1 (12-ounce) package frozen unagi (contains one eel)
1 teaspoon prepared wasabi (if you can only find the powdered kind, mix it with a little water according to the package directions)
4 pinches of finely julienned celery root, shallow-fried until crisp (optional)
Salt
4 pinches julienned scallion greens

a little of the sauce and dot with a few very small bits of wasabi. Season the fried celery root (if using) with salt, then top the unagi with it and the scallion and serve immediately.

You can easily make a more wintery, rich dish by doing a celery-root puree instead of the remoulade—roast or boil the peeled and chopped root, then puree it with cream and a little butter—or even try a flan (see page 86 for a corn custard, and substitute cooked and pureed celery root for the corn). Since karashi *isn't readily available in most places across the country, I've substituted dry mustard powder here. If you are fortunate enough to find the real thing, you can use the same amount. Japanese hot mustard is quite spicy, though, so proceed with caution.*

FRIED MUSSELS
WITH OVERNIGHT TOMATOES, HARISSA, AND SAFFRON SULTANAS

SERVES 4

FOR THE OVERNIGHT TOMATOES:

4 ripe, large beefsteak tomatoes, halved, stem base removed

2 tablespoons olive oil

2 large garlic cloves, sliced

4 sprigs each fresh thyme and tarragon

Salt and black pepper

Harissa to taste (recipe follows—store-bought harissa can be substituted)

FOR THE SAFFRON SULTANAS:

2 tablespoons sultanas (golden raisins)

About 3 tablespoons white wine

Pinch of salt

Pinch of saffron threads

FOR THE FRIED MUSSELS:

1 cup all-purpose flour

1 teaspoon ground coriander

1 teaspoon ground cumin

1 teaspoon ground cinnamon

½ teaspoon turmeric

Salt and black pepper

28 extra-large mussels, shucked

Neutral-flavored vegetable oil

TO SERVE:

1 tablespoon sliced fresh parsley

People are constantly asking me where I get my inspiration. I usually reply that it can be found anywhere: travel, books, a childhood meal, an ingredient I've never tasted, or a new technique. Often I'm inspired by the people I work with, especially cooks who come from faraway locales and have access to foreign food cultures that are sometimes completely unfamiliar to me.

This dish happens to have its roots right here in the West Village of New York; it was inspired by Toby, an old fishing buddy I met on the Hudson River the summer before Jen and I opened *annisa*, when we were still looking for spaces and writing our business plan. Since then, Toby has occasionally stopped by *annisa* to dine at the bar, which is where I like to chat with regulars when I need a break from the kitchen. On one visit, he told me of his fried mussels—if I recall correctly, they're simply breaded and shallow-fried. It was such a brilliant idea. At the same time, it's an obvious preparation if you consider that other bivalves, such as oysters, are often cooked like this. I was excited to take a common ingredient and showcase it in a way that was new to me.

The resulting creation takes the strong-flavored mussels and treats them to the Mediterranean and North African flavors of saffron, tomato, raisins, cinnamon, cumin, and coriander. The recipe for harissa, a chile paste associated with North Africa, is borrowed from a Palestinian intern, who passed on her mother's instructions for making the condiment, explaining that it is also produced in her homeland.

Make the overnight tomatoes: Preheat the oven to 300°F. Put the tomatoes in a bowl and toss with the oil, garlic, herbs, and salt and pepper to taste. Arrange on a baking sheet, cut side down, hiding any loose herbs or garlic underneath the tomato halves. Bake for 15 minutes. Remove the skins and return the tomatoes to the oven. Turn the oven temperature to as low as it goes (you can let the tomatoes sit overnight with the heat from the oven pilot light) and bake until the tomatoes are dried and concentrated and have lost three-quarters of their volume. Discard the herbs and garlic and roughly chop the tomatoes. Season with harissa. Taste and adjust the seasonings. Keep warm or reheat just before serving.

Make the saffron sultanas: Put the raisins in a small saucepan with enough wine to just cover. Add the salt and saffron and simmer over medium heat until reduced and glossy.

Make the fried mussels: Combine the flour, spices, and salt and pepper to taste in a shallow bowl. Dredge the mussels in the flour mixture. In a heavy pot, heat 2 inches of oil to 375°F. Fry the mussels until golden. Drain on a paper towel.

To serve: Place the fried mussels on top of a bed of the tomato mixture, garnished with the sultanas and parsley.

> *Like Toby's, the mussels in this recipe are also good shallow-fried, a technique that saves on oil—one inch of it in a skillet is enough. The process for cooking the tomatoes renders them concentrated and flavorful, like the essence of tomato in sauce form. They're wonderful on toast for a quick canapé or rustic bruschetta, or with eggs, so make extra.*

HARISSA

MAKES 1½ CUPS SAUCE

1 pint spicy red chiles, chopped in a
 food processor
1 heaping tablespoon kosher salt
Olive oil

Combine the chiles and salt and put in a clean 1-quart ceramic bowl. Let ferment at room temperature, uncovered, for 1 week, stirring every other day. Add enough oil to cover the surface of the mixture to prevent oxidation, then cover the bowl and refrigerate. The harissa can be kept in an airtight container in the refrigerator for up to 2 months.

CHAPTER THREE

FROM THE SEA

INSPIRATION: FISHING

The first fish I ever caught was taken in the Hudson River on the west side of Manhattan. I used a soft plastic lure with a lead head jig—a very realistic-looking fake fish with a hook coming out of its back; its tail trills as you reel it in, mimicking a swimming bait fish.

This was the summer before I opened *annisa*. I had always been fascinated with the idea of fishing, but up until then I hadn't had the time or wherewithal to learn. Fearless Jennifer, my then partner, had taken us to Kmart in Ohio and bought rods and reels, and my mother's boyfriend, Ivan, had taught us how to cast. With plenty of time to kill (no pun intended) while we were looking for restaurant spaces, we became part of a small motley fishing community centered on Pier 40, where Houston Street hits the river. The major players were Matt Umanov, a guitar-store owner who is actually allergic to fish and whom I met at the bait vending machine (yes, these exist and look just like soda dispensers); Toby, who was in charge of the pier's redevelopment program (at the time, they were going to turn it into a park and had architects from all over the world visiting to submit their bids for the structure); Candy, a caterer, and her musician husband, Dave, who worked for Matt; Brian, a construction worker who lived above the Rocking Horse Tavern; Jerry, a laundromat owner straight out of a kinder, gentler *Sopranos*; a mother (no one can remember her name, sadly) whose son played soccer on the roof of the pier; and Annis, who, back then, was twelve years old (he subsequently became a chain-smoking superintendent in the neighborhood). Often, someone would fire up the barbecue, cook some hot dogs, and pop open some beers, and a spontaneous party would occur. It was one of the few places since high school where I felt as though I "fit in."

I think I was the only person who caught anything in that fateful first-fish day. Plenty of the river dwellers were biting, but none were being landed.

When my fish finally hit, it didn't fight very hard, but once I got it to the pier's edge it was so heavy that I had to adjust the drag on the reel in order to lift my catch over the edge. It was a decent-sized fish, silver and speckled, and I had no idea what it was. I also had an incredibly difficult time detaching it from the lure. Luckily, one of the Parks Department's interns was there, and had a fish classification book and a good pair of pliers. We eventually identified it as a weakfish, a sea trout–like creature named for its lips, which tend to tear when you hook them. I had no interest in eating the spoils of my victory, but the intern said he would take it home and cook it, which made me feel better that it had died while my inexperienced hands tried to extract it from the lure. Candy, or someone from the pier, took a picture, and we went home.

In the days that followed, I was stopped by no fewer than two strangers, once on said pier, and once at the tackle shop about a mile away. "You're the one that caught that *fish*!" As it was the only fish I'd ever nabbed, I was quick to figure out what they were talking about. Being new to fishing, I gave a factual recounting of the landing and subsequent species identification. But after the second encounter, I was beginning to think I had accomplished something special.

A week later, we returned to the pier and found a picture of me, holding the fish, posted on the glass door that led to an indoor area where the architect's designs were being displayed. I recall thinking, "Wow, I don't remember it being that big," and feeling sort of proud. Then Candy came up and said, "*Some fish*! How are you holding up that monster with one hand?" After getting a few seemingly humble acknowledgments from me, she finally stuck it to me: "Photoshop, baby!"

I. SHELLFISH

SHELLFISH AND KIMCHI STEW

SERVES 4

2 tablespoons neutral-flavored vegetable oil

2 teaspoons sesame oil

1 small onion, chopped (about ⅔ cup)

3 cloves garlic, sliced

1½ cups kimchi, with juice

1 piece kombu, rinsed

¼ cup dried anchovies (*iriko*)

12 littleneck or Manila clams, scrubbed

20 mussels, scrubbed

12 large shrimp, shelled and deveined

8 large sea scallops, cleaned

1 cup daikon or silken tofu cut into bite-size pieces

1 cup zucchini cut into bite-size pieces

2 squid bodies, cleaned, cut into bite-size pieces, and scored

3 tablespoons fish sauce, or to taste

2 tablespoons soy sauce, or to taste

1 tablespoon sugar

Several grinds of black pepper

2 tablespoons thinly sliced (on a bias) scallion greens

I love soups and stews. This one isn't anything anyone taught me; it's an amalgam of what I thought was needed to make it taste the way I imagined it should, and can be prepared with whatever you have on hand—fish, shellfish, tofu cubes, or some combination thereof. I used to serve it for staff meals, because it was a great way to use the off-cuts of fish that weren't getting placed on diners' plates. Nothing goes to waste. You can also add any leftover kimchi you have lying around. (Buying new kimchi is okay too.) No matter what I toss in, everyone seems to love the end result. Perfect for home cooking, it's a one-pot pleaser that can be put together in thirty minutes.

First, you sweat the usual enhancers, onions and garlic—lots of it—plus the kimchi in some sesame oil. Next, you pour in the major components of your cooking liquid—water and its flavorings. For those, instead of creating a regular dashi, the kombu or kelp-broth used as the basis for most Japanese stews and noodle dishes and one of my favorite ingredients, I combine kombu with dried anchovies to give the stock some saltier, fish-derived complexity. You bring everything to a boil and then let it simmer. At the end, the seafood goes in, along with some vegetables—daikon (Japanese radish) and zucchini. You finish the dish with fish sauce, sugar, soy, and some reserved kimchi juice and garnish with some fresh green scallions.

Even better than the daikon is its green-topped Korean equivalent, the moo. *The latter is denser, which is why I prefer it, but the Japanese variety is a lot easier to find. In the recipe, I suggest tofu as a substitute for the radish. It can be an alternative, but you should feel free to add both. If you're going to include the tofu and you feel like taking an extra but worthwhile step, you can fry it first—make sure you dredge it in cornstarch for a crisp outer layer that shatters when eaten—and save it to use as a garnish so it doesn't get soggy.*

In a large pot, heat the vegetable and sesame oils and add the onion. Cook over medium heat until softened, then add the garlic and stir. Add the kimchi and stir, then add 6 cups water, the kombu, and dried anchovies and bring to a boil. Simmer for 8 minutes, then remove the kombu, cut it into thin strips, and return it to the pot. Add the clams and simmer for 3 minutes, then add the mussels, shrimp, scallops, and daikon and bring to a boil. Add the zucchini, then the squid, and season with the fish sauce, soy sauce, sugar, and pepper. When the squid and zucchini are just cooked through, remove from the heat. Garnish with the scallions and serve.

GRILLED CUTTLEFISH IN ITS OWN INK
WITH QUINOA AND MUSSELS

In French, the following appetizer might have been called *seiche en deuil*, or "cuttlefish in mourning," as it is a whole cuttlefish dressed in black—that is, served with a sauce made from its own dark ink. But in ancient times the color black was associated as much with rebirth as with death. The story goes that, thousands of years ago, Egyptians saw that the black mud from the Nile was very fertile; leftover embedded seeds of plants that had died in the silt would sprout and grow quickly there. The mud's engendering powers were associated with its color. Thus, that hue is prevalent in funerary scenes. Anubis, a god of the underworld, is depicted as a black dog, or a jackal-headed figure with an ebony face, and helps to resurrect the deceased in the afterlife. In a related reference, the word *chemistry* comes from the Egyptian *kemet*, or "black land." The ancient people of the Nile were exceptionally gifted at combining raw materials to make medicine; the term "black magic" was a simple reference to Egypt.

This preparation, which inadvertently touches on these themes of blackness and rebirth, was originally inspired by a snack I had at the Boqueria, a large covered marketplace in Barcelona. I'm not sure they were actually eggs, but the Spaniards call them *huevos de chocos* (cuttlefish eggs). As I experienced them that day, they were the oval parts found inside the cuttlefish, simply sautéed in olive oil and finished with lemon and parsley. In

SERVES 4
FOR THE MUSSELS:
2 tablespoons olive oil
1 shallot, minced
2 cloves garlic, chopped
½ cup white wine
1 pound Prince Edward Island mussels
1 bay leaf
1 sprig fresh thyme
1 sprig fresh tarragon
1 sprig fresh parsley
1 sprig fresh cilantro
FOR THE CUTTLEFISH:
4 small, fresh cuttlefish, gutted, ink sacs removed (your fishmonger can do this) and reserved, or cleaned squid plus 1 tablespoon frozen squid ink
(CONTINUED)

FOR THE CUTTLEFISH (CONT'D):

2 cloves garlic, finely chopped

3 sprigs fresh thyme

2 tablespoons lemon juice

3 tablespoons olive oil

FOR THE QUINOA SALAD:

1 cup quinoa

2 tablespoons plus 1 teaspoon salt

1½ tablespoons lemon juice, or to
   taste

½ tablespoon lime juice

Large pinch grated lemon zest

Small pinch grated lime zest

⅓ cup extra-virgin olive oil

1 tablespoon chopped fresh chives

1 heaping teaspoon chopped fresh
   cilantro

Black pepper to taste

TO GRILL AND SERVE:

Salt and black pepper to taste

1 tablespoon extra-virgin olive oil

1 tablespoon butter

Lemon juice to taste

addition to these "eggs," I use quinoa, a grainlike seed originally cultivated by the Inca. The lime and cilantro echo the quinoa's Andean roots while providing bracing acidity and herbal greenness to bring out the sweetness of the cephalopod. The mussels simply accentuate the cuttlefish's oceanic notes.

For me, this study in cuttlefish, at least today, reads as a Spanish-influenced representation of an Egyptian theme because it incorporates eggs (even if figurative) and seeds into a black-stained dish. It taps into an even larger theme: Food itself is at the juncture of death and life. Through the act of eating—taking what's no longer alive to nourish ourselves—death is transformed into life. Cuisine, in a way, is "chemistry"—a mixing and manipulating of raw ingredients to create a new, delicious whole. At its best, cooking—what's written into a recipe, or tasted on the spoon—is layered in flavor and in meaning. A dish is a text: taste, interpret, and it may tell you a story.

Make the mussels: Heat a small saucepan over high heat, add the oil and shallot, then lower the heat to medium and cook until translucent but not browned. Add the garlic and stir. Add the wine and increase the heat to high. Add the mussels, bay leaf, and herbs and cover. Cook until the mussels open and are cooked through, about 3 minutes. Remove the mussels to a plate and cool, then extract the meat from the shells and set aside. Pour the cooking liquid through a fine-mesh sieve into a bowl and put in the refrigerator until cold.

Make the cuttlefish: Remove the tentacles from each cuttlefish in one piece; extract the beak. Peel the body cavity, then open it from the belly with a sharp knife and score the outside fairly deeply but not all the way through. Remove and save the "eggs" (the two white oval pieces inside the body cavity). Remove the ink sacs and soak them in ¼ cup cold mussel cooking liquid. Remove the sacs then drain their ink into the mussel liquid, pressing with a ladle or spoon until dry. Place the sacs back in the same liquid, stir, and strain again in order to extract as much ink as possible. Discard the empty ink sacs. Put the cuttlefish bodies, tentacles, and "eggs" in a bowl, and add the garlic, thyme, lemon juice, and oil. Set aside to marinate for at least an hour, or up to overnight, refrigerated.

Make the quinoa salad: Rinse the quinoa well 3 times in cold water to remove bitterness. In a large saucepan, bring 2 quarts of water to a boil and add 2 tablespoons of the salt. Add the quinoa and cook at a hard simmer for 10 minutes or until al dente—the quinoa should be soft with a little popping texture and still hold up as individual grains. Drain in a fine-mesh sieve and let cool to room temperature. Transfer to a bowl and stir in the lemon and lime juices and zest, oil, chives, and cilantro and season with the remaining 1 teaspoon of salt and the pepper.

Grill the cuttlefish: Brush off any extra marinade from the cuttlefish, then season on both sides with salt and pepper. Place the bodies on a hot grill, scored side down, along with the tentacles. Cook until nicely marked, then turn 45 degrees and mark again. Turn over and finish the cooking (once it completely curls and is no longer translucent, it's done), then place on a warm plate.

Meanwhile, heat a small sauté pan over high heat. Add the oil, and when smoking, add the cuttlefish "eggs," lower the heat to medium-high, and cook until lightly browned. Turn and finish the cooking on the other side. Remove to the warm plate with the rest of the cuttlefish. Add 3 tablespoons of the reserved mussel liquid and the mussels to the pan and heat through. Remove to the warm plate with the cuttlefish. Add the cuttlefish ink to the pan and heat over high heat. Add the butter and swirl to emulsify. Season to taste with pepper, lemon juice, and salt, if necessary (the mussel juice has much natural salinity).

To serve: Place an off-centered mound of the quinoa salad on each serving plate. Let the grilled cuttlefish body naturally curve over the quinoa, and place the tentacles at the head of the body so that the cuttlefish looks as it would normally, when whole. Place a puddle of the sauce on the other side and decorate with the mussels and cuttlefish "eggs."

GRILLED SHRIMP
WITH TAMARIND, ROASTED PEPPER, AND CHILE

SERVES 8 AS AN APPETIZER OR 4
AS AN ENTRÉE

1½ pounds head-on large shrimp,
  peeled, deveined, tail feathers left
  on, 8 heads reserved

1 teaspoon garlic paste (from about
  2 cloves)

1 to 2 tablespoons *nam prik pao* (Thai
  chile–tamarind paste)

3 tablespoons neutral-flavored
  vegetable oil

FOR THE SAUCE:

2 yellow bell peppers

1 tablespoon neutral-flavored
  vegetable oil

3 tablespoons tamarind pulp (see Note)

1 teaspoon *nam prik pao*, or to taste

1½ teaspoons sugar

½ teaspoon salt

A few grinds black pepper

FOR THE QUINOA SALAD:

1 cup quinoa

2 tablespoons plus ¼ teaspoon salt

3 tablespoons lemon juice

3 tablespoons olive oil

1 tablespoon thinly sliced (on a bias)
  scallion greens

1 tablespoon chopped fresh mint

A few grinds black pepper

FOR THE SHRIMP HEADS (OPTIONAL):

½ cup cornstarch

Pinch of salt and a few grinds of
  pepper

Neutral-flavored vegetable oil

(CONTINUED)

I'm not sure exactly where this recipe comes from. It uses Thai ingredients, but doesn't register as Southeast Asian; once you factor in the quinoa salad and a roasted yellow pepper sauce, you're left with something distinctly American. That sauce dates the dish—pepper purees were big in the 1990s—but twenty years later this brightly colored example still works. What wasn't typical of that culinary era is quinoa. No one knew what it was back then. Now, it's everywhere and in different forms—along with traditional white, there's Inca red and wild black. I can't remember how I was introduced to the grain; by another restaurant's menu, perhaps, or maybe my Central American prep cook brought it to me. While others approach quinoa like rice, I have my own technique: After rinsing them, I boil the seeds in ample water to help remove any residual bitterness, then drain them. Making sure the quinoa isn't overcooked will keep it fluffy.

The quinoa, simply dressed with olive oil, lemon, and chive, becomes a bed for the shrimp. These clean, fresh notes don't distract from the yellow pepper's acidic sweetness or the shrimp's pungent spice, both of which the quinoa absorbs. Tamarind is the secret ingredient. Its juice lends the yellow pepper some sour complexity, and once it's combined with Thai chile to form the paste known as *nam prik pao*, the tree-grown fruit gives the shrimp a distinct, bold burst of sharp heat. The ideal quick dinner, this requires little effort and yields tons of flavor. The shrimp's seasonings can be slathered on right before grilling; there's no need to marinate. And the seafood can always be broiled if that's preferable to firing up a grill.

Toss the shrimp with the garlic, *nam prik pao*, and oil and set aside.

Make the sauce: Heat a broiler to high. Coat the peppers with the oil and place them under the broiler. When the tops are blackened, turn and blacken the other sides. Place in a bowl, cover with plastic wrap, and let steam for 5 minutes. Peel and remove the seeds, saving any accumulated juices. Put the flesh in a blender and pour the juices through a sieve into the blender. Add the remaining ingredients and blend until smooth.

Make the quinoa salad: Rinse the quinoa 3 times in cold water to remove bitterness. In a large saucepan, bring 2 quarts water to a boil and add 2 tablespoons of the salt. Add the quinoa and cook at a hard simmer for 10 minutes or until al dente—the grains should be soft with a little popping

FOR GRILLING:

½ **teaspoon salt**

A few grinds black pepper

texture and still hold up as individual grains. Drain in a fine-mesh sieve and let cool to room temperature. In a bowl, toss the quinoa with the remaining salt, the lemon juice, oil, scallions, mint, and pepper.

Make the shrimp heads, if desired: Heat 1 to 2 inches of oil in a shallow, straight-sided pan to 350°F. Season the cornstarch with the salt and pepper. Dredge the heads in the cornstarch and fry, turning once, until crisp. Drain on a paper towel and keep warm (a toaster oven set at 250°F will work).

Season the shrimp with salt and pepper and grill or broil until the thickest part is just slightly translucent at the very center (shrimp are best when not overcooked). They should get nice char marks, the grill should actually sizzle, and when you see the shrimp slightly curl, you know they're starting to cook and then it's only a matter of 1 or 2 minutes more. Serve with the sauce, quinoa salad, and fried heads (if using).

NOTE: Either use ready-made Thai tamarind pulp, or soak 3 tablespoons of a block of tamarind in 3 tablespoons hot water and push it through a fine-mesh sieve to remove seeds and fibers.

> *The shrimp would make a great hors d'oeuvre on its own, or with the puree served on the side as a dipping sauce. If you can't find head-on shrimp, use cleaned shrimp and skip the fried-head garnish.*

RAGOUT OF LOBSTER, STEAMER CLAMS, AND CORN
WITH CHANTERELLES AND TARRAGON

Lobster was always my favorite ingredient. Every year, growing up, I ate it on my birthday. A pound and a quarter was never enough. While it's difficult for me to eat that much now, I still love the coral-shelled delicacy. In my opinion, butter and lobster are just fantastic together. That was always my preferred way to enjoy seafood, simply with drawn butter, as it's done at clambakes. I also enjoy old-fashioned lobster rolls made with mayonnaise.

Here is a dish that uses the entire crustacean. The fresh, rich, sweet meat is the ragout's main component and is sautéed in a little butter with some clams, chanterelles, and corn cut off the cob; the shell flavors the stock that thickens the stew, and the tomalley forms a sauce.

Everyone loves this sauce, even people who think they won't. Many people who have seen but not tasted the tomalley are understandably made nervous by it—it's the green part of the shellfish that looks similar to brains. Creamy and delicious, it's actually an organ that performs the duties of both the liver and pancreas; I have loved it since I was a kid. Although I enjoy eating this straight, combining the tomalley with cream and butter creates something that tastes like the essence of lobster and makes this ragout a little more special.

Put the potato in a small saucepan and cover with water. Bring to a boil, add ½ teaspoon of the salt, and cook until a piece breaks apart when stuck with a fork; drain and set aside.

Fill a pot large enough to hold the lobsters with 4 inches of water and bring to a rapid boil. Add the remaining 2 tablespoons salt and the corn. Cover and cook until tender, about 3 minutes. Remove the corn and submerge it in a very large container of ice water to cool.

Remove any rubber bands from the lobster claws and add the lobsters to the boiling water. Cover and cook until just bright red all over, about 8 minutes.

SERVES 4

1 purple potato, cut into ¼-inch dice (optional)

½ teaspoon plus 2 tablespoons salt, plus more for seasoning

4 (1¼-pound) live female lobsters

3 ears corn, shucked

Tomalley, extracted from the lobsters (about 2 tablespoons)

About 2 tablespoons heavy cream (use as much cream as tomalley)

20 live steamer clams (about 2 pounds)

½ cup chanterelle or other wild mushrooms (optional)

5 tablespoons butter

Black pepper

A few drops of lemon juice

½ teaspoon finely choppped fresh tarragon

1 teaspoon chopped fresh chives

Sugar as needed

If you don't want to deal with a whole, live lobster, you can buy the meat already removed from its shell. Just make sure you go to a supplier you trust (preferably one who also sells lobster stock).

Meanwhile, cut the kernels from the corn cobs and set aside. When the lobsters are done, submerge them in the ice water. Extract the meat, reserving any tomalley (the green stuff) and roe (the red stuff). In a small bowl, add the cream to the tomalley and stir with a fork to break up and form a smooth sauce. Push through a fine-mesh sieve if chunky. Finely chop the roe and set aside.

Remove all but ½ inch of water from the pot and reserve it for washing the clams. Bring the water in the pot back to a boil and add the clams. Cover and steam until open, about 3 minutes. Shuck by removing the brown outer skin, rinsing in the reserved water. Set the clams aside. Pour the cooking liquid through a fine-mesh sieve into a bowl, leaving any sediment behind.

In a sauté pan over high heat, cook the chanterelles in 1 tablespoon of the butter until the edges are brown and crisp. Season with a pinch of salt and a few grinds of pepper. Add the corn and 6 tablespoons of the strained clam/lobster cooking liquid. Bring to a boil. Add 2 tablespoons of the remaining butter and swirl to melt. Add the clams and toss to heat through, then remove the pan from the heat.

Place 3 tablespoons of the clam/lobster juice in another small pan and add the chopped roe and lemon juice. Bring to a boil and swirl in the remaining 2 tablespoons butter. Taste and adjust the seasoning if necessary. Add the lobster and reheat over very low heat, turning once.

Add the herbs to the corn. Taste and adjust the seasoning with salt, pepper, and sugar if necessary. Mound the corn mixture in the center of each of 4 large serving plates. Ring with the lobster roe and the tomalley sauce. Dot with the purple potatoes. Place the lobster on top of the corn and serve.

PAN-ROASTED SEA SCALLOPS
WITH UNI, BACON, AND MUSTARD GREENS

For our elimination challenge in the first Champions' Round of *Top Chef*
Masters, we were each asked to present our fellow competitors with a signature dish—subsequently, one of our opponents would have to reinvent
and make the dish his or her own. As none of my true signatures could
have been done in the two hours allotted, I chose this rich scallop entrée,
because it's indicative of my cooking. The seared golden mollusk sits on
a white potato puree, surrounded by a ragout of orange sea urchin, dark
mustard greens, and burgundy-hued bacon. Although the shellfish is the
star, the salty cured meat is the lynchpin; with the bitter greens, the bacon
recalls the Southern collards-and-pork pairing; with the same leaves' mustardy notes, it draws on that condiment's ability to enhance pig parts; with
the briny sea urchin, it calls a chowder to mind; and, with the sweet scallop,
it references a staple of New American cuisine.

My potato puree is based on David Bouley's. His is composed of fingerlings and butter in equal amounts, plus a bit of heavy cream. I apply less
butter and combine fingerlings with Idaho potatoes, which maintain fluffi-
ness and make for a more foolproof outcome. When Hubert Keller reinter-
preted my dish on that television show, I don't remember his straying much
from the original, but I believe he substituted peas for the mustard greens.
Home cooks have a chance to put their own twist on things; for example,
caviar could be used in place of sea urchin, or that component could be
left out entirely.

Make the potato puree: Put the potatoes in a pot, cover with water, and
bring to a boil. Add 1 teaspoon of the salt and cook until the potatoes are
tender. Drain well and pass through a food mill. In a small saucepan, heat
the cream and the butter over medium to medium-high heat until the
butter is melted and the cream is steaming, then whisk the mixture into
the potatoes until well blended and smooth; do not overwhisk, which will
make the potatoes gluey. Season with the remaining salt and pepper.
Cover and set aside in a warm place.

Make the scallops: Heat a pan large enough to hold all the scallops in one
well-spaced layer. Add the oil, and when it's smoking, add the scallops

SERVES 4
FOR THE POTATO PUREE:
½ cup peeled and roughly chopped fingerling potatoes
1 small Idaho potato, peeled and roughly chopped
3 teaspoons salt
⅓ cup heavy cream
½ cup (1 stick) butter
A few grinds black pepper
FOR THE SCALLOPS:
1 tablespoon neutral-flavored vegetable oil
1½ pounds extra-large sea scallops, connector muscle removed (3 or 4 scallops per person)
1 teaspoon salt
Black pepper to taste
FOR THE SAUCE:
1 tablespoon Cognac
¼ cup lobster stock or clam juice
2 tablespoons small bacon lardons, cooked to render fat
¼ cup wide-stem Chinese mustard greens cut (on a bias) into bite-size pieces
¼ cup (½ stick) butter
1 teaspoon chopped fresh chives
Pinch of chopped fresh tarragon
20 pieces sea urchin
1 teaspoon lemon juice, or to taste
¼ teaspoon salt, or to taste
Black pepper to taste

and season with the salt and pepper. Lower the heat to medium-high and cook until golden brown. Turn and cook to desired doneness. (I like them medium-rare, about 2 minutes per side.)

Meanwhile, make the sauce: Heat a small sauté pan over medium-high heat. Add the Cognac, bring to a boil, and cook for 30 seconds to cook off some of the alcohol. Add the stock and lardons and bring to a boil. Add the mustard greens and butter and stir to emulsify. Add the chives and tarragon, then the sea urchin and a little lemon juice to taste. Taste and adjust the seasonings, adding the salt and pepper.

To serve: Place the potato puree in the center of each of 4 large serving plates. Circle the puree with the sauce and try to distribute the lardons and mustard greens evenly. Top the puree with the scallops and serve.

There are endless different kinds of mustard greens and any of them would work in this recipe. You have, to name a few, the red frilly variety, the green frilly type, and the Chinese type called gai choy *that are either small- or, as I prefer for this preparation, wide-stemmed. Those stems are often pickled or, as here, braised. The cooking process tames the sharpness. They retain their mustardy bite but won't overpower the other ingredients. Although quite strong, broccoli rabe, a cousin of these greens, is a viable alternative; if you choose it here, a little bit will be enough.*

II. FISH

STEAMED FISH
WITH SCALLIONS AND GINGER

The most memorable steamed fish I had was one I caught while visiting my sister, who was renting a house up in Bar Harbor, Maine. I was just learning to fish, and had wandered to the fishing pier, down a long flight of log stairs and through a pine forest to a deep, rock-lined portion of the coast. While Jen used a bait net to grapple with an uncooperative lobster, I threw out a weighted line bearing a plastic worm with a bright-yellow spiral tail, let it hit bottom, and slowly retrieved, stopping every two or three feet. On the third leg of my retrieve, *bam!* The rod bent over, and—*jerk, jerk jerk*—I had caught my first sea bass. But this isn't a big fish story; it only took a few minutes to land the bass, and up it came, in all its one-and-a-half-pound, beautiful green, black, and azure glory, its spine glistening, alternately flexing and relaxing in the clean Maine air. I returned to my sister's house, where I scraped and gutted my singular catch on the rock outside, then did this quick and easy preparation along with some steamed rice.

All told, the fish went from ocean floor to table in about an hour. For starters, we had some briny, metallic, Belon-like oysters that we had harvested from a nearby cove at low tide, as well as some blue mussels and periwinkles. Then everyone had a bit of the bass, including my six-year-old niece, Ilana, who, appropriately, ate one of the eyes, which in China are considered a special treat.

This is the recipe of my mom's that I make the most. It's classic Chinese cooking; something that she, in turn, learned from her mother. The ginger brightens the bass, making it seem cleaner and sweeter, much in the same way an acidic element like citrus would. The scallions and soy lend body and depth. The same treatment works for a fillet if you are dining alone or cannot procure an entire fish. It is healthy and clean, and, as such, honors the memory of my mother the doctor. I serve a fancified version of this dish at *annisa* on Mother's Day; I use sautéed micro peashoots and sugarsnap peas, and a bright green scallion oil. I think she would have been proud.

Put the fish in a shallow, heatproof dish. Season lightly with salt and pepper inside and out. Disperse the scallions and ginger on top, underneath, and inside the fish. In a separate bowl, combine the remaining ingredients and pour over the fish. Place the dish with the fish on a rack above boiling water in a suitable pot and cover the pot. Cook until a small knife or skewer can be easily inserted into the thickest part of the body of the fish, 6 to 7 minutes. Serve.

SERVES 4

1 (1½-pound) whole white-fleshed fish, such as black sea bass, scales removed, gutted, flesh scored (on a bias) in 2-inch intervals down to the bone

Salt and black pepper

¼ cup thinly sliced (on a bias) scallion greens

1 heaping tablespoon finely julienned fresh ginger

¼ cup soy sauce

3 tablespoons peanut oil

Dash of sesame oil

Pinch of sugar

Any firm, white-fleshed fish will do, or even salmon or a richer fish such as hamachi (also known as Japanese amberjack or yellowtail). While I wouldn't recommend tuna—the preparation would dry it out—rich tuna belly might work. Once, on a photo shoot out on Long Island, a food stylist tried the recipe with bluefish and I was pleasantly surprised by the results. When in doubt, you can't go wrong with black sea bass, which is easy to find.

SALT-BROILED SPANISH MACKEREL

WITH HEIRLOOM TOMATOES, HIJIKI, AND SWEET ONION

For this low-maintenance late-summer dish, I was inspired by the Spanish mackerels I've had in Japanese izakaya restaurants, which are most easily compared to pubs. The focus is on drinking, but there's always some simple, delicious food served. On many occasions at such establishments, I've happily eaten a broiled piece of the fish placed beneath a salad of raw onions or beside some grated daikon and a side of ponzu sauce. The sweet sharpness of the former cuts the mackerel's oiliness. The radish's dry astringency has a similar effect, while the sauce's soy-vinegar base brings both salt and acid into the equation to counter the fish's fattiness and tie the other ingredients together with a brightening burst of flavor.

My interpretation integrates the onions and daikon, then takes things in another direction with tomatoes and hijiki seaweed. These also balance the mackerel's richness, but there's a different combination of flavors working together. The tomatoes have a subtle, earthy sweetness that's both fruity and vegetal. Sea plants tend to be carriers of umami, which is one reason I like to use hijiki. In this case, though, it also provides a great contrast in color when juxtaposed with the yellow sauce and the jewel tones of the tomato salad. Hijiki has a distinct twiglike shape and character—lots of minerality and, underlying that, a muted nuttiness that reminds me of a buckwheat noodle. It's readily available in health food stores or at Whole Foods, and it's a dried item, so you can get it at any time of year.

The hijiki is simply dressed in the vinaigrette. I use Vidalia onions here; conveniently, they hit their peak at the same time as heirloom tomatoes. These onions are so sweet that you can enjoy them as is without fear. As a crisp, playful garnish, I slice a few rings and give them a quick shallow-fry. That's an optional step, though, for a more dramatic presentation.

Make the dressing: Put all the ingredients in a blender, or use a hand blender, and blend until smooth. Transfer to a bowl and set aside.

Make the tomato sauce: Put all the ingredients with 3 tablespoons of the dressing in a blender, or use a hand blender, and blend until smooth.

SERVES 4

FOR THE DRESSING:

¼ cup dashi, or ¼ cup warm water mixed with ⅛ teaspoon Hon Dashi (see Note)

1½ tablespoons lemon juice

3 tablespoons rice vinegar

3 tablespoons soy sauce

2 tablespoons chopped Vidalia or other sweet onion

1 tablespoon roughly chopped daikon

¼ teaspoon chopped garlic

A few grinds of black pepper

FOR THE TOMATO SAUCE:

1 yellow tomato, peeled and seeded

¼ teaspoon salt

A few grinds of black pepper

FOR THE HIJIKI SALAD:

¼ cup hijiki, soaked in 1 cup cold water for 15 minutes and drained well

1 tablespoon neutral-flavored vegetable oil

½ teaspoon salt

A few grinds of black pepper

FOR THE TOMATO SALAD:

1 quart various heirloom tomatoes cut into bite-size pieces

⅓ cup thinly sliced (on a mandoline) Vidalia onion

(CONTINUED)

FOR THE TOMATO SALAD (CONT'D):

2 tablespoons julienned scallion

2 tablespoons neutral-flavored
   vegetable oil

1½ teaspoons salt

A few grinds of black pepper

FOR THE FRIED ONION (OPTIONAL):

4 very thin slices Vidalia or other
   sweet onion

¼ cup cornstarch

Pinch of salt

FOR THE MACKEREL:

4 (5½-ounce) Spanish mackerel fillets,
   skin on, scored

2 tablespoons neutral-flavored
   vegetable oil

1 teaspoon salt

Black pepper to taste

TO SERVE:

1 tablespoon julienned scallion greens

Make the hijiki salad: In a small bowl, combine all the hijiki salad ingredients with 3 tablespoons of the dressing.

Make the tomato salad: In a bowl, combine the tomatoes, onion, scallion, and salt and pepper. Add the oil to the remaining dressing, mix well, then combine with the tomato salad.

Make the fried onion, if desired: Toss the onion slices in the cornstarch to coat well. Heat 1 inch of oil to 350°F and fry the onion slices until crisp and browned at the edges. Drain on a paper towel and season immediately with the salt.

Make the mackerel: Coat the mackerel with the oil and season both sides with salt and pepper. Place skin side up under the broiler on the highest setting, as close to the heat source as possible. Cook until the skin is browned and crisp and the fish is almost cooked through. Timing will depend on the fish's thickness and the heat of your broiler.

To serve: Divide the tomato salad among 4 serving plates, circle with the tomato sauce, and place a few mounds of hijiki salad around the edges of the tomato salad. Top with the mackerel and then with the fried onion (if using) and a pinch of the scallion.

NOTE: Hon Dashi is an instant dashi powder, available at Asian grocery stores. It usually contains MSG.

> *I usually look for the smaller cherry- or grape-size heirlooms for the salad—they're often the sweetest—and a larger yellow tomato for the pureed sauce. In general, yellow tomatoes tend to be lower in acid than the red, which, epitomized by the well-known beefsteak Brandywine strain, tend to have that classic "tomato" flavor. Green tomatoes possess a characteristic mild tartness that makes them a favorite for jam. The orange heirlooms are sweeter than their counterparts but, unlike the green, still emit a pronounced earthy aroma.*

GRILLED BLUEFISH WRAPPED IN GRAPE LEAVES
WITH CHARRED GRAPES

Bluefish is the most underrated fish gracing tables today. So what if it's the *only* fish that I've been able to both catch and cook myself in recent years? To be fair, my angling skills are still in development and I have only a small skiff. (Honestly, excuses aside, I'm not a great fisherman, but it's not for lack of enthusiasm.) On Moriches Bay, it is not unusual to snag a whole brace of these omega-3 powerhouses for a big feast or, if you want to save them for later enjoyment, curing and smoking.

As its meat is very soft, anchoa (another common bluefish moniker) can easily fall apart on the grill. The grape leaves in the following recipe solve this problem by holding the flesh together; they also give the dish a briny, vegetal Mediterranean flavor. Along with the dill, they evoke Greek and Turkish cuisines, while the anchovy-lemon-garlic dressing presents a more universal combination, but with an Italian edge. The sharpness of the red onion and garlic, along with the acid from the lemon, balance and bring out the sweetness of the fish. The grapes, once grilled, provide a sugared and smoky counterpoint, and the herbs a fresh brightness.

Season the bluefish on both sides with salt and pepper and wrap each with two overlapping grape leaves. Brush the exterior with olive oil and place on a hot cleaned and oiled grill, seam side down. Cook for about 3 minutes, until you have nice grill marks, then turn over. Grill until just cooked through, when a cake tester is easily inserted into the thickest part of the fish and is warm to the touch after being left in the fish for 30 seconds. Toss the onion and grapes with a little oil, salt, and pepper and grill until a little shriveled and, ideally, a bit charred on the edge if your grill is very hot. If you can't get your grill that high, don't wait until they're charred, just until they're a little shriveled, or they'll be overcooked. Put the onion and grapes in a bowl and toss with the garlic, lemon juice, anchovies, ⅔ cup extra-virgin olive oil, chives, and dill. Taste and adjust the seasonings, then serve over the grilled fish still wrapped in the grape leaves.

SERVES 4

4 (5½-ounce) bluefish fillets (freshest catch possible), skin removed

Salt and black pepper

8 grape leaves, large veins removed

Olive oil, for grilling

1 small red onion, cut into ¼-inch-thick rounds

1⅓ cups large red grapes, halved, seeded if applicable

1 large clove garlic, smashed to a paste

6 tablespoons lemon juice

2 anchovy fillets, smashed to a paste

⅔ cup extra-virgin olive oil

1 tablespoon chopped fresh chives

1 tablespoon chopped fresh parsley and/or dill

SALT-BROILED WEAKFISH
WITH JAPANESE YAM, SPICY COD ROE, AND MEYER LEMON CONFIT

SERVES 4

FOR THE YAMS:

2 small *satsumaimo* (Japanese sweet potatoes), white sweet potatoes, or large boiling potatoes, peeled and cut into bite-size pieces

3 tablespoons olive oil

2 sprigs fresh thyme

4 slices lemon

Salt and black pepper

FOR THE WEAKFISH:

4 (5½-ounce) weakfish fillets, skin on, scored

Salt and black pepper

Neutral-flavored vegetable oil (about 2 tablespoons)

FOR THE SALAD:

1 tablespoon lemon juice

1 clove garlic, smashed but left whole

2 tablespoons extra-virgin olive oil

Salt and black pepper to taste

5 ounces potato stems or mesclun

TO SERVE:

1 heaping tablespoon julienned scallion greens

1 teaspoon Meyer lemon or regular lemon confit, finely diced (optional; see Notes)

(CONTINUED)

After my prank-inspiring first catch, I subsequently found out that weakfish, or tide runners as they're called among Long Island anglers, are delicious, slightly oily, yet mild when fresh. That oiliness works well with the high acidity in the following dish. I realize that weakfish isn't an option at most fish markets, only those near my beach house, but Spanish mackerel is easy to find and a wonderful choice. While many of the following ingredients are Asian, the flavors—those of lemon, olive oil, garlic, and fish roe—are purely Mediterranean. If you can't find *mentaiko* (marinated pollock roe), tarama (the cured Greek codfish roe used to make taramasalata), which is available in jars (made by the Kronos company) in many regular grocery stores, can be substituted. The potato stems are a springtime vegetable found in Chinese cuisine, but are delicious when used as a simple, sweet salad green and echo the yam theme.

Make the yams: Put the yams in a sauté pan with the oil, thyme, lemon, water to cover, and salt and pepper to taste. Simmer until cooked through and the water has evaporated. Set aside to cool to room temperature. If using tarama, add it to the potatoes and toss to evenly distribute.

Make the weakfish: Season the weakfish with salt and pepper and lightly coat with oil. Put on a baking sheet skin side up and put under the broiler set to high as close to the heat source as possible. Broil until browned, bubbly, and crisp and just cooked through.

Spanish mackerel isn't the only alternate fish. Feel free to substitute any oily, full-flavored fish such as hamachi, kingfish, or Boston mackerel (those last two would need to be balanced with a little more acid), or skinless tuna. If using tuna, a quick sear in a sauté pan would be a better cooking method than salt-broiling.

Make the salad: Combine the lemon juice, garlic, oil, and salt and pepper in a bowl. Add the potato stems and toss to coat. Season with additional salt and pepper, as needed, to taste. Remove and discard the garlic.

To serve: Arrange a quarter of the salad in the center of each of 4 serving plates. Sprinkle with the scallion, lemon confit (if using), some of the yam mixture, and a few rounds of *mentaiko*. Decorate the outside of the plate with the scallion oil (if using), *mentaiko* removed from the sac (or bits of tarama, if using), and the *shichimi togarashi*. Top the yams with the fish fillets. Serve immediately.

NOTES: To make scallion oil, roughly chop, blanch, and shock 1 bunch scallions and squeeze out the excess water. Put them in a blender or food processor with ½ cup neutral-flavored vegetable oil and salt and pepper to taste. Puree until smooth. Use immediately.

Lemon confit can be bought in specialty stores, but it is easy to make at home: Take halved lemons and a copious amount of salt, toss them together, and press the lemons into a clean, dry Mason jar so that the resulting juice rises above the lemons. Cover and leave at room temperature until soft, about 1 month. Spices such as coriander, cinnamon, and bay leaf may be added.

Alternatively, you can make a quick lemon confit by scoring the sides of a few lemons, submerging them in a salt-heavy brine with the optional spices, and simmering until soft. Let cool before using.

TO SERVE (CONT'D):

1 sac *mentaiko*, cut into rounds, plus 1 piece *mentaiko* removed from the sac, or 4 tablespoons jarred tarama, plus extra for garnish

Scallion oil (optional; see Note)

1 pinch *shichimi togarashi* (Japanese "seven-spice" powder) or red pepper flakes

---

Shichimi togarashi, *or Japanese "seven-spice" powder, is made from ground chiles, hemp seeds, aonori flakes (or green seaweed), black sesame seeds, sansho pepper, mandarin orange peel, and poppy seeds. If you cannot find this blend, omit it or use any ground red chile in its place, taking into account the difference in heat.*

SALT-BROILED SPANISH MACKEREL

WITH FRESH CHICKPEAS, SUNCHOKES, AND WARM ORANGE-ANCHOVY VINAIGRETTE

SERVES 4

Extra-virgin olive oil

2 cups sunchokes, washed and cut into large-bite-size pieces

Salt and black pepper

4 (5½-ounce) Spanish mackerel fillets, skin on, scored

2 tablespoons finely diced red onion

1 teaspoon julienned garlic

½ teaspoon julienned lemon zest

½ teaspoon julienned orange zest

½ teaspoon finely sliced anchovy fillet

¼ teaspoon red pepper flakes

3 tablespoons lemon juice

¾ cup orange juice

1 cup fresh chickpeas, shelled, large ones briefly blanched and shocked, small ones raw (or use canned)

1 tablespoon chopped fresh chives

Spring's fresh chickpeas are what make this dish exciting. They're green and, compared to the ubiquitous dried ones, less starchy, sweeter, and more beanlike—that is, they have a more vegetal quality. I discovered their greatness when a purveyor came to *annisa* and dropped off a sample bagful. I brought some with me to my beach house on Long Island and served them just like this.

For most recipes, I am happy to suggest alternative ingredients if the originals can't be found; this is an exception. Without the fresh chickpeas, something is lost. Other than tracking down your star legume, however, the rest is practically effortless. I start with the bottom layer, sunchokes, which I sauté and then pan-roast, skin on, for texture and added nutty sweetness. Spooned above those, the chickpeas are barely cooked—warmed, really— to showcase their freshness. I create a syrupy, citrusy sauce for the fish, because the fruits' acids will cut through the mackerel's fattiness and lend a bright, zingy kick. Bolstered by salty anchovies, the liquid takes on an almost sweet-and-sour character that is checked by the heat of red pepper flakes. It's to this just-cooked sauce that I add the beans at the last possible moment. The fish, which I grill but could just as easily broil, is perched on top of the sauced beans and finished sunchokes.

Preheat the oven to 500°F. Heat an ovenproof sauté pan over high heat. Add 2 tablespoons of oil, then the sunchokes, and season with ½ teaspoon salt and a few grinds of pepper. Place in the oven for 2 to 3 minutes, until browned, then turn and roast on the other side for a minute or two; sunchokes cook quickly. Remove to a plate and keep warm.

Preheat the broiler to high. Season the Spanish mackerel with salt and pepper on both sides and coat with oil. Put on a baking sheet and place under the broiler as close to the heat source as possible. Broil until the skin is browned and bubbly and the fish is almost cooked through.

(Alternatively, grill skin side down until grill marks appear browned, then turn 45 degrees to make crosshatch marks, then flip and finish on the other side.)

Add ¼ cup of oil, the onion, garlic, lemon and orange zests, anchovies, and red pepper flakes to the same pan in which the sunchokes were roasted, and cook over medium heat until soft. Add the lemon and orange juices and cook until reduced and syrupy. Season with salt and pepper. Add the green chickpeas and stir for 15 seconds, just until warmed through—they are already cooked at this point. Divide the sunchokes among 4 plates, and then spoon the green-chickpea mixture over the top. Sprinkle with the chives and top with the fish.

While the larger chickpeas benefit from a quick blanch, the little dark-green ones are best enjoyed raw. Yes, of course you can substitute the canned variety; you will still eat well. But I think you're better off making a different Spanish mackerel dish such as the ones on page 119. You can easily swap that fish for another variety. I chose the white-fleshed Spanish mackerel for its firmer, steakier texture, which is the essential trait—fattiness, too— since the sauce has such bold flavors: the sweetness of orange, the bracing tartness of lemon, and the saltiness of anchovies. Swordfish, for example, would be a good option, but it's more expensive and its status on the overfished list remains uncertain (it was banned for a few years, although some say it's alright now, at least for American eaters).

SAUTÉED FILLET OF HALIBUT

WITH FENNEL AND WHITE ANCHOVIES

SERVES 4

FOR THE FENNEL SALAD:

1 bulb fennel, trimmed, tops cut off,
   fronds reserved and chopped

1 teaspoon chopped fresh chives

4 white Spanish anchovy fillets, or
   2 regular anchovy fillets, chopped

2 teaspoons lemon juice

2 tablespoons extra-virgin olive oil

¼ teaspoon salt

Black pepper to taste

FOR THE SAUCE:

1 cup blood orange or regular orange
   juice

½ teaspoon lemon juice

⅓ cup extra-virgin olive oil

Pinch of salt

A few grinds of black pepper

FOR THE HALIBUT:

4 (6-ounce) halibut fillets

1 teaspoon salt

Black pepper to taste

1 tablespoon Wondra flour (optional)

3 tablespoons neutral-flavored
   vegetable oil

This is an excellent weeknight dish, because it's not too demanding. Its primary influence is Italian: Using lemon and olive oil to flavor fish and pairing that with fennel is common to that cuisine. The white anchovies, or boquerones, are Spanish and, unlike their oil-packed Italian counterparts, salted then pickled. They lend a vinegary element to the blood orange sauce and give it a vinaigrette-like quality. At the restaurant, I use the mild halibut as a canvas for contrasting preparations of citrus and fennel. Braised with water, butter, salt, lemon, and a bit of sugar, the vegetable becomes tender, sweet, and subtly fragrant; it's also taken raw and tossed with just-squeezed lemon juice, the anchovies, and chives, which collectively draw out its almost-spicy sharpness, its green brightness, and its distinct licorice notes. The crunchy salad sits atop the fish, while the soft, braised component rests beneath, as a base. For the home cook, one application of fennel is plenty; there's no need to include the braised portion, and skipping it will save you time. The sauce, however, is essential. Featuring two types of citrus, it's a mixture of reduced orange juice, which, once cooked down, gets concentrated, and fresh lemon juice, which adds the extra acid needed to counter the fruit's sweetness, the fish's brininess, and the fennel's anise.

Halibut, which you can also grill, is a flat fish. For annisa, *I buy a West Coast variety, not because it's better, per se, but because the East Coast version is overfished. Then, yes, you have to ask the carbon-footprint question. This is the problem with ethics. I decided it was better to take my halibut from a sustainable source and apologize for the airplane fuel than to enable a resource's depletion. Diversity is important to me as a chef; if I stick to the extant list of local, sustainable ingredients, my menu will be limited, and that doesn't support my multicultural point of view. However, when you create the demand for a product, theoretically the result should be increased biodiversity locally. I've seen this happen with vegetables, and I'd like to think the same could be true for fish. If there's a sustainable halibut farm out west, there's no reason it's not feasible to have one over here on the other side of the country too.*

Make the fennel salad: Thinly slice the fennel bulb, put it in a bowl, and add 1 tablespoon of the chopped fennel fronds, the chives, and anchovies. Add the lemon juice and oil. Season with the salt and pepper, toss to combine, and set aside.

Make the sauce: Put the orange juice in a saucepan and cook over medium-high heat until syrupy and reduced to about 3 tablespoons. Transfer to a bowl and whisk in the lemon juice. When cool, slowly whisk in the oil in a thin stream to emulsify, then season with the salt and pepper.

Make the halibut: Heat a sauté pan over high heat. Season the fillets on both sides with the salt and pepper, then dust lightly with the Wondra (if using). Add the oil to the pan. When it is smoking, add the fillets, whitest side down, and lower the heat to medium-high. Cook until golden brown, then turn. Cook briefly on the other side until cooked to medium, or until a toothpick can be easily inserted into the thickest part of the fish.

To serve: Spoon a pool of the sauce on each serving plate, top with the halibut, then top the halibut with the fennel salad. Serve immediately.

SLOW-COOKED SALMON
WITH SMOKED PAPRIKA AND SAVOY CABBAGE

Salmon is particularly good for slow cooking, especially if you love the texture created by that process; the fish's flesh becomes meltingly tender. This dish tends to scare people off because the salmon's deep pink color gives the impression that the meat is raw. It isn't. Another reason people may find this preparation daunting is that it's often associated with a complicated-sounding technique—cooking sous-vide in an immersion circulator. In a professional kitchen, chefs use special machines to ensure controlled cooking without any changes in temperature, but you can easily get the same results at home without any of those gadgets.

In this recipe, you're essentially placing the fish in a buttery bath and roasting it at a low temperature for about 15 minutes. It's a recipe that will appeal to those who love smoked salmon; the smoked paprika gives it that distinct flavor. The sauce's crème fraîche and lemon supply a balancing tangy, acidic note that's reminiscent of the cream cheese that frequently complements lox. Then there's the savoy cabbage, wilted in, again, butter, which draws out the vegetable's sweetness. This is a reference to Eastern European cuisine—both cabbage and salmon are among its staples.

Preheat the oven to 225°F.

Make the sauce and salmon: In a wide ovenproof saucepan, melt the butter over medium heat and add the shallot; cook until soft and translucent. Add the smoked paprika and stir. Add the wine and cook until it is reduced by three-quarters. Add the crème fraîche and increase the heat to medium-high. Whisk in the butter, little by little, to emulsify. Remove from the heat and add the lemon juice, 1 teaspoon of the salt, and the pepper. Season the salmon with the remaining ½ teaspoon of salt and the pepper, submerge in the sauce, then place in the oven. Cook for about 15 minutes, until a toothpick is easily inserted into the thickest part of the fish.

Make the cabbage: Heat a sauté pan over medium-high heat, add the butter, and swirl. Add the cabbage and sauté until wilted. Add 1 tablespoon of water if necessary to prevent browning. Season with the salt and pepper. Divide among 4 serving plates and sprinkle with the chives. Top with the fish and spoon the sauce around the cabbage.

SERVES 4

FOR THE SAUCE AND SALMON:
1 tablespoon butter
1 shallot, minced
2 tablespoons smoked paprika
½ cup white wine
2 tablespoons crème fraîche
¾ cup (1½ sticks) cold butter, cut into small pieces
½ teaspoon lemon juice
1 teaspoon salt
Black pepper to taste
4 (5½-ounce) salmon fillets, skin removed

FOR THE CABBAGE:
2 tablespoons butter
2 quarts thinly sliced light-green savoy cabbage leaves
1½ teaspoons salt
Black pepper to taste
1 tablespoon chopped fresh chives

ROASTED FILLET OF HAKE
WITH A TWO-ARTICHOKE GRATIN AND MEYER LEMON

SERVES 4

FOR THE GRATIN:

2 ounces cleaned hake belly

Salt

1 cup heavy cream (plus more, as
  necessary, to cover)

1 large pinch fresh lemon-thyme or
  regular thyme leaves

1 bay leaf

2 large artichokes, dark-green outer
  leaves removed, bottoms and stems
  peeled, choke removed, ⅓ inch thick

1½ cups sunchokes, peeled and sliced
  ⅓ inch thick

1 clove garlic, finely chopped

1 tablespoon extra-virgin olive oil

Black pepper to taste

FOR THE MEYER LEMON VINAIGRETTE:

3 tablespoons Meyer lemon juice

1 tablespoon Dijon mustard

3 tablespoons extra-virgin olive oil

3 tablespoons neutral-flavored
  vegetable oil

¼ teaspoon salt

Black pepper to taste

FOR THE HAKE FILLETS:

4 (5½-ounce) hake fillets

½ teaspoon salt

Black pepper to taste

(CONTINUED)

Reduced to its most basic form, this is a piece of fish on a gratin. That was where I started when creating this entrée, although the initial premise isn't mine. I borrowed it from Pierre Franey, whose recipe for *flétan boulangère* was one I followed in college, long before I'd gone to cooking school. I was already a Francophile, and his food was always Franco-forward; that was the only style of fine-dining back then, in the 1980s. Published in his *New York Times 60-Minute Gourmet*, Franey's was a quick, one-dish dinner, a gratin that included halibut, or *flétan*. In French, *boulangère* is feminine for "baker," and in this context it refers to the sprinkling of bread crumbs that covers the casserole. Wine, butter, garlic, onions, and potatoes were the other ingredients involved; they were mixed together and positioned around the fish.

A traditional gratin is often cooked with cream, whose sugars bubble up and brown to produce that irresistible top layer that characterizes the dish. I relied on that technique for my interpretation of the Franey original. I also used another source of inspiration, brandade, as the French call it, or, as it is known in Spain, bacalao. This delicacy is a whipped mixture of pureed salt cod, olive oil, and potato and has the consistency of a mash. Different regions have their own versions; some add milk, others garlic. I wanted to incorporate the brandade's flavors in a revisited adaptation of Franey's easy masterpiece. What differentiates the following preparation from its models is that I swap in hake fillets and hake belly for cod or halibut, artichokes and sunchokes for potatoes.

To give the fish some necessary acid, I make a Meyer lemon vinaigrette. (In a pinch, regular lemon would do.) If you're feeling lazy, the gratin's cream will suffice as a sauce; just remember to squeeze some lemon over the top of the fish before serving.

Make the gratin: Season the hake belly with ½ teaspoon of salt and put it on a rack over a baking dish or plate in the refrigerator overnight. Preheat the oven to 450°F. Put the salted hake belly in a small saucepan, add the cream to cover, and add the lemon thyme and bay leaf. Simmer until the hake belly is cooked through. In a large bowl, combine the hake belly mixture with the artichokes, sunchokes, garlic, oil, ½ teaspoon of salt, and the pepper. The hake should break up into smaller pieces as you stir. Transfer to an 8-by-8-inch baking dish and bake until bubbly and browned on top, about 25 minutes.

Make the Meyer lemon vinaigrette: In a small bowl, mix the lemon juice with the mustard, then slowly whisk in the oils in a thin stream to emulsify. Season with the salt and pepper.

Make the hake fillets: Season the fillets with the salt and pepper and dust lightly with the Wondra. Heat a sauté pan over high heat and add the oil. When the oil is smoking, add the fillets, whitest side down. Reduce the heat to medium-high and cook until golden brown, then turn the fillets and cook until a toothpick can be easily inserted into the thickest part of the fillet.

To serve: Place a mound of the gratin in the center of each serving plate. Top with the hake fillets and surround with the vinaigrette. Decorate the vinaigrette with the lemon thyme and lemon zest and serve immediately.

FOR THE HAKE FILLETS (CONT'D):
1 teaspoon Wondra flour
2 tablespoons neutral-flavored vegetable oil
TO SERVE:
1 teaspoon fresh lemon-thyme leaves
1 teaspoon julienned Meyer lemon zest

I made a dish like this one at Maxim's; I took it in a Provençal direction. My gratin contained potato and garlic, and I surrounded it with a tomato sauce and an olive tapenade. Either of those condiments would be appropriate on my hake-and-artichoke plate.

No one has found a hassle-free way to prep the artichoke. I recommend you pull off all of the leaves until you get to that white-gold part of the vegetable, then extract the hairy section from the center.

MISO-MARINATED SABLE
WITH CRISP SILKEN TOFU IN A BONITO BROTH

SERVES 4

FOR THE SABLE:

3 tablespoons sake

3 tablespoons mirin

½ cup saikyo miso (sweet white miso)

3 scallion whites, sliced lengthwise to
   make fans

Splash of yuzu juice

4 (6-ounce) sable (black cod) fillets,
   skin on

FOR THE BROTH:

1 quart dashi (page 231)

¼ cup mirin, boiled to cook out some
   of the alcohol

¼ cup soy sauce

1 teaspoon yuzu juice

FOR THE KOMBU:

Cooked kombu from dashi, cut into
   ¼-inch-thick strips

2 tablespoons dashi

1 tablespoon soy sauce

1 tablespoon mirin

1 tablespoon sugar

FOR THE TOFU:

Neutral-flavored vegetable oil

½ cup cornstarch

1 teaspoon salt

Black pepper to taste

1 (14-ounce) package silken Japanese
   tofu, cut into 4 rectangles

(CONTINUED)

When I first opened *annisa*, **I had an incredibly talented Japanese cook** named Aki. He really loved food, and though he spoke very little English (it was kind of amazing that we were able to communicate), I couldn't have managed without him. It wasn't easy to find staff back then; we were, relatively speaking, a tiny operation and didn't have lots of money.

Among the many things Aki contributed to the restaurant, he is responsible for at least two of the components in this recipe, a true collaboration that remains on the menu. The marinade, which lends the sable (also called black cod) a distinctly sweet, meaty quality, was his and it's one used often in Japan for rich fishes such as this. Items like miso-broiled cod are now ubiquitous at Asian-fusion places; they all rely on a similar marinade. He also, separately, showed me how to make the kombu that I decided to add to this entrée. It brings a vegetable to the plate along with extra umami and a pleasing chewy texture. Dried sea kelp, as previously noted, is the main ingredient in dashi, the broth on which mine is based. I incorporated dashi here because broths were in back then, but also because it makes sense with the fried tofu. In Japan, this way of preparing the bean curd is associated with *agedashi tofu*, a dish that sets the tofu in dashi.

Here, the tofu takes the place of a starchy side, in that it's bland, soft (in its silken interior), and crisp (the dredged exterior). It simultaneously mimics and contrasts the sable's buttery texture without introducing competing flavors. Elsewhere, as the vegetarian dish on page 73 illustrates, the same tofu can become the main ingredient.

Marinate the black cod: In a small saucepan, bring the sake and mirin to a boil to cook off some of the alcohol. Let cool to room temperature, then combine with the miso, scallions, and yuzu juice. Cover the fish liberally on both sides with the marinade. Cover and put in the refrigerator to marinate for 2 to 3 days.

Make the broth: Season the dashi with the mirin, soy sauce, and yuzu juice. Keep warm.

Make the kombu: Simmer the kombu in the dashi, soy sauce, mirin, and sugar until lightly syrupy. Drain and set aside.

Make the tofu: Place 2 inches of oil in a large saucepan and heat to 350°F. Season the cornstarch with the salt and pepper and dredge the tofu in the mixture. Fry until crisp. Drain on a paper towel and keep warm.

To serve: Wipe any excess marinade from the fish and place the fish skin side up in a shallow baking dish with ½ inch of water. Place under a preheated broiler and cook until caramelized but not burned, then turn the oven to 500°F and bake until a toothpick inserted in the thickest part of the fish passes through without resistance.

Scatter a dozen or so strips of the kombu in each of 4 warmed serving bowls, along with a heaping tablespoon of tobiko and a large pinch of scallions. Add ¾ cup of hot broth to each bowl and place a tofu square in the center. Top with the fish and serve immediately so the tofu doesn't get soggy.

TO SERVE:
4 heaping tablespoons red
  tobiko (flying fish roe)
¼ cup julienned scallion
  greens

A sable's pin bones are at the center of the fillet near the head bones and are very hard to remove with the usual tweezers. Aki taught me to do it after the fish has been cooked, because the bones come out much more easily. On the line, that isn't efficient, so we are forced to cut them out beforehand. At home, luckily, you can adhere to Aki's method. His marinade works well on other oily fishes like salmon and baby bluefish.

SAUTÉED FILLET OF SKATE

WITH CARAMELIZED APPLES AND CHICKEN LIVER

SERVES 4

FOR THE SAUCE:

4½ tablespoons butter

1 onion, finely diced

3 tablespoons brandy

¾ cup chicken stock (page 231)

½ teaspoon salt

Black pepper to taste

FOR THE APPLES:

2½ tablespoons neutral-flavored
   vegetable oil

1½ tablespoons butter

1½ cups finely diced Granny Smith
   apples

2½ tablespoons sugar

Pinch of salt

FOR THE CHICKEN LIVERS AND SKATE:

4 tablespoons neutral-flavored
   vegetable oil

1 tablespoon butter

6 ounces chicken livers, finely diced

4 (5½-ounce) skate fillets

Salt and black pepper to taste

Wondra flour

1 lemon, halved

TO SERVE:

1 tablespoon chopped fresh chives

My introduction to skate took place when I was a child, during a summer spent on Cape Cod, where, with my older brother and sister, I ran into a fisherman. He was an old salt, his arms deeply tanned and wrinkled from the sun, his beard scraggly and speckled with dried seawater. We asked what he had been catching. "Skate," he replied. Not familiar with the fish, we inquired further and he told us, "In New England we call skate poor man's scallops." He explained that "back in the day," people on the Cape would cut out rounds of skate meat as a substitute for scallops because the two species shared a common sweetness. What he didn't tell us is that skate is notoriously difficult to work with when whole.

I learned that lesson the hard way, and at the same time realized the true value of the fish. In the fall of 1999 I had a lot of free time on my hands. *Annisa* wasn't open yet and I was just learning the art of angling. Jen and I had driven all the way from Manhattan to Shinnecock Canal on Long Island because we heard that striper fishing was particularly good there. After a few hours and a rough time of it, I landed my skate.

I am by no means squeamish, but this fish broke me. None of my extensive culinary training prepared me for what followed. It was the skate that would not die. It took hours; multiple gashes in the head; a three-and-a-half-hour airless trunk ride from Long Island back home to Manhattan, and a drag-out struggle on the cutting board. We gave up the good fight and decided to let the skate die while we watched TV in the next room. Since that traumatic experience, I have not personally killed another skate, but it's often on the menu at *annisa*. It is robust and, yes, sweet-flavored, but to call it "poor man's scallop" is inaccurate and doesn't do justice to the distinct character of the fish.

Make the sauce: Heat a saucepan over high heat. Add 3 tablespoons of the butter and swirl. Add the onion and lower the heat to medium. Cook, stirring occasionally, until golden brown. Add the brandy, then the stock, and bring to a boil. Cook until reduced by one-third, then swirl in the remaining 1½ tablespoons butter. Season with the salt and pepper and keep warm.

Although the skate stands up to the chicken liver (the "poor man's foie gras"), too much liver will overpower the dish. So don't overdo it.

Make the apples: Heat a sauté pan over high heat and add the oil. When just smoking, add the butter and apples and sauté for about a minute. Add the sugar and salt and cook until caramelized. Remove to a warm plate.

Make the chicken livers and skate: Heat two large sauté pans over high heat. Add 1 tablespoon of the oil and the butter to one pan and the remaining 3 tablespoons of oil to the other. On a plate, season the livers and skate with salt and pepper and dust lightly with Wondra. When the oil in the pans is smoking, add the livers to the pan with the oil and butter and the skate, whitest side down, to the other pan. Lower the heat to medium-high and cook until golden brown. Turn the skate and finish cooking on the other side. Squeeze lemon juice over the fish.

To serve: Pour some sauce in the center of a serving plate, followed by the skate. Top with the chicken livers, apples, and chives.

ROASTED FILLET OF COD
WITH STEAMER CLAMS AND PISTACHIOS

Chatham cod is delicious but, sadly, overfished. Although the population is recovering, I now use either ling cod or hake, which are more plentiful.

One of my all-time favorite things to do is to go clamming. I first learned to dig for steamer clams on Cape Cod; my stepfather used to take us to Chatham each summer to stay in an old Cape house with a well out front. I love everything about it, from being by the water to the simple pleasure of digging, not to mention the delicious end results. The experience for me is pure primal gratification coupled with an excitement that must be like gambling. I'm always thinking, "*Just one more...*" and can never quite pull myself away from the mud to go home.

Clams remind me of my time spent in New England and, along with pistachios, my childhood—they're two basic ingredients that I ate often and happily when I was little, but prior to this I had never experienced them in tandem. Maybe, subconsciously, that's what caused me to put them together in a dish. In retrospect, there is something about the sweet earthiness of both the steamer clam and the pistachio that makes this a great pairing. This wouldn't work as well with other kinds of clams; the steamer belly holds much of that earthy nuttiness that goes with the pistachio. In addition, the richness of the pistachio brings out the sweetness of the clam, thereby performing the same function as drawn butter in the classic combination. New England meets the Middle East (or California).

Put the steamer clams in a high-sided sauté pan with 1 cup water, cover, and bring to a boil. Cook for 3 minutes, or until the clams open. Remove with a slotted spoon and pour the liquid through a sieve lined with a coffee filter or rinsed and squeezed cheesecloth to remove any sand or grit. Shuck the steamers and remove the outer membrane from the siphons. Rinse in warm water to remove sand. Set the clams and liquid aside.

Put the potatoes in a saucepan and cover with cold salted water. Bring to a boil and cook until tender; drain and keep warm.

Put 1 cup of the reserved clam liquid in a saucepan and add the pistachios. Bring to a boil and immediately whisk in the butter. Season with pepper. The sauce should not need any extra salt.

Season the fillets on both sides with salt and pepper and dust lightly with the Wondra. Heat a sauté pan over high heat, add the oil, and when the oil is smoking add the fillets, white side down. Lower the heat to medium and cook until deep golden brown, then turn the fillets and cook until a toothpick can be easily inserted into the thickest part of the fillet.

To serve: Add the clams to the sauce and heat gently. Divide the potatoes among 4 serving plates, mounded in the center. Ring with the sauce, dividing the clams evenly. Sprinkle with the chives and top with the cod.

SERVES 4

2 pounds steamer clams, rinsed

½ cup sliced fingerling or other small, waxy potatoes such as Red Bliss

Salt

⅓ cup shelled pistachios, ground

2 tablespoons butter

Black pepper to taste

4 (6-ounce) Chatham cod, ling cod, or hake fillets

1 tablespoon Wondra or all-purpose flour

3 tablespoons neutral-flavored vegetable oil

TO SERVE:

1 tablespoon chopped fresh chives

ROASTED MONKFISH AND ITS LIVER
WITH LOBSTER AND SAVOY CABBAGE

SERVES 4

SERVES 4

FOR THE MONKFISH LIVER:

4 ounces monkfish liver, cleaned,
   veins and other foreign bits removed
   (see sidebar)

½ teaspoon salt

Black pepper to taste

Splash of sake

FOR THE LOBSTER SAUCE:

1½ cups white wine

1 shallot, minced

1 clove garlic, smashed

1 tomato, roughly chopped

1 quart lobster stock (page 231)

1 sprig fresh tarragon

1 (1¼-pound) lobster, steamed and
   shelled, tomalley, shells, and head
   reserved

Lobster shells and head

1 cup (2 sticks) cold butter, cut into
   pieces

Salt and black pepper to taste

½ teaspoon lemon juice, or to taste

FOR THE CABBAGE BUNDLES:

4 outer leaves savoy cabbage, thick
   lower part of the center rib removed

4 small pinches of grated lemon zest

A few drops of lemon juice

2 teaspoons chopped fresh chives

1 teaspoon chopped fresh tarragon

(CONTINUED)

This is a two-part dish. Resting on a bed of sautéed cabbage, there's a piece of the monkfish, roasted, with a shiso leaf and a sliver of steamed *ankimo* (monkfish liver) on top. Then there's a butter-poached lobster bundled in a cabbage leaf. Each component has its own sauce: The first has a lobster base and is a refined version of a *sauce américaine*—the usual thickener, rice, is left out; the second is a blend of heavy cream and lobster's green tomalley, the digestive gland that performs the functions of a liver and pancreas combined. The poor man's lobster sits beside the real thing; cabbage and butter unite the two and draw out the seafood's inherent quiet sweetness. Often compared to foie gras, the coral-colored *ankimo*, a prized ingredient in Japan, is a wintertime specialty and lends a gentle oceanic note that brings complexity to the monkfish. The tomalley offers the flavors of lobster in concentrated form. Both organs enhance their respective proteins and give the plate extra lusciousness.

Make the monkfish liver: In a bowl, season the cleaned liver with the salt and pepper and splash with a little bit of sake. Tightly roll in a sheet of plastic wrap and tie both ends to form a firm sausage. Wrap with aluminum foil to help keep its shape and steam for 18 minutes, or until cooked through. Let cool to room temperature, then put in the refrigerator to chill for at least 4 hours (you can do this the day before and chill it overnight). Cut into ½-inch-thick disks.

Make the lobster sauce: Put the wine, shallot, garlic, and tomato in a saucepan and cook over medium to medium-high heat until reduced and thick. Add the stock, tarragon, and lobster shells and cook until reduced to ¼ cup. Pour through a fine-mesh sieve and return to the pan. Right before serving time, heat over medium-high heat, whisk in the butter, little by little, to emulsify, and season with lemon juice, salt if necessary, and pepper.

Make the cabbage bundles: While the sauce is reducing, blanch the cabbage leaves in boiling salted water for 30 seconds and plunge into an ice bath. Dry the leaves on towels. Place one-quarter of the lobster (1 claw or ½ tail cut lengthwise) on each cabbage leaf and sprinkle with the lemon zest and juice, chives, tarragon, salt, and pepper. Dot with a little butter and roll into a round bundle, like a burrito, then re-form into a ball to resemble a little cabbage. Keep refrigerated.

Make the tomalley sauce: Over medium heat, heat the cream and tomalley until the mixture just comes to a boil, and blend using a hand blender until smooth. Season with a pinch of salt and pepper.

Make the monkfish and cabbage: If you are using thick pieces of the fish and/or desire it well done, preheat the oven to 450°F. Heat an ovenproof sauté pan over high heat. On a plate, season the monkfish with ½ teaspoon of salt and the pepper and dust lightly on all sides with the flour. Add the oil to the pan, and when just smoking, add the monkfish. Lower the heat to medium-high and brown on all sides. Finish cooking in the oven as needed. Set aside on a warm plate to rest while you sauté the cabbage: Heat a sauté pan over high heat, add the butter, then the cabbage, and season with ½ teaspoon of salt. Lower the heat to medium and sauté until softened but not browned. Add a splash of water if necessary. Remove from the heat and add the chives.

To serve: Place a mound of the shredded cabbage on one side of each warmed serving plate. Place the monkfish on top of the cabbage. Surround with the lobster sauce and top the monkfish with a shiso leaf, then a disk of monkfish liver. Steam the cabbage bundles for 5 to 6 minutes to heat through. On the other side of the plate, streak a line of the tomalley sauce and center a bundle on top of it. Serve immediately.

The ankimo *(monkfish liver) is surprisingly easy to prepare; your fishmonger can clean it for you, or you can do that yourself—simply pull out the veins and any foreign bits. Alternatively, your local sushi bar can probably sell you a few slices of already steamed monkfish liver.*

FOR THE CABBAGE BUNDLES (CONT'D):
Salt and black pepper to taste
1 tablespoon butter, cut into 4 cubes
FOR THE TOMALLEY SAUCE:
Heavy cream (as much as you have tomalley)
Lobster tomalley (from above)
Salt and black pepper
FOR THE MONKFISH AND CABBAGE:
4 (4-ounce) monkfish fillets, cleaned
Salt
Black pepper to taste
1 tablespoon Wondra flour
2 tablespoons neutral-flavored vegetable oil
2 tablespoons butter
3 cups shredded savoy cabbage
2 tablespoons chopped fresh chives
TO SERVE:
4 fresh shiso leaves

SAUTÉED FILLET OF BROOK TROUT

WITH ITS SMOKED ROE, SORREL, AND RÖSTI POTATO

SERVES 4

FOR THE ROE:

¼ cup trout roe (see sidebar)

FOR THE RÖSTI POTATOES:

2 Idaho potatoes, peeled

2 teaspoons salt

Black pepper to taste

¼ cup neutral-flavored vegetable oil

FOR THE SORREL SAUCE:

1 shallot, sliced

1 cup white wine

2 ounces sorrel, large stems removed,
   roughly chopped

¼ cup crème fraîche

½ cup heavy cream

¼ teaspoon salt

Black pepper to taste

FOR THE TROUT:

2 whole (10-ounce) boned trout, skin
   on, scaled and filleted

½ teaspoon salt

Black pepper to taste

3 tablespoons neutral-flavored
   vegetable oil

TO SERVE:

1 Persian, Kirby, or hothouse
   cucumber, cut into thin triangles
   (about ⅔ cup)

1 teaspoon lemon juice

(CONTINUED)

There is a French dish called *saumon à l'oseille*, **which is salmon with a** sorrel cream sauce. Although many traditional places have it on their menus, it's a signature of the Maison Troisgros. That renowned restaurant perfected a special, lighter version of this salmon that Gilbert Le Coze served twenty years ago at New York City's Le Bernardin when he was still its chef and I was a college student having a fancy dinner there with my girlfriend's parents. The salmon was thinly sliced and placed under a broiler for just a second. The barely cooked fish was topped with a butter sauce and garnished with a simple chiffonade of sorrel. The herb was raw; you could tell because it was still bright green. Sorrel leaves have so much natural acid that as soon as they hit a hot pan, they turn dark.

The entire meal was unforgettable. We had Perrier-Jouët Champagne and, to start, I ordered sea urchins because they were something I'd never tried before. They were wonderful, but Le Coze's replication of the Troisgrois salmon was the most impressive. Years later, it inspired me to pair a fillet of sautéed brook trout with a simple, frothy sauce of sorrel, shallots, white wine, and crème fraîche. My other model was the Eastern European combination of smoked fish, potato, and cream, or its trendy reincarnation as the popular hors d'oeuvre of smoked salmon and sour cream on a latke (potato pancake). Here, along with the trout and the tangy, creamy sorrel foam, there's the fish's cold-smoked roe and rösti—the Swiss pan-fried potato cake.

Make the smoked roe: If smoking the trout roe, soak 2 cups of hickory-wood chips in water overnight; drain. Put the roe in a cup embedded in a container filled with plenty of ice. Smoke the roe with a stovetop smoker following the manufacturer's instructions, or make a small fire to one side of your grill. When the fire has turned to glowing embers, top with the soaked wood chips. Place the container of ice with the roe to the other side of the grill and cover the grill, opening the vents just a little. Smoke for 20 minutes. The ice should keep the roe from cooking. Refrigerate the roe until ready to use.

Make the rösti potatoes: Working quickly to prevent oxidation, grate the potatoes and put them in a clean kitchen towel. Season with the salt and pepper and mix, then wrap and squeeze to remove as much liquid as possible. Heat a small nonstick sauté pan over high heat. Add the oil and when it is hot, add the potatoes and press with a spatula to form a cake. Lower the heat to medium-high and cook until browned, then turn, adding more oil if necessary, and cook the other side until browned and crisp. Remove to a warm plate.

Make the sorrel sauce: Put the shallot and wine in a saucepan and cook over medium to medium-high heat until reduced by two-thirds. Add the sorrel, crème fraîche, and cream and bring to a boil. Season with the salt and pepper and keep warm.

Make the trout: Heat two sauté pans over high heat. Season the fillets with the salt and pepper. Divide the oil between the pans and when smoking, add the trout, skin side down, and press with a spatula to keep the fillets flat. Lower the heat to medium-high and cook until browned and crisp. The trout should be almost cooked through by this time. Turn and immediately remove from the pan.

To serve: Combine the cucumber with the lemon juice, salt, and pepper. Cut the rösti into 4 pieces and place one in the center of each serving plate. With a hand blender, froth the sauce and spoon 2 tablespoons around the rösti on each plate. Top the rösti with the fish, then with the cucumber. Top with the smoked roe and a few chives. Decorate the plate with the purple potato (if using). Serve immediately.

TO SERVE (CONT'D):
¼ teaspoon salt
Black pepper to taste
12 fresh chives, cut into 2-inch lengths
1 small purple potato, finely diced,
    cooked in salted water (optional)

This is a springtime dish; that's when both the brook trout and the sorrel are in season. The herb's leaves are long, shaped like arrow-heads. It's a perennial plant—at least the variegated example in my garden seems to come back every year. The fish's roe is easily cold-smoked; you place it on a bed of ice above the wood chips that are heated from beneath. If that's a step you don't have time for, you can leave the eggs as is.

CHAPTER FOUR

MEAT

INSPIRATION: MY MOTHER

Last spring my mother, Molly, passed away. She was a wonderful cook who loved to eat. Don't get me wrong, she wasn't a glutton; she was thin and fit. As a physician, she was concerned with maintaining a well-balanced, healthy diet, one that would allow her to eat her favorite cruciferous vegetables and her beloved pork fat—in moderation, of course.

As she butchered, she would often talk about how, when growing up in Malaysia, she would have to slaughter and pluck the chickens for dinner by breaking their necks, dipping them in scalding water, and pulling off the feathers in pillowy handfuls. Or she would describe the animal's anatomy in medical terms as if performing an autopsy or dissecting a specimen, a habit that laid the foundation for my belief that death is a fact of life, and meat a delicious by-product.

In Asia and many other parts of the world, whole animals are prized. At Chinese New Year, a whole fish or a whole chicken, head and tail—or beak and feet—intact, is traditionally served to represent the beginning of one year and the end of another.

For family celebrations, my mother sometimes made one of my favorite dishes—a whole roasted duck that, pre-cooking, is filled with a brew of soy sauce, soybean paste, Shaoxing cooking wine, sugar, garlic, and dried tangerine peel, then stitched shut with kitchen twine. A Franco-centric chef might call it *canard à l'orange à la chinois*, but it hails from the good old *1,000 Recipe Chinese Cookbook*, which is like a Chinese *Joy of Cooking* and I think pretty authentic. That dish is one of many culinary lessons my mom taught me.

"Finish what's on your plate" was another. "There are starving people in China." I used to wish I could take my half-eaten chicken drumstick and overnight it across the Pacific from our suburban kitchen in Michigan. It could have been French culinary school that forced me to change my ways; France's cuisine was born out of poverty, and nothing gets tossed. But really it was a trip through rural China that turned me into my mother and made me staunchly anti-waste. I realized that it isn't about the gnawed-on drumstick left unfinished; it is about appreciation for the food and respect for its source. It's all precious.

This lesson has had a stronger impact on my approach to cooking than any borrowed recipe. When I sew up a duck full of tangerine-infused sauce, I am thinking of my mother. When I turn one bird into four different dishes, leaving no bone behind, I think of it as paying homage not just to my mom, or even to our shared cultural heritage; I practice a time-honored, universal approach to food.

I. POULTRY

TURKEY WITH SPICY BLACK BEANS
IN TOFU DUMPLINGS

SERVES 4

3 (14-ounce) packages firm tofu, cut
    into 1½-inch cubes

8 ounces ground turkey

½ bunch scallions, green parts only,
    thinly sliced on a bias

½ teaspoon finely chopped garlic

2 teaspoons Chinese fermented black
    beans, roughly chopped

2 teaspoons Szechuan chunky chile
    sauce (*doban djan*)

1½ tablespoons soy sauce

½ beaten large egg

½ tablespoon cornstarch

½ teaspoon salt

Black pepper to taste

FOR THE DIPPING SAUCE:

1 tablespoon Szechuan chunky chile
    sauce (*doban djan*)

2 tablespoons rice vinegar

2 tablespoons plus 2 teaspoons soy
    sauce

1 tablespoon thinly sliced (on a bias)
    scallion whites

This homey meal borrows its flavors from my mother's *mapo dofu*, **a** Chinese dish comprised of ground meat (traditionally, it would probably be pork, but at our house in Detroit beef was used instead) and chunks of tofu cooked with garlic, ginger, some kind of chile sauce, and Chinese fermented black-bean sauce. Cornstarch was used as a thickener, and the hashlike mixture would be served over rice and strewn with some chopped scallion greens. One of the first things I learned to make, it's quick (takes less than twenty minutes) and economical, and it got me through lots of hungry nights in college. It turns up at staff meals too; apparently, a lot of my cooks know how to prepare it.

Here is a healthier adaptation of my mother's dish. I choose ground turkey over pork or beef, and after stuffing that into hollowed-out tofu, I steam the bundle. Inspired by a similar dim sum item, it's basically a wrapperless dumpling. There's no waste because the tofu that's scooped goes into the turkey filling and is seasoned with the condiments my mother added so many years ago. As a final perk, it's kid-friendly; children will enjoy helping you make and eat it.

With a melon baller, hollow out the tofu cubes, reserving 1 cup of the balls and putting them in a large bowl. To the balls, add the turkey, scallions, garlic, black beans, chile sauce, soy sauce, egg, cornstarch, salt, and pepper and mix thoroughly (the tofu will break up). Liberally stuff into the tofu cubes so that the mixture is rounded above the tofu. Steam for about 5 minutes, until cooked through.

Make the dipping sauce: Combine all the ingredients and serve in 4 small dipping bowls alongside the tofu dumplings, which can be plated 3 per person.

MY AUNTIE BETH'S
CHICKEN PAPRIKASH

My nanny, Sister Elizabeth Angel, was very much like a mother to me. Hungarian born, from Budapest, she was orphaned at the age of eleven and was sent to live in a convent. She stayed with us for a total of eight years—from the time I was three until I was twelve; there was a gap somewhere in the middle when she had to go back to the nunnery to maintain her standing with the church.

When, unlike my older siblings, I was too young to be allowed out on my own with friends, I would often have Sister Elizabeth all to myself. We would watch *The Galloping Gourmet* on her black-and-white TV while she sat on her massage chair and crocheted.

From her, I learned how to forage for wild berries and dandelion leaves, how to chop wood and build a fire, and how to make chicken paprikash, a favorite childhood dish. Inexpensive, fast, and filling, this was one of the first meals I learned to cook. I've made it over and over again throughout the years. When I lived in France, I substituted crème fraîche for the sour cream. Oddly, it is much like my mother's chicken curry, where the paprika is replaced by curry powder, the parsley by a bay leaf simmered into the curry, and the sour cream and flour by a smaller quantity of coconut milk. My mother's curry had potatoes in it and was served with coconut rice. Different, but equally comforting and nostalgic for me.

SERVES 4

3 tablespoons sweet Hungarian paprika

2 teaspoons salt, plus more for seasoning

Black pepper to taste

8 chicken thighs with skin, trimmed of excess fat

3 tablespoons neutral-flavored vegetable oil

1 large onion, chopped

1 cup sour cream

3 tablespoons all-purpose flour

2 tablespoons chopped fresh parsley

1 pound dried egg noodles, cooked

Combine the paprika, 2 teaspoons of salt, and pepper, then toss with the chicken to coat. Heat a pot over medium-high heat, add the oil, then add the onions. Lower the heat to medium-low and cook until translucent. Add the chicken and turn to coat with the oil. Add just enough water to cover; simmer for 20 minutes.

In a small bowl, combine the sour cream and flour. Add to the pot and stir. Increase the temperature and bring to a rapid boil; boil, stirring constantly, for 5 minutes, breaking up any lumps. Season to taste with salt and pepper and sprinkle with the parsley. Serve over hot egg noodles.

CHICKEN POT PIE
WITH SALSIFY, FAVA BEANS, AND MORELS

SERVES 4

FOR THE BISCUIT TOP:

1½ cups all-purpose flour

1½ tablespoons sugar

1 tablespoon baking powder

Large pinch of salt

5 tablespoons butter, softened

¾ to 1 cup heavy cream

FOR THE FILLING:

2 tablespoons plus ½ cup (1 stick)
   butter

1 small onion, diced

1 clove garlic, chopped

1 bay leaf

1 sprig fresh thyme

6 chicken thighs, skinless

1 cup fresh or dried morel or other
   mushrooms, cleaned and cut into
   bite-size pieces (see Notes)

½ cup all-purpose flour

1½ cups salsify, peeled and cut into
   bite-size lengths, or artichoke hearts
   or chopped sunchokes

2 tablespoons chopped fresh chives

1 cup shucked and peeled fava beans
   (see Notes), or shelled peas

3 tablespoons salt

Black pepper to taste

Quintessential American comfort food, the chicken pot pie can be adapted to any season. It's not unlike the fancier sounding vol-au-vent served in France. That term refers to the light (it translates literally to "windblown"), hollow puff pastry case that can be filled with many things, including, quite often, chicken. I learned how to make that specific dish abroad and have never prepared it in the States. Here, I cook pot pies. I love it when people make them for staff meals.

This particular version is a springtime creation. Instead of the potatoes, peas, and carrots you see on the boxes in the grocery's freezer section, I chose salsify, a root vegetable whose flavor many compare to that of an artichoke; the green fava bean, which is arduous to work with but well worth it; and the sweet, meaty morel mushroom. Frequently combined, theirs are the earthy flavors of the season. For the pot pie, you don't need to do much to these ingredients—the morels further enhance the stock in which the chicken thighs were boiled; the salsify gets peeled, chopped, and cooked in a roux before the stock is added; and the favas, once shucked and shelled, get tossed in at the end with the chives and chicken meat. And it doesn't have to be poultry. I've made this dish, in miniature form, using rabbit legs (in a course that presented that animal in three different forms). And you can always swap your vegetables to coincide with what's available.

A roux is one of the mainstays of French cooking; it's a thickening agent and based on a simple 1:1 ratio of fat to flour. Butter is the most traditional fat selected and the one I prefer for this recipe. You will see a roux described by its color, which is determined by how long you cook it. The longer it spends on the stove, the darker your flour gets. A toasty roux will impart a stronger, nuttier flavor. In this case, that's not what I'm looking for. I want a lighter-hued, or blond, roux just to give my stock some body. Thickness is something to keep in mind if you're planning to bake the dish again in its shell (it's an easy item to make in advance and freeze). If you are going to reheat it, you actually want to start with a sauce that's a little too thick—it will thin out when it's placed in the oven a second time as all the vegetables will release their water.

Make the biscuit top: In a large bowl, combine the flour, sugar, baking powder, and salt, then cut in the butter. Add the cream, starting with ¾ cup, and stir just until the dough forms a ball. You may have to use up to 1 cup cream, depending on the humidity. Do not overwork the dough. Enclose in plastic wrap and refrigerate for at least 30 minutes. This can be done a day in advance.

Make the filling: Melt 2 tablespoons of the butter in a pot and add the onion. Cook over medium heat until softened and translucent, about 5 minutes. Add the garlic, bay leaf, and thyme and stir. Add the chicken thighs and enough water to cover. Bring to a boil, skim off any foam and scum, and simmer for 1 hour, skimming as needed and adding water to keep the thighs covered if necessary. Remove the thighs from the broth and let cool slightly, then remove the meat and cut into bite-size pieces. Remove and discard the thyme and bay leaf. There should be about 1 quart of broth in the pot; if not, cook until it is reduced to 1 quart. Add the mushrooms and bring to a boil.

Meanwhile, in a separate pot, melt the remaining ½ cup of butter over medium heat and whisk in the flour. Cook, without browning, for 3 minutes, whisking constantly. Add the salsify and cook for 1 minute. Slowly whisk in the morels and the stock mixture, whisking constantly to prevent lumps. Simmer, stirring occasionally, for 4 to 5 minutes, until the mixture is quite thick. Add the chives, fava beans, and chicken meat and season with the salt and pepper. Transfer to an 8-inch square (or 2-quart) baking dish. Preheat the oven to 375°F.

Roll the biscuit dough out to ⅓ inch thick and use it to cover the chicken mixture to form a pie. Cut 4 slashes in the top to allow the release of steam. Bake until the top is browned and cooked through, about 30 minutes. Let cool slightly before serving.

NOTES: To reconstitute dried mushrooms, cover with warm water and allow to steep for 20 minutes, then strain.

To clean fresh fava beans, remove from the pods, then peel off the thin, light-green covering, reserving the pea-green centers.

PAN-ROASTED DUCK BREASTS

WITH CHESTNUT PUREE AND HONEY GASTRIQUE

SERVES 4

FOR THE RED WINE SAUCE (OPTIONAL):

½ cup red wine

¼ cup port wine

1 shallot, chopped

2 cups duck demi-glace (see Note)

1 sprig fresh sage

¼ teaspoon salt

Black pepper to taste

FOR THE CHESTNUT PUREE:

2 tablespoons butter

½ pound roasted peeled chestnuts

1 cup heavy cream

1 teaspoon salt

Black pepper to taste

FOR THE DUCK AND THE HONEY
GASTRIQUE:

2 Long Island duck breasts, split, skin
   scored in a checkerboard pattern

1 tablespoon salt

Black pepper to taste

2 tablespoons butter

4 fresh sage leaves

¼ cup red wine vinegar

¼ cup chestnut honey

FOR THE BRUSSELS SPROUTS:

16 to 20 large Brussels sprouts,
   cleaned, blanched in salted water,
   shocked, and cut in half

1 tablespoon butter

1 tablespoon neutral-flavored
   vegetable oil

½ teaspoon salt

What I love about duck is that there are endless possibilities with every single part of this delicious bird. I've braised tongues and feet, stuffed duck necks, made confit of gizzard and heart, and used the rendered fat in numerous ways—poached fish in it, whisked hollandaise full of it, formed pastry dough with it; the liver (and the other f-word) seems tame after that. I've even had grilled duck testicles! Oddly, they didn't sell very well at the restaurant where we prepared them; they were big and delicious (is that why they walk that way?). One chef, whom I won't name, swears they taste just like duck semen. Such is the banter in a professional kitchen.

Here, the most commonly served part of the bird—the breasts—I pair with roasted chestnuts. I make a simple chestnut puree, with some salt, pepper, and cream. After I render the fat in the skin at a low temperature and turn the breasts over and increase the heat to sauté them, they get placed on the puree. Over those, I drizzle a chestnut-honey gastrique, a syrupy sauce that sounds much more complicated than it is. It refers to a reduction of vinegar and caramel—replaced here by the subtler honey. It's quick work; just pick up the unwashed pan in which you cooked the breasts, so that the natural duck juices left behind can give their flavor to the sauce. Since greens are good for you and add a different color and some balancing bitterness to the plate, I like to braise a few Brussels sprouts in a bath of water and, to make them taste extra good, a touch of duck fat or butter.

Make the red wine sauce, if desired: In a saucepan, combine the wines and shallot and bring to a boil. Lower the heat to medium-high and cook until reduced and syrupy, then add the demi-glace. Simmer, skimming occasionally, until reduced and thickened to a sauce consistency, and well flavored. Add the sage sprig and simmer another minute, then pour through a fine-mesh sieve into a bowl. Season to taste with salt and pepper. This can be made several days in advance and reheated.

Make the chestnut puree: Put the butter in a saucepan and cook over medium heat until browned, frothy, and fragrant of nuts, then add the chestnuts and cream and bring to a boil. Transfer to a food processor and blend until smooth. Season with the salt and pepper. Keep warm, covered, until use.

Make the duck and the honey gastrique: Season the duck breasts with salt and pepper on both sides. Heat a sauté pan large enough to hold the duck breasts in a single layer (or use two pans) over high heat. When hot, add the duck breasts, skin side down, to the dry pan and immediately lower the heat to low. Cook, pouring off fat as necessary so that only the skin cooks, until it is browned and crisp (it should be about half the size it was at the start). Increase the heat to medium-high and turn the duck over. Add the butter and sage leaves and cook on the other side for another 1 to 2 minutes for medium-rare (or 5 to 6 minutes for well-done), basting the meat with the browned butter. Remove to a warm plate to rest and reserve the sage leaves for garnish. Pour the fat from the pan, then add the vinegar, scraping any browned bits up from the pan. Add the honey and cook until reduced and syrupy.

Make the Brussels sprouts: Put the Brussels sprouts in a sauté pan with the butter and oil and season with salt. Cook over medium-high heat until caramelized and cooked through.

To serve: Place a dollop of the chestnut puree in the center of each serving plate, slice the duck breasts against the grain and place on top, and garnish with the reserved sage leaf. Circle with the red wine sauce (if using) and drizzle with the honey gastrique. Top the sauce with a few Brussels sprouts.

NOTE: D'Artagnan makes a duck demi-glace that works well here; see Resources, page 233.

The breast of a Long Island duck is like that of a chicken except flatter and more square. To remove the breast from a whole duck, make an incision down the center of the breastbone: You will see a line that separates the two breast muscles where the cartilage is. Cut just to one side of this bone, straight down, until you hit the breast plate, separating it all the way from the tip of the body to the neck area. Then turn your knife almost horizontally, perhaps at a 90-degree angle, and cut along the plate until you separate the meat from the bone. Squab, another gamy fowl, would work beautifully in this recipe as well.

BREAST OF DUCK
WITH HOISIN AND FIGS

Here, basically, is westernized Peking duck. I taught this dish to a class of home cooks at the New School in Manhattan because it's easy and looks impressive. You take the bird's breast and render it, skin down, over low heat until the fowl's outer layer browns and crisps up. Next, you flip the meat over and let the flesh cook to a desired doneness—mine is medium-rare. With that, you present a quick beggar's purse—a package of confit duck leg and fresh fig bundled in a mu shu wrapper that is tied with a blanched scallion ribbon. In cooking school, where I learned to make these types of purses, a crêpe served as the container for whipped crème fraîche and caviar, or a protein salad filled with, for example, lobster. This Chinese-style rendition is a lot easier and, once executed, might be compared to a savory bun. The mu shu wrapper is virtually the same as a traditional Peking pancake only larger, and the inclusion of crackling skin, scallion, and a hoisin-based sauce makes this a reworking of the original.

The fig, like any other duck-friendly fruit, underscores the sweetness of the hoisin and cuts the fatty, gamy notes. In the following recipe, I include a small pile of sautéed spinach on the side for some balancing vegetation, but the greens are interchangeable; for that class, I steamed some yu choi, an Asian green. An even quicker option entails slicing some raw cucumber and scallion for a salad dressed with a little soy and rice vinegar. Another choice would be to exclude the greens altogether; they are not mandatory.

Score the skin of the duck breasts to facilitate the melting of fat. Season both sides with salt and pepper. Heat a large sauté pan over high heat. When hot, add the duck breasts, skin side down, and immediately lower

SERVES 4

2 boneless breasts of Long Island (also known as pekin) duck, split

Salt and black pepper to taste

FOR THE SAUCE:

¼ cup hoisin sauce

½ teaspoon sesame oil

Black pepper to taste

FOR THE BEGGAR'S PURSES:

1 scallion, green part only

4 fresh figs

1 confit duck leg, meat shredded

Salt and black pepper to taste

1 tablespoon thinly sliced (on a bias) scallion greens

4 mu shu wrappers (optional)

TO SERVE:

Neutral-flavored vegetable oil

1 clove garlic (optional)

1 bunch spinach, stemmed and washed (optional)

Salt (optional)

You can either buy your confit meat, or do something homemade by slow-roasting duck legs in your oven at 300°F for 2½ hours, or until tender. If the season for figs has passed, dried figs or even prunes will also work. So would peaches or lychees, which, because of their floral qualities, add a layer of complexity. Other options include plum, or a combination of apricot and almond. In addition, you can simplify this recipe by omitting the mu shu wrapping and serving the stuffed figs as they are.

the heat to the lowest setting. As fat accumulates, pour excess from the pan. You will need to degrease the pan several times before the fat in the skin is fully rendered. When the skin is light brown and shrunken, but the meat still raw, remove to a rack, skin side up, and let cool.

Make the sauce: In a small bowl, whisk the hoisin sauce with 2 to 3 tablespoons of water, the sesame oil, and pepper.

Make the beggar's purses: Blanch the scallion, shock in ice water, and shred into 4 long strings. Cut the tips off the figs and, starting from the top, make 3 incisions two-thirds of the way down to the base of the fig to open the fig up like a flower. In a small bowl, combine the confit with the thinly sliced scallion and salt and pepper and stuff the figs with the mixture. Wrap each in a mu shu wrapper and tie with the scallion strings to form beggar's purses.

To serve: Just before serving, heat a sauté pan over high heat and add 2 tablespoons of oil. When smoking, add the duck breasts, skin side down, then immediately lower the heat to medium-high. Recrisp to a dark brown, turn, and cook to desired doneness.

Meanwhile, steam the beggar's purses over boiling water until hot in the center, about 5 minutes. If making the spinach, heat a sauté pan over medium-high heat. Add 2 tablespoons of oil, then the garlic, and swirl. Do not brown the garlic. Add the spinach and sauté until wilted, adding 1 tablespoon water if necessary. Season with salt and drain. Serve with the sauce, duck breasts, and beggar's purses.

PAN-ROASTED FARM CHICKEN

WITH SHERRY, WHITE TRUFFLE, AND PIG FEET

This requires some technique, but it isn't that hard. It's more of a time commitment than anything else, and it's the pig feet that demand the most minutes. It's also the pig feet that make the dish stand out. Recently, this portion of the pig has started to show up on more menus as part of an offal trend. People seem to think it's either cool or weird—or cool because it's weird. But it's an ingredient that has been used around the world for ages, most often in peasant cuisine, where nothing is wasted. The trotter is both cheap and full of flavor. At the famous Au Pied de Cochon, a Parisian restaurant named for this very part, I once had the most delicious example. It was a foot (*pied*) that had been braised until its meat was falling off the bone, then reshaped into its original form, coated in cornmeal, and, finally, fried and served with mustard sauce.

If you work with a good chicken, it will be juicy and stand out on its own, especially its crisp, roasted skin; the pig makes it that much better. The sauce is a puree of caramelized onions, scented with sherry and white truffles. Since fresh white truffles aren't always easy to find (or afford), I opt for white-truffle butter, which you can order from D'Artagnan (see Resources, page 233). I use caramelized onions as a thickening agent; they pick up on the stuffing's leeks and provide yet another layer of savory richness.

Make the pig feet: In a small saucepan, blanch the pig feet in boiling, heavily salted (about 2 tablespoons salt) water seasoned with the lemon juice for 3 to 5 minutes; drain and discard the water.

> *If you don't want to go the extra mile with the pig feet, or if you don't eat pork, you can skip the hoof and stuff the chicken with the sautéed leeks and mushrooms. In spring, you can serve this with some asparagus or more leeks (also known, in France, as "poor man's asparagus"). You can substitute whatever mushrooms are in season or whichever ones you prefer if you don't want to use chanterelles.*

SERVES 4

FOR THE PIG FEET:

2 pig feet, split lengthwise

Salt

1 tablespoon lemon juice

1 small onion, diced

1 clove garlic, chopped

2 tablespoons butter

½ cup white wine

About 2 quarts chicken stock (page 231)

1 bay leaf

1 sprig fresh thyme

5 whole black peppercorns

FOR THE STUFFING:

3 tablespoons butter

2 leeks, cleaned, white parts only, diced (about 3 cups)

2 teaspoons instant polenta, or 2 tablespoons bread crumbs

⅓ cup chanterelle mushrooms (about 2 ounces), brushed clean, cut into bite-size pieces, and sautéed (see Note)

2 teaspoons mixture of chopped fresh thyme, chives, and tarragon leaves

½ teaspoon salt

A few grinds of black pepper

3 teaspoons Dijon mustard

FOR THE SAUCE:

3 tablespoons butter

(CONTINUED)

FOR THE SAUCE (CONT'D):

2 onions, chopped

½ cup sherry

½ teaspoon salt

A few grinds of black pepper

¼ cup white-truffle butter

FOR THE CHICKENS:

2 whole chickens, halved, rib cage
   removed, legs and wing tips and
   second wing joints removed and
   reserved for another use (leave
   the wing "drumstick" attached),
   leaving the skin of each chicken half
   attached

Salt and black pepper

1 tablespoon neutral-flavored
   vegetable oil

20 asparagus spears

2 tablespoons butter

In a large pot over medium-low heat, sweat the onion and garlic in the butter until soft and slightly caramelized. Add the wine and cook until reduced by three-quarters. Add the pig feet and enough stock to cover. Bring to a boil, skim any foam that rises to the top, and lower the heat to a simmer. Add the bay leaf, thyme, and peppercorns and simmer for 3 hours, or until the pig feet are soft and the meat is falling off the bones, adding more liquid as necessary to keep the pig feet covered. Remove the pig feet and pour the stock through a fine-mesh sieve. When the pig feet are cool enough to handle, remove and discard all bones and dice the remains.

Make the stuffing: Heat a pot over medium heat and add the butter. When melted, add the leeks and cook, stirring, until softened but not browned. Add ¼ cup of the strained stock, stir in the polenta, and simmer for 3 minutes, until thickened. Add the sautéed chanterelles, chopped pig feet, and herbs and stir well. Season with the salt, pepper, and mustard. Set aside to cool to room temperature.

Make the sauce: Heat a pot over medium-high heat. Add the butter and swirl, then add the onions and cook, stirring occasionally, until golden brown. Add the sherry and cook until reduced and syrupy. Add about 1 cup of the remaining strained stock and bring to a boil. Cook to reduce slightly, then puree in a blender. Add the salt and pepper. Just before serving, bring back to a boil in the saucepan and whisk in the truffle butter.

Make the chickens: When the stuffing is completely cool, preheat the oven to 500°F. Place one-quarter of the stuffing into each chicken half, against the meat (the side that was against the rib cage). Roll up, wrapping the skin completely around to close. Season with salt and pepper. Heat a large ovenproof sauté pan over high heat. Add the oil and when smoking, add the chicken. Cook on high heat for 1 minute, then place in the oven. Roast, turning the chicken twice to be sure each side has become a crisp golden brown.

Put the asparagus in a large sauté pan with the butter, enough water to cover, and ½ teaspoon salt. Bring to a boil and cook until tender, then drain. Serve the stuffed chicken halves with the sauce and asparagus.

NOTE: Sauté the mushrooms in 1 tablespoon of butter and season with ⅛ teaspoon of salt and a few grinds of black pepper.

PAN-ROASTED GUINEA HEN
WITH ITS LIVER AND CRAYFISH

As you might have noticed, my culinary training in Paris has had a big influence on how I approach things as a chef. Here is another example, and it draws on two of French cuisine's timeless pairings, one familiar—lobster and foie gras; the other, less so—chicken liver and crayfish. Both are variations on the same theme—the union of a crustacean and a particular organ of fowl. In cooking school, I remember making a chicken-liver flan with a crayfish sauce, and then a similar custard (without the sauce) in French chef David Bouley's kitchen at his eponymous restaurant, where I began working right after I graduated from college. When I re-created it, I developed it from memory, and, I thought, a Paul Bocuse version. (Years later, I revisited the Bocuse recipe and realized mine looks nothing like it.)

Rich, gamy chicken livers multiply the lushness of an egg-based creamy flan. The depth builds when you add a classic crayfish reduction, which, flavored with the crustacean's shells and thickened with rice, is based on a *sauce américaine*. The seafood's sweet, briny character brings another layer of intensity. When I think of crawfish and rice, my mind goes to Creole cooking. Both ingredients are important parts of Louisiana culture. In New Orleans' (and its food's) honor, I use its "holy trinity"—celery, onion, and green pepper—in this truly American sauce, and I add one of that city's favorite spices, cayenne, for heat. Sautéed okra makes a perfect side.

Make the crayfish sauce: Heat 2 tablespoons of the butter in a large sauté pan over high heat. Add the crayfish, stir, then add the brandy and sauté until bright red. Remove the crayfish from the pan and extract the tail meat, reserving the meat, and shells and heads separately. To the pan, add the onion, green pepper, celery, carrot, and garlic. Reduce the heat to low and cook, stirring, until vegetables are wilted and onion is translucent, about 5 minutes. Add the cayenne and stir, then add the reserved heads and shells plus the tomato, rice, wine, thyme, and bay leaf. Cook until reduced by half, then add enough water to cover and simmer until well flavored, about 1 hour. Place all in a blender with 1 teaspoon of salt and puree. Pour through a fine-mesh sieve into a bowl, extracting as much vegetable pulp as possible. The result should be thick like a sauce. If it is still not thick, return to a clean pot and cook to reduce until thickened.

SERVES 4

FOR THE CRAYFISH SAUCE:

4 tablespoons butter

2 pounds crayfish

2 tablespoons brandy

½ cup chopped onion

¼ cup chopped green bell pepper

¼ cup chopped celery

¼ cup chopped carrot

1 clove garlic, smashed

½ teaspoon ground cayenne

½ cup chopped tomato

3 tablespoons long-grain rice

1 cup white wine

1 sprig fresh thyme

1 bay leaf

Salt

½ teaspoon lemon juice, or to taste

Black pepper to taste

FOR THE FLANS:

2 teaspoons minced shallots

1 clove garlic, smashed

2 tablespoons duck fat or butter

1 tablespoon brandy

½ cup guinea hen livers (from below; supplement with chicken livers if necessary)

½ cup heavy cream

1 large egg

1 teaspoon salt

Black pepper to taste

(CONTINUED)

FOR THE GUINEA HENS:

2 small guinea hens, breasts removed
   with first joint of wings attached,
   skin on (frenched, legs and thighs
   reserved, livers reserved for flans
   above)

1 teaspoon salt

Black pepper to taste

4 tablespoon neutral-flavored
   vegetable oil

TO SERVE:

1 tablespoon butter, plus more for
   reheating the crayfish

12 okra pods, trimmed

Salt

12 fresh tarragon leaves (optional)

Whisk in the remaining butter and lemon juice, then season to taste with salt and pepper.

Make the flans: Preheat the oven to 300°F. In a sauté pan, sweat the shallots and garlic in the duck fat over medium-low heat, then add the brandy and cook to reduce by half. Add the mixture, along with the livers, cream, egg, salt, and pepper, to a food processor and blend until smooth. Pour through a fine china cap or your finest sieve. Divide among 4 buttered 3-ounce molds, and put in a hot water bath (see page 16). Cover the pan and bake until puffed and set, 20 to 25 minutes. Set aside in a warm place (a toaster oven set to 250°F will work).

Make the guinea hens: Preheat the oven to 500°F. Season both sides of the breasts, legs, and thighs with the salt and pepper. Heat two large ovenproof sauté pans over high heat. Add 2 tablespoons oil to each and when smoking, add the breasts to one pan, skin side down, and the legs and thighs to the other, also skin side down. Place in the oven and roast for 3 to 4 minutes, until golden brown and crisp. Turn and return to the oven to roast on the other side until just cooked through, another 3 to 4 minutes. The legs will take a few minutes more than the breasts. Remove to a warm plate.

To serve: In a medium sauté pan, heat the butter and sauté the okra until al dente and just bright green. Season with ½ teaspoon of salt. In the same pan, reheat the crayfish tail meat with a little butter. Place a puddle of the sauce on a plate, unmold a flan to one side of the sauce, then top the flan with the crayfish and three tarragon leaves (if using). Place the roasted guinea hen to the other side of the sauce and serve with the okra.

> *If you want to do something over-the-top, you could consider deep-frying a few spears of okra and using those as a garnish. Its crunchy exterior provides an excellent textural contrast to everything else on the plate.*

CHICKEN WINGS
WITH KOREAN CHILE

When it comes to wings, I truly believe you have to deep-fry them. You can bake them, of course, but I love wings because they include my favorite part of the chicken, what I refer to as the forearm, and it's deep-frying that gets the end of the wing crispy, sticky, and perfect. The other amazing thing about the wing is that flavorful, tender piece of flesh in between the radius and the ulna (the two thin parallel bones in the flat joint); frying enhances this, too, as the section's fat helps to crisp up the skin around it.

At Maxim's, we always had lots of forearms on hand; they were the by-product of whatever chicken dish we were serving to diners. My cook, Juan, would coat them in a mixture of ketchup, sriracha, and red wine vinegar after frying them. They were fantastic. He'd serve them Buffalo-style with a blue-cheese sauce.

When the deep-frying is done, you can add the sauce or seasonings of your choice to your wings. Here, I take them in a Korean direction with a combination of *gochujang* (Korean chile paste), garlic, ginger, and sesame seeds. A quick pickle of cucumbers and daikon radish provides a sweet, cooling agent to counteract the chile's heat and gives you something to crunch on.

Make the pickles: Heat the vinegar and sugar in a small saucepan just until the sugar melts, then pour over remaining pickle ingredients in a bowl and stir. Let sit for 1 hour before serving. (The pickles can be made in advance and kept in an airtight container in the refrigerator.)

Make the chicken: Fill a large pot halfway with the oil and heat to 375°F. Season the wings with salt and pepper and deep-fry just until they float. Drain on paper towels.

Make the sauce: Combine all the ingredients in a large bowl. When the wings are done, toss them with the sauce and serve with the pickles.

> *My other favorite parts of the bird are, like the wings, the fattiest— the legs and the tail. You could actually apply this recipe to the latter (yes, it's technically the chicken's butt) and turn an often wasted bit of poultry into something delicious.*

SERVES 4

FOR THE PICKLES:

1 cup rice vinegar

2 tablespoons sugar

1 Kirby cucumber, unpeeled, halved lengthwise and cut into ⅓-inch-thick half moons

As much daikon as cucumber, peeled, halved lengthwise, and cut into ⅓-inch-thick half moons

3 cloves garlic, smashed

1 teaspoon salt

FOR THE CHICKEN WINGS:

3 pounds chicken wings

Salt and black pepper

1 quart neutral-flavored vegetable oil (or more as necessary)

FOR THE KOREAN CHILE SAUCE:

½ cup ketchup

⅓ cup *gochujang* (Korean chile paste)

3 tablespoons sugar

1½ tablespoons soy sauce

1½ tablespoons rice wine vinegar

½ teaspoon sesame oil

1 teaspoon toasted sesame seeds

1 teaspoon finely chopped garlic

Pinch of finely chopped ginger

Several grinds of black pepper

II. MEAT

KOHLRABI AND FLANK STEAK STIR-FRY

My mother used to serve kohlrabi in stir-fries when I was growing up. The first time I saw the plant growing, she had taken me to visit some older woman who, I think, may have belonged to the Quaker meetinghouse where I had to spend many Sunday mornings sitting silently in a circle. The woman's home was somewhere near Cranbrook, a local private school whose environs had the only hills in town. She had a large garden on the side of one of those hills with all sorts of vegetables growing in it. Her kohlrabies were huge. Maybe I just thought they were huge because I was small, but I swear, now, I can never get them to grow that big without their turning tough and fibrous, like pieces of wood.

I remember marveling at the plant's shape—like the Oriental Pearl Tower, Shanghai's famous space-needle skyscraper. The stalk grows up from the ground; in the middle, a big, protruding bulb seems impossibly perched, and on top, a leafy plant blossoms. The stalk and globe are light green, and the latter is what you peel and eat. The dark leafy greens are also edible and packed with nutrients.

Heat a wok or large sauté pan over high heat for 2 to 3 minutes. Add the oil and when smoking, add the kohlrabi and onion. Stir until softened but not fully cooked through, 1 to 2 minutes. Add the garlic and ginger and stir, then add the flank steak. Stir until the meat has started to brown. Add the Shaoxing and bring to a boil. Add the soy sauce, oyster sauce, and sugar and stir. Add the cornstarch slurry, stirring until thickened. Season to taste with pepper. Serve over rice.

SERVES 4 AS A MAIN COURSE

4½ tablespoons neutral-flavored vegetable oil

1½ large bulbs kohlrabi, peeled and cut into ¼-inch-thick, 2-inch-long matchsticks

1 medium onion, sliced

3 cloves garlic, finely chopped

1½ teaspoons julienned fresh ginger

1½ pounds flank steak, thinly sliced across the grain

2½ tablespoons Shaoxing cooking wine (or substitute dry sherry)

4½ tablespoons soy sauce

1½ tablespoons oyster sauce

1½ teaspoons sugar

3 tablespoons cornstarch mixed with ½ cup water

Black pepper

Steamed white rice

Kohlrabi is also delicious eaten raw, in a slaw, or straight up. While she was preparing her stir-fry, my mom used to hand us a few slices of the vegetable uncooked, sprinkled with a bit of salt. That was the way I liked it best, crunchy and sweet, simple and refreshing.

MY MOTHER'S BBQ SPARERIBS

SERVES 4

1 side pork spareribs

Salt and black pepper

1 cup ketchup

1 cup hoisin sauce

Before she retired, my mother put in long hours as a pathologist in charge of the blood bank at our local hospital in Troy, Michigan. One of the few female physicians of her time, she had to work extra hard, but she always managed to come home and cook well-balanced dinners that included a variety of dishes for my brother, sister, and me. This was one of our favorites; it's also one of the first (and easiest) things she taught me to make.

I have no idea where she first discovered these BBQ ribs. They require equal amounts of Chinese hoisin sauce and ketchup, the old-fashioned American version. It almost sounds like something you'd find on the back of a bottle of Heinz 57. I've tried more complicated Korean recipes, but my mom's produces results that are just as good. Her pork ribs were one of the most popular items on the menu at my restaurant bar Q. They were also a hit at a staff meal, served with sticky rice and sautéed Asian greens.

Preheat the oven to 400°F. Season the spareribs on both sides with salt and pepper. In a small bowl, combine the ketchup and hoisin. Put the ribs in a shallow baking dish and pour the ketchup-hoisin mixture over the ribs, turning to coat both sides evenly. Cover the baking dish with aluminum foil and bake for 25 minutes, then remove the foil and continue to cook for another 20 minutes.

> *My mother prepared this with meatier spareribs, but I like using the more tender baby backs just as much. The sauce is versatile and can be applied to short ribs or chicken, too. A quick sear on the grill before slathering on your sauce and putting the ribs in the oven will capture the char flavor. In summer, if you are doing an outdoor barbecue, grilled corn is a nice accompaniment.*

BONELESS BARBECUED SPARERIBS
WITH KOHLRABI, PEANUT, AND BASIL

I love to look through old cookbooks for forgotten recipes that might spark new ideas, and there is a treasure trove at my neighbor Jerry's house. His late wife, who came from Germany, was a passionate cook and had collected many such books over the years. I was recently perusing one of these and came across a recipe for stuffed kohlrabi. I didn't know that this was a vegetable common in Germany; perhaps that's how it came to my childhood table, and not, as I'd initially thought, via Asia or Tennessee (where my mother went to school).

It's easy to assume that kohlrabi is a Chinese ingredient; you find it in Chinatowns across the United States and in many Chinese dishes here, including stir-fries like the ones my own mother made. It's an equal-opportunity plant in terms of where it will grow—in almost any climate—but it came to us in its current form and denomination from Germany. *Kohlrabi* is a combination of two words—one for cabbage, the other turnip—and is also known as German turnip. Flavor-wise, there's no turnip here, though. The cabbage, however, is accurate. Like broccoli, cauliflower, Brussels sprouts, collards, and kale, kohlrabi is a wild cabbage descendent, which explains its flavor profile.

The kohlrabi in Jerry's wife's book was stuffed with pork and echoes—or foreshadows—the following recipe. When I created this dish, I used kohlrabi as a nod to the American South, instead of selecting a more Southeast Asian ingredient such as green papaya. Perhaps it is a nod to Germany as well. Such is the American experience.

Make the marinade: Put the fish sauce, sugar, garlic, lemongrass, and pepper in a food processor and process until finely chopped. Transfer to a baking dish, add the ribs, and turn to coat all sides. Put in the refrigerator to marinate overnight.

Make the stuffing: Combine all the ingredients in a bowl. Transfer to a pastry bag fitted with a wide round tip.

SERVES 4

FOR THE MARINADE AND SPARERIBS:

1 cup fish sauce

2 cups sugar

5 large cloves garlic

1 stalk lemongrass, dry outer leaves removed, cut into 1-inch lengths

Black pepper to taste

1 side pork spareribs, top cut off at the end of the rib bone

FOR THE STUFFING:

1 pound ground pork

1 cup blanched and shocked glass noodles, chopped

¼ cup grated carrot

⅓ cup reconstituted and cleaned dried tree-ear mushrooms

1 large egg

¼ cup chopped scallions

About 3 tablespoons oyster sauce, or to taste

1 tablespoon sriracha chile sauce

Sugar, salt, and black pepper to taste

FOR THE NUOC MAM SAUCE:

¼ cup fish sauce

¼ cup lime juice

2 tablespoons rice vinegar

2 tablespoons sugar

(CONTINUED)

Make the nuoc mam sauce: Combine all the ingredients in a small bowl. Taste and adjust the seasonings.

Make the peanut sauce: Combine the peanut butter, hoisin sauce, 1 tablespoon of the nuoc mam sauce, and 2 tablespoons water in a bowl. Taste and adjust the seasonings.

Make the ribs: Preheat the oven to 350°F. Cover the baking dish with the ribs and marinade with aluminum foil and bake for 1½ to 2 hours, until the bones start to come away from the meat. Remove the ribs from the baking dish and let cool. Pull the bones out and stuff the spaces that remain with the ground-pork mixture. Return to the baking dish and bake, uncovered, for 20 minutes, or until the stuffing is cooked through. Scrape the marinade from the ribs and pour the juices from the baking dish through a fine-mesh sieve into a bowl. Cut the ribs into 4 equal portions.

To serve: In a bowl, combine the kohlrabi and basil and season with salt, pepper, and nuoc mam sauce. Place the peanut sauce and strained rib juices in the center of each large serving plate. Place one rib portion on top of each. Top with the salad and serve.

FOR THE NUOC MAM SAUCE (CONT'D):
1 clove garlic, smashed to a paste
2 Thai bird chiles, finely chopped
FOR THE PEANUT SAUCE:
½ cup chunky peanut butter
1 tablespoon hoisin sauce
TO SERVE:
2 heads kohlrabi, peeled and thinly sliced
Several Thai and opal basil leaves
Salt and black pepper

Some say the word sparerib *evolved from the German* rippenspeer, *which translates to "spear rib," because this cut of pork was often cooked on a spear or spit. In any case, this is a part of the pig enjoyed the world over. It comes from the belly side of the rib cage and benefits from the slow cooking this recipe entails. Before you marinate the spareribs, consider marking them on a hot grill for a bit of char; let them cool to room temperature before adding them to the marinade.*

GRILLED HANGER STEAK
WITH KOREAN FLAVORS AND SPICY POTATO PANCAKES

SERVES 4

FOR THE STEAK AND MARINADE:

¼ cup soy sauce

¼ cup sugar

1 teaspoon finely chopped garlic

1 tablespoon finely chopped scallion
    white

½ teaspoon toasted sesame seeds

Black pepper to taste

4 (6-ounce) trimmed hanger steaks

FOR THE POTATO PANCAKES:

3 large Idaho potatoes, peeled

1 teaspoon Korean ground chile
    (*gochu garu*) or any mild ground
    chile

2 tablespoons thinly sliced (on a bias)
    scallion greens

Salt and black pepper to taste

½ cup neutral-flavored vegetable oil

FOR THE SALAD:

1 teaspoon soy sauce

1 teaspoon rice vinegar

Pinch of sugar

1 tablespoon neutral-flavored
    vegetable oil

A few drops of sesame oil

A large handful of mixed greens,
    preferably an Asian mesclun

Salt and black pepper to taste

(CONTINUED)

Here's a French classic—steak frites—via Seoul. When I opened Mirezi in the mid-'90s, I was sent to Korea to take a week of cooking classes and to meet the head honchos of the company that owned the new pan-Asian restaurant. One of the recipes I learned was the marinade for bulgogi, which some might call Korea's national dish. It's composed of thin cuts of beef, grilled and served with lettuce wraps. This is an American take on that specialty and my first "signature" dish, if there ever was such a thing. I use a hanger steak, a classic bistro cut of meat that is full flavored with a slightly sweet liverlike note that pairs nicely with the garlic, sugar, and soy. Not only is it one of the cow's more economical parts, but it's tender, too; in fact, it was once called "butcher's steak," as butchers would keep it for themselves.

Instead of French fries, I decided to reinterpret that side so that it would complement my Asian-influenced beef. Koreans have all different kinds of pancakes, including one made from mung beans and another, *pajun*, a wheat- and/or rice-flour example with endless stuffing variations. I thought it would be interesting to try a potato version with scallion and, as a reference to the pancake's origins, Korean chile.

Make the steak and marinade: Combine the soy sauce, sugar, garlic, scallion, sesame seeds, and pepper and pour over the steaks. Cover and put in the refrigerator to marinate for at least 4 hours, turning once halfway through, or overnight.

Make the potato pancakes: Working quickly to prevent oxidation, grate the potatoes on the largest holes of a box grater or in a food processor. Put in a clean kitchen towel and squeeze to extract as much liquid as possible. Place in a bowl and combine with the Korean ground chile and scallion. Season with salt and pepper. Heat a 12-inch sauté pan over high heat. Add half of the oil and when lightly smoking, add the potatoes, divided into 4 even balls. Press down to form round cakes about ½ inch thick. Lower the heat to medium-high and cook until the cakes are deep golden brown. Turn and add the remaining oil if necessary (the potatoes will absorb some oil) and brown the other side. Drain on paper towels.

Make the salad: Combine the soy sauce, vinegar, and sugar in a bowl and whisk in the oils. Dress the greens with the vinaigrette and season with salt and pepper.

Make the sauce, if desired: In a small bowl, combine all the ingredients.

To serve: Remove the steaks from the marinade and scrape off any excess marinade. Season with pepper and a little bit of salt. Rub both sides with a little oil and grill to desired doneness. Reheat the potato pancakes, if necessary, in a 375°F oven. Place one in the center of each large serving plate and ring with 1 tablespoon of the sauce (if using). Slice the steaks against the grain and arrange over the top of the pancake. Garnish the top with the salad and serve.

> It's important to have a clean, well-oiled grill that isn't too hot. Because of the sugars in the marinade, the meat tends to caramelize quickly and stick, which causes it to burn before it has finished cooking. A properly prepped grill will help prevent the sticking.

FOR THE SAUCE (OPTIONAL):
2 tablespoons *gochujang* (Korean chile paste)
2 tablespoons water
1 scant tablespoon sugar

TO SERVE:
Salt and black pepper to taste
Neutral-flavored vegetable oil

CRISP ROTISSERIE PORK

SERVES 4

FOR THE MARINADE AND PORK:

1 cup sour orange juice, or ⅔ cup
    lime juice

2 tablespoons finely chopped garlic

1 teaspoon ground cumin

1 tablespoon red pepper flakes

1 tablespoon dried oregano

3 tablespoons olive oil

4 pounds pork belly, boned, skin on

1 heaping tablespoon salt

Black pepper to taste

FOR THE BLACK BEANS:

2 tablespoons olive oil

1 small onion, chopped

3 cloves garlic, chopped

1 teaspoon ground cumin

1 sprig fresh thyme

1 bay leaf

2 cups dried black beans, soaked
    overnight in water

1 quart chicken stock (page 231), plus
    more if needed

Salt and black pepper to taste

FOR THE RICE:

Pinch of saffron

¼ cup white wine

1½ tablespoons olive oil

1 small shallot, minced

1 clove garlic, finely chopped

1 ripe medium tomato, finely chopped

1 cup long-grain white rice

1½ cups chicken stock (page 231) or
    water

1 teaspoon salt

Black pepper to taste

This dish couldn't be easier. In the country, when I have company, I often set the pig up on the rotating spit (although you can do this in an oven, too) and let it roast while I take my guests clamming. The meat needs at least three and a half hours of cooking and will still be delicious, if not more meltingly tender, after four and a half hours. If all goes well, we return with both steamers and hardshells. We eat the hardshells raw, before our pork dinner, and soak the rest of the shellfish overnight so we can enjoy it for the next day's lunch.

Just by changing the marinating liquid or dry seasonings, you can create entirely different styles of pork: Rub it down with Chinese five-spice powder and serve it in steamed buns, or make a porchetta by applying garlic, rosemary, and fennel pollen. I've prepared it in many ways, but this approach, a Cuban one, reminds me of my college days, when I lived above La Rosita, a sliver of a restaurant that served outstanding roast pork with sides of rice and beans.

Make the marinade and pork: Combine the sour orange juice, garlic, cumin, red pepper flakes, oregano, and oil and place in a shallow baking dish with the pork, turning to coat all sides. Let marinate, skin side up, for 2 hours at room temperature or up to overnight in the refrigerator. Remove the pork from the marinade. Season both sides with the salt and pepper. Roll into a tight cylinder with the skin facing out, tie tightly with butcher twine at 2-inch intervals. If you have a rotisserie, place the pork onto it, set over a drip pan and cook over low heat for at least 3½ hours, until tender throughout and crisp. Toward the end of the cooking, stop the rotisserie but leave the heat on. Blast the pork with high heat, and the pig skin will puff up and bubble. Turn the pork once the skin puffs up and repeat until every inch of the skin is exposed to the heat, and you end up with a crisp, chicharrón-like crust.

If you don't have a rotisserie, preheat the oven to 300°F. Place the pork on a rack over a baking dish with 1 inch of water in it and cover with aluminum foil. Bake for 3 hours, then remove the foil and bake for 1 hour longer. Finish under the broiler to crisp the skin, as described above, or increase the oven temperature to as high as it goes; watch as the pork continues to cook, until its skin puffs.

Make the black beans (this can be done the day before): Heat a pot over medium heat. Add the oil, then the onion, and cook until soft and translucent, 3 to 5 minutes. Add the garlic and stir, then add the cumin, thyme, and bay leaf and stir again. Drain the beans and add them to the pot along with the stock. Bring to a boil, skim off any foam that rises to the top, then lower the heat to a simmer and cook until the beans are very soft and falling apart, about 45 minutes, adding more stock as necessary to keep the beans covered. The liquid should be thickened and somewhat soupy. Season with salt and pepper.

Make the rice: Soak the saffron in the wine. Heat a pot over medium heat. Add the oil, then the shallot and garlic, and cook until soft and translucent, 3 to 5 minutes. Add the saffron-wine mixture and tomato and cook until the tomato is reduced to a thick sauce. Add the rice and stir, then add the stock, salt, and pepper. Bring to a boil, stir, then cover and lower the heat to the lowest possible setting. Cook for 20 minutes, then fluff with a fork. Serve alongside the beans and pork.

BRAISED PORK WITH GIGANTES

SERVES 4

FOR THE PORK:

2 tablespoons olive oil

1 small onion, chopped

1 large clove garlic, chopped

2 pounds pork belly, boned, skin on,
   cut into 4 pieces

1 tablespoon salt

Several grinds of black pepper

About 6 cups chicken stock
   (page 231)

FOR THE GIGANTE BEANS:

1 cup gigante beans, soaked
   overnight in water

1 bay leaf

2 teaspoons salt

FOR THE CLAMS:

1 slice bacon, chopped

½ teaspoon finely chopped garlic

1 tablespoon finely chopped shallot

1 sprig fresh thyme

⅔ cup white wine

20 Manila or littleneck clams

FOR THE CILANTRO PESTO:

1 teaspoon seeded and finely
   chopped jalapeño chile

1 clove garlic

1 cup packed cilantro leaves

¼ cup olive oil

½ teaspoon salt

TO SERVE:

1 tablespoon butter

1 tablespoon lime juice

The initial influence for this comforting cold-weather rendition of pork and beans is Mexican. At the restaurant, this comes through in the garnish, a homemade chicharrón made by slow cooking in oil at a low temperature, then deep-frying some of the pig's skin. I love the contrast of pork textures—the crisp crackling on top of the melting, tender confited belly. For the home cook, this is an unnecessary step (or it could be accomplished by chopping a bag of pork rinds). Although you could use any white bean, such as Great Northern, I choose the gigantes because they're creamy and, as their name tells you, big. Indigenous to Greece, they're dried and available year round in specialty markets and gourmet groceries. These beans are easy to work with; you soak them overnight, cook them separately, and finish them in the pork's braising liquid. To turn the final product a beautiful shade of green and intensify its flavor, I make a garlic-cilantro pesto and, at plating time, stir it into each bowl to create a sauce. You could be more rustic about it, and incorporate the pesto into the cooking pot and let diners serve themselves, family style.

If you want to bring more depth and complexity to this stew, you could easily add some clams. Pork and clams, or seafood, is a ubiquitous pairing globally. For example, in New England you'll find creamy chowder of bacon and clams; in Korea, *bossam*, a classic dish, combines fresh oysters and steamed pork; and in Spanish cuisine there are endless recipes with chorizo and clams or other seafood. If you wanted to turn this into a Spanish entrée, you might prepare it with a fish—hake—and a parsley sauce. You could just as easily give it a Chinese twist by braising the pork belly in an oyster sauce with white soybeans, and for something more Japanese, swap in edamame or red azuki beans and a dashi broth with perhaps some daikon radish.

Any braising cut of pork will do. You could opt for the shoulder or a shank if you just want a simple weeknight supper. The pesto is a versatile condiment, so you might want to make extra. It's great spooned onto most meats or, with a little lime added, fish.

Make the pork: Heat a large saucepan over medium heat, add the oil, then the onion, and cook until translucent and soft. Add the garlic and stir. Season the pork belly all over with the salt and pepper and add it to the pan. Add enough stock to cover. Bring to a boil, skim off any foam that rises to the top, then simmer for 3 to 3½ hours, until very tender, skimming occasionally and adding water as necessary to keep the pork covered. Remove the pork to a dish and cook until the liquid is reduced to 2 cups. Set the pork and braising liquid aside.

Make the gigante beans: Drain the beans, put them in a saucepan, and add enough water to cover. Add the bay leaf, bring to a boil, and skim. Lower the heat to a simmer and cook for 40 minutes, or until soft. Add the salt and cook for another 5 minutes. Remove from the heat and set aside.

Make the clams: Heat a pot over high heat. Add the bacon and stir. Lower the heat to medium-high and cook for 1 minute, until some of the fat is rendered but the bacon is not crisp. Add the garlic, shallot, and thyme and stir. Cook until just soft, then add the wine and the clams and cover. Cook for 4 to 5 minutes, just until the clams open. Remove the clams and set the clams and pan aside. When cooled, remove the clams from their shells and discard the shells. Do not wash the pan.

Make the cilantro pesto: In a small food processor or blender, puree all the ingredients.

To serve: In a large pot, reheat the pork in 1 cup of the braising liquid. Add the remaining cup of braising liquid to the pan with the clam broth. Drain the beans, add to the clam broth, and bring to a boil. With a slotted spoon, divide the beans among 4 soup plates. Bring the remaining liquid in the pan to a boil again, add the pesto, and stir. Add the butter and whisk to emulsify. Add the clams and reheat. Season with the lime juice and spoon around the beans. Top the beans with the pork and serve.

GRILLED LAMB TENDERLOINS
WITH CURRIED GOLDEN RAISINS AND A SPINACH TIMBALE

SERVES 6

FOR THE CURRY OIL:

½ teaspoon black mustard seeds

½ cup neutral-flavored vegetable oil

1½ teaspoons curry powder

FOR THE LAMB SAUCE:

1 small onion, roughly chopped

3 cloves garlic, smashed

2 tablespoons clarified butter
  (see Notes)

1 cup red wine vinegar

1 large beefsteak tomato, roughly
  chopped

1 roasted lamb shank

2 quarts veal stock (page 232)

½ teaspoon salt

Black pepper to taste

FOR THE SPINACH TIMBALE:

4 whole cloves

4 green cardamom pods

1 bay leaf

6 whole black peppercorns

3 tablespoons clarified butter
  (see Notes)

1 medium onion, sliced

1 teaspoon chopped fresh ginger

1½ teaspoons chopped garlic

1 teaspoon ground cumin

½ teaspoon ground coriander

(CONTINUED)

My mom was from Malaysia. Like her, most of that country's inhabitants are Chinese—part of a substantial number of people who left the Fujian province for life in Kuala Lumpur. They continue to identify themselves as Chinese, linguistically and nationally, and are singled out by the Malaysian government as such; there are laws created specifically to control what you can or can't own as a Chinese person. This is a measure taken to preserve the native population and its progeny. The crossroads of Asia, Malaysia doesn't have one holistic, defining cuisine. Instead, there are four types of cooking styles, and each of those is a hybrid. There's Malay, which shares a lot with Indonesian food but bears traces of Chinese, Indian, and Thai cooking as well; then there's Malaysian Chinese food, whose strongest influence is the cuisine of mainland China but has its distinguishing marks and more regionally appropriate produce; third, there's Malaysian Indian cooking, which, though its roots lie in India, has been shaped by the other dominant ethnic cultures that Malaysia comprises; and finally there's Nyonya food, which is the cuisine of my mother's upbringing and combines Chinese ingredients with Southeast Asian spices; like my mom, it's technically a Chinese-Malay entity.

This dish owes a lot to Nyonya food, but it's an improvised amalgam that can only be explained as what makes sense on my palate. It started with the spinach timbale—comprised of dark, leafy greens, a heady blend of spices known as garam masala, and creamy yogurt. Then I decided on a main protein; the lamb's particular funkiness stands up to and complements the timbale's bold flavors. Next came the garnishes. The curried sultanas counter the lamb's muskiness with an earthy sweetness. For a final, crowning touch, I borrowed a Malaysian specialty that is unfamiliar to most people, *roti jala*, which translates to "net bread," and is a thin, lacy savory pancake often served with a curry. Made with coconut milk for mild sweetness, it is pretty to look at and provides the plate with some starch.

FOR THE SPINACH TIMBALE (CONT'D):

¼ teaspoon ground cayenne

1 teaspoon garam masala

2 bunches spinach, blanched,
    squeezed dry, and chopped

5 to 6 chicken bones and/or wings,
    roughly chopped

1 cup full-fat Greek yogurt

2 large eggs

2 large egg yolks

1½ teaspoons salt

Black pepper to taste

FOR THE RAISINS:

¼ teaspoon black mustard seeds

1 tablespoon clarified butter
    (see Notes)

1 teaspoon Madras curry powder

½ cup chicken stock (page 231)

¼ cup golden raisins

Salt and black pepper to taste

FOR THE *ROTI JALA*:

1 cup coconut milk

1 large egg

1 cup all-purpose flour

1 teaspoon salt

About 1 tablespoon clarified butter
    (see Notes)

2 teaspoons nigella (*kalonji*) seeds

1 tablespoon chopped fresh chives

FOR THE TENDERLOINS:

2½ pounds lamb tenderloins, 2 or 3
    per person (see Notes)

2 teaspoons salt

Black pepper to taste

Make the curry oil: Sweat the mustard seeds in a small amount of the oil in a saucepan over medium heat until they begin to pop, then add the curry powder. Stir and cook for a minute, then add the remaining oil. Stir. Remove from the heat and let stand overnight to allow the spices to settle to the bottom. Use the clarified oil from the top.

Make the lamb sauce: Sweat the onion and garlic in 1 tablespoon of the clarified butter in a medium stockpot over medium-low heat. Add the vinegar and cook until almost completely reduced. Add the tomato, lamb, and stock and simmer, skimming occasionally, until well flavored and thickened, about 4 hours. Pour through a fine-mesh sieve into a bowl. Season with the salt and pepper and finish with the remaining 1 tablespoon of clarified butter. Reserve the braised lamb shank for another use, such as in a ragout for pasta or a dinner for one.

Make the spinach timbale: Preheat the oven to 300°F. Cook the cloves, cardamom, bay leaf, and peppercorns in the clarified butter in a medium sauté pan over medium-low heat until they are fragrant and the cardamom pods puff slightly. Tie the spices in a piece of cheesecloth and return the sachet to the pan. Add the onion and cook until translucent and soft but not browned. Add the ginger and garlic and cook until soft. Add the cumin, coriander, cayenne, and garam masala and cook until fragrant. Add the spinach, chicken bones, and ¼ cup of the yogurt. Cook, covered, for about 20 minutes. Remove and discard the bones and cheesecloth bag with spices. Transfer the spinach mixture to a food processor and puree. Add the remaining yogurt, eggs, and egg yolks, blend, then season with the salt and pepper. Transfer the mixture to 6 (4-ounce) ramekins sprayed with nonstick cooking spray and set in a hot water bath (see page 16). Cover the pan with alumium foil and bake until just set, about 30 minutes.

Make the raisins: Cook the mustard seeds in the butter in a small saucepan over medium-low heat until they begin to pop. Add the curry powder and cook until fragrant. Add the stock and raisins and simmer until the raisins are reconstituted and the liquid is almost completely reduced. Season with the salt and pepper.

Make the *roti jala*: In a large bowl, combine the coconut milk and egg. Add the flour and salt. Add about 6 tablespoons of water to create a very thin crêpe-batter consistency (so it won't puff up too much). Use a small tea strainer with wide holes or perforate a plastic cup by punching small holes through the bottom. Heat a sauté pan over medium heat and rub with a thin layer of the butter. Add a pinch of nigella to the pan, followed by a pinch of chives. Drizzle the batter through the tea strainer to make lacy pancakes. Alternatively, dip your fingertips in the batter and, keeping them spread apart, drizzle the batter over the bottom of the pan. When golden brown, flip and brown the other side, starting on medium heat and lowering the heat if it browns too quickly. They should be crisp on the edges, but soft and crêpelike in the center. Apply butter to the pan after each pancake is done; set finished pancakes aside and keep warm.

Make the tenderloins: Season the tenderloins with the salt, pepper, and 3 tablespoons of the curry oil and grill (or sauté over high heat) to desired doneness. (Feel it with your thumb and first finger; if it's as firm as your cheek, it's rare; if it's as firm as your deltoids when relaxed, it's medium-rare; if it's as firm as your nose, it's medium; as firm as your forehead, well-done.) Let rest, then cut into 1-inch-long pieces.

To serve: Place a spinach timbale in the center of each large serving plate. Circle the timbale with the raisins, the lamb sauce, and a drizzle of the curry oil. Surround the timbale with the lamb and top the timbale with a *roti jala.*

NOTES: For this recipe you'll need about ½ cup (1 stick) butter, clarified to yield about 7 tablespoons clarified butter (see page 16). Alternatively, you can use ghee.

D'Artagnan packs lamb tenderloins in 2½-pound packs, which can be ordered online. See Resources, page 233.

This recipe has many components, but none is especially challenging to prepare. And although it's the perfect showstopper, you can easily make it more casual if you keep the spinach mixture in loose form by omitting the eggs and skipping the pureeing step; you don't need to form it into a fancy timbale. I like working with the tenderloin, because it's not too gamy. If your butcher doesn't carry it, or it's not your first choice, any grillable cut of lamb will do.

DRY-AGED RIBEYE
WITH RACLETTE-STUFFED RÖSTI POTATOES

SERVES 4

FOR THE LEEKS:

2 tablespoons butter

2 leek whites, cleaned and thinly
   sliced (about 1½ cups)

½ teaspoon chopped fresh chives

½ teaspoon chopped fresh parsley

½ teaspoon chopped fresh thyme
   leaves

½ teaspoon chopped fresh tarragon
   leaves

¼ teaspoon salt

A few grinds of black pepper

FOR THE SAUCE:

2 tablespoons grainy mustard

3 tablespoons crème fraîche

Pinch of salt

A few grinds of black pepper

FOR THE RIBEYES:

2 dry-aged ribeye steaks, bone in,
   2 inches thick

2 tablespoons neutral-flavored
   vegetable oil

Salt and black pepper to taste

FOR THE RÖSTI POTATOES:

4 large Idaho potatoes, peeled

Salt and black pepper to taste

¼ cup neutral-flavored vegetable oil

5 ounces raclette cheese, grated

TO SERVE:

12 cornichons

The meat-and-potatoes theme has countless possible variations. Previously, I offered a Korean twist on a classic bistro version (page 166). This time, I look to the American steakhouse and traditional Swiss cuisine. Ribeye has tons of flavor and is nice and fatty, especially the surrounding well-marbled cap of muscle, the spinalis dorsi. The hanging process results in a stronger-tasting, gamier piece of meat that, when its flavor is at its best, might remind you of foie gras.

Although it's delicious when grilled and left on its own, it's hard to imagine a steak without a side. My preferred accompaniment is a rösti—a Swiss potato pancake made from the grated tuber—stuffed with sautéed oniony leeks and raclette. People often confuse raclette with fondue, but they're not the same thing; native to Switzerland and France, raclette is both a cheese and the hot dish made from that cheese. It's a cow's-milk product of the "stinky" kind, which means it's wonderfully funky and pungent; it has character. Raclette is what fills the rösti and brings out the ribeye's richness. It's not so different from serving a steak with Roquefort; subtler, or just less expected. I place the raw cheese in the center of the pancake and it melts during the cooking process. Like the salad dressing that coats my midday lettuces, the mustard–crème fraîche sauce offers an acidic counterpoint to the rest of the full-bodied food on the plate.

Make the leeks: Heat a sauté pan over high heat. Add the butter and swirl. Lower the heat to medium, add the leeks, and stir. Cook until very soft and wilted but not browned. Add the herbs and season with the salt and pepper. Remove to a bowl.

Make the sauce: In a small bowl, combine the mustard and crème fraîche and season with the salt and pepper.

Grill or broil the ribeyes: Rub the steaks with the oil and season liberally with salt and pepper on both sides. Grill or broil to desired doneness and let rest on a warm plate while you make the potatoes.

Make the rösti potatoes: Working quickly to prevent oxidation, grate the potatoes on the large holes of a box grater or in a food processor, season with salt and pepper, and toss to combine. Immediately put the potatoes in a clean kitchen towel and squeeze, twisting to extract as much liquid as possible. Heat a 10-inch nonstick sauté pan over high heat. Add the oil and when hot, add half of the potatoes. Press with a spatula to form a cake the size of the bottom of the pan. Add the leek mixture and spread almost to the edges. Do the same with the raclette, then add the remaining potatoes to cover. Press with a spatula to form an enclosed potato cake stuffed with the leeks and cheese. When the bottom is browned and crisp, flip. Add more oil as necessary and cook the other side until golden and crisp. Remove to a cutting board and cut into wedges. Slice the steaks and serve with the potatoes, cornichons, and sauce.

For the rösti, you might consider adding some pro-sciutto as well as the leeks. And while dry-aging gives the beef additional meati-ness, it's not necessary. A regular ribeye will do.

PAN-ROASTED FILET OF BEEF
WITH SANSHO PEPPERCORN SAUCE

Even if you haven't heard of steak au poivre, you've probably seen "Steak with Peppercorn Sauce" on the menu at your local French restaurants and bistros. They're one and the same—filet of beef covered in a reduction made with cream and crushed peppercorns. When I was a little girl, my parents used to take me to a place in Windsor, Canada, for my favorite exe-cution of this classic dish. The restaurant, La Cuisine, wasn't that far away; it was on the border, just southeast of Detroit. The drive was worth it. The steaks were served bloody rare, and the sauce was that perfect blend of Cognac, shallots, cream, peppercorns, and maybe some demi-glace. It was the epitome of steak au poivre, and I loved it.

This is my ode to that dish, with some Japanese influence. The fea-tured pepper is sansho, a more floral spice that isn't, actually, a pepper. It's piquant and numbing, not unlike a Sichuan peppercorn (which would make a fine substitute). I order the tiny berries jarred, in pickled form, and toss them into my sauce at the last minute. The sauce is so easy and takes no time to make; I prepare it in the same pan that I use to cook the steaks. While they're resting, I sauté some shallots, to which I add mirin (a Jap-anese cooking wine), demi-glace, and foie gras mousse. The fat in the mousse's cream, the sweetness of the mirin, and the unctuous, gamy liver work well with the filet, a leaner cut with a more delicate flavor than others.

SERVES 4

4 (6-ounce) filets mignons of equal thickness
Salt and black pepper to taste
3 tablespoons neutral-flavored vegetable oil
1 teaspoon chopped shallot
2 tablespoons mirin
1 cup veal demi-glace
4 tablespoons foie gras mousse
1 tablespoon pickled sansho peppercorns

The sansho's earthy, fragrant, stealthy heat balances the richness of the other ingredients and gives everything a surprising kick. At the restaurant, I used to garnish the filet with glazed baby Japanese turnips; it was an elegant way to let diners know that this was not their usual steak au poivre.

Heat a large sauté pan over high heat. Season the steaks with salt and pepper. Put the oil in the pan and when smoking, add the steaks. Cook over high heat for 1 minute, then lower the heat to medium-high. Cook until deep brown, 2 to 3 minutes, then turn and cook to desired doneness. (Feel it with your thumb and first finger; if it's as firm as your cheek, it's rare; if it's as firm as your deltoids when relaxed, it's medium-rare; if it's as firm as your nose, it's medium; as firm as your forehead, well-done). Remove to a warm plate. Pour off any excess fat from the pan. Add the shallot to the pan and stir over medium-high heat. Add the mirin and cook until it is reduced by half. Add the demi-glace and cook to reduce by half again. Add the mixture to a quart container or a beaker and, using a hand blender, incorporate the foie gras mousse. Add the sansho peppercorns, and serve the sauce with the steaks.

> *If you can't find foie gras mousse, you can puree bits of foie gras in a blender with the demi-glace and some cream along with the shallots and mirin that deglazed the pan in which you cooked the steak.*
>
> *If the sansho isn't an option, pink or green peppercorns would be nice too; they will just yield a Western dish instead of one with Eastern influences.*

BRAISED SHORT RIBS
WITH CAULIFLOWER AND CAPERBERRIES

My first memorable short rib was eaten in the 1990s at Lespinasse, a fancy establishment in New York City's St. Regis Hotel. Gray Kunz was the chef and had received four stars from Ruth Reichl, who was the restaurant critic for the *New York Times* back then. Born in Singapore, he was admired for his application of French technique to Asian ingredients, including some Malaysian ones I'd grown up with. I went with my friend Scott and we ordered the parallel tasting menu. The service was fabulous, but that wasn't what made this one of the most unforgettable meals. For each course, the Swiss chef would present two dishes; one would showcase a luxurious item such as lobster, while the other would take something related but less expensive, squid perhaps, and highlight that. Both were equally delicious, and that made a big impression; with that brilliant meal, Kunz showed me that although much depends on the ingredients, a great chef can do some-thing beautiful with anything.

That night, the final savory course was his signature, beef short ribs. At that time, that cut of meat wasn't seen on menus, but with the arrival of this dish, the braising meat started showing up in restaurants soon thereafter.

Thanks to Gray Kunz, I too have continued to put various forms of short ribs on my menus, including this wintertime main course from *annisa*. The recipe has Italian influences—there is salty Parmesan cheese, fragrant sage, and briny, sour caperberries—but the liquid in which the beef braises is more French in spirit, and a puree, although found in both cultures along with plenty of cream and butter, is perhaps more common to France. To bring out the cauliflower's nuttiness, the stems get roasted before being pulverized. The garnishing florets, also roasted, emphasize that flavor and offer a textural contrast.

Make the short ribs: Heat a casserole over high heat. Add the oil. Season the short ribs with 2½ teaspoons of salt and pepper to taste, and when the oil is just smoking, add them to the pan and brown on all sides. Add the wine, shallot, garlic, bay leaf, and thyme and cook until the liquid is reduced by three-quarters. Add the veal stock and the chicken stock, bring to a boil, skim off any foam that rises to the top, and lower the heat to a simmer. Cook, skimming occasionally, for 3 to 3½ hours, until the meat is falling from the bone, adding water as necessary to keep the meat covered. Remove the meat to a plate and continue reducing the liquid until slightly thickened. Add the sage 5 minutes before the sauce is finished, then strain. Reserve the sage leaves. The resulting sauce should

SERVES 4

FOR THE SHORT RIBS:
2 tablespoons neutral-flavored vegetable oil
4 (4-inch-square) pieces beef short ribs, bone in, excess fat removed (4 pounds, trimmed)
Salt and black pepper to taste
1½ cups red wine
1 shallot, sliced
2 cloves garlic, smashed
1 bay leaf
1 sprig fresh thyme
3 cups veal stock (page 232)
3 cups chicken stock (page 231)
1 sprig fresh sage

FOR THE CAULIFLOWER PUREE:
2½ cups roughly chopped cauliflower
1 tablespoon olive oil
¼ cup (½ stick) butter
¼ cup heavy cream
½ teaspoon salt
Black pepper to taste

FOR THE ROASTED CAULIFLOWER:
¾ cup cauliflower florets (little ones)
8 fresh sage leaves
2 tablespoons olive oil
¼ teaspoon salt
Black pepper to taste

TO SERVE:
12 shavings Parmesan cheese, removed with a vegetable peeler
1 teaspoon julienned orange zest
1 teaspoon lemon zest
12 caperberries, or 1 tablespoon capers

just coat the back of a spoon and should be free of any accumulated fat or scum. Season with pepper and salt, if necessary, to taste.

Make the cauliflower puree: While the short ribs are cooking, preheat the oven to 400°F. Toss the cauliflower pieces with the oil in a small ceramic baking dish and roast for about 20 minutes, until tender and slightly caramelized. Put the butter in a saucepan and cook over high heat until browned and nutty smelling. Add the cream and heat through. Put the roasted cauliflower and the cream mixture, along with the salt and pepper, in a food processor and process until smooth.

Make the roasted cauliflower: Toss the florets with the sage, oil, salt, and pepper in the same baking dish in which the other cauliflower was roasted. Roast until browned, 15 to 20 minutes.

To serve: Divide the cauliflower puree among 4 serving plates, top each serving with a short rib, then with roasted florets and reserved sage leaves, and finish with the Parmesan shavings and a few pieces of mixed orange and lemon zests. Surround with the reduced braising liquid and garnish with the caperberries.

ROASTED PORK TENDERLOIN
WITH GUANCIALE AND PEAS

This combination of ingredients is one that celebrates subtle, earthy flavors. Pork and peas always make a delicious pair, but the sugar, salt, black peppercorns, and herbs—thyme, among others—used to cure guanciale (hog jowls) renders it an especially well-suited match for those sweet, green orbs, which are presented as a puree here. The tenderloin isn't the fullest-flavored cut of pork, so serving it with Italian cured pork cheeks (a.k.a. face bacon) accentuates its porcine notes and provides nuance. Plus, adding another part of the pig is another way to pay tribute to that animal.

Fried gnocchi are the dish's starchy complement. I can't take credit for them. That belongs to Jen (who, to remind you, tested most of the recipes for this cookbook and shared this one with me when we opened *annisa* together). It's a simple preparation that calls for only a small amount of flour; the rest of the dough consists predominantly of potato. After a quick bath in boiling water, the dumplings are sautéed a bit in reserved guanciale fat for crispness, a hint of nuttiness, and an extra shot of something porky. Sugarsnaps, pea shoots, and fresh mint form a salad to garnish the tenderloin and emphasize the puree's main ingredient.

Make the gnocchi: Preheat the oven to 400°F. Prick the potato all over with a fork to allow steam to escape and wrap in aluminum foil. Bake until soft, about 55 minutes. Peel and roughly chop or break up into pieces, then pass through a food mill while still hot. Let cool slightly, then sift the flour over the top and add the egg, chives, salt, and pepper. Mix until uniform. Bring a pot of water to a boil and add ample salt. On a floured board, roll the dough into ½-inch-thick ropes, then cut into 1-inch lengths. When the water is boiling, add the gnocchi. As soon as the gnocchi float, remove to a plate and toss with the oil. This can be done up to 1 day in advance. Keep the gnocchi wrapped and refrigerated until use.

Make the pea puree: Put all the ingredients in a blender and process until smooth. Push through a fine-mesh sieve using a rubber spatula, pushing through as much pulp as possible. Taste and adjust the seasonings.

SERVES 4

FOR THE GNOCCHI:
1 large Idaho potato
2 tablespoons all-purpose flour
⅓ beaten large egg
1 tablespoon chopped fresh chives
Salt and black pepper to taste
1 tablespoon extra-virgin olive oil

FOR THE PEA PUREE:
1½ cups shelled peas, blanched in salted boiling water and shocked in ice water, or frozen peas (thawed)
½ cup chicken stock (page 231)
½ teaspoon salt
A few grinds of black pepper
1 teaspoon sugar, or to taste

FOR THE PORK:
4 (6-ounce) pieces trimmed pork tenderloin
½ teaspoon salt
Black pepper to taste
2 tablespoons neutral-flavored vegetable oil

FOR THE SALAD:
12 sugarsnap peas, blanched, shocked, and split lengthwise along the curved side to reveal the seeds
2 cups pea shoots or baby lettuce
4 fresh mint leaves, sliced
(CONTINUED)

FOR THE SALAD (CONT'D):
Salt and black pepper to taste
1 teaspoon lemon juice
1 tablespoon extra-virgin olive oil
TO SERVE:
⅓ cup finely diced guanciale

Make the pork: If you want to cook the pork more well done than medium-rare, preheat the oven to 450°F. Heat a large sauté pan over high heat. Season the pork with the salt and pepper. Add the oil, and when just smoking, add the pork. Lower the heat to medium-high and brown on all sides. Once this is done, the tenderloin should be medium-rare. If you desire it more well done, transfer to the oven to finish, or continue to cook it on the stovetop over medium heat, turning the meat continually so it cooks evenly. Let the pork rest on a warm plate while you finish the rest of the dish.

Make the salad: Combine all the ingredients in a large bowl.

To serve: Heat a (preferably) nonstick sauté pan over high heat, then add the guanciale. Lower the heat to medium-low and cook to render the guanciale until browned on the sides but not crisp throughout. Drain on a paper towel, leaving the resulting rendered fat in the pan. Increase the heat to high. When hot, add the gnocchi and cook until crisp and browned.

Reheat the pea puree and divide it among 4 serving plates. Top with the pork tenderloin and surround with the guanciale bits and gnocchi. Top the pork with the salad and serve.

Because tenderloin doesn't have much fat, it shouldn't be cooked through or it will become dry. Medium-rare is my ideal doneness, but people like my mother, who was afraid of trichinosis, are put off by any residual pinkness in their pork meat. Since there have been no cases of that disease since the 1970s, I think we're safe. Bill Niman, who was at the forefront of humanely raising Berkshire pigs, was a smaller producer when I created this recipe (and has since sold the company). Although the Niman business has expanded, the pigs continue to have more fat and flavor than mass-bred animals and are still locally and humanely raised. Niman Ranch (see Resources, page 233) sells its guanciale online, but if you need a quick fix and your butcher doesn't stock that item, pancetta and bacon are both fine substitutes.

BRAISED PORK CHEEKS IN CARAMEL
WITH CARROTS AND LOTUS ROOT

My first job as executive chef was in the early '90s at a little French-Vietnamese restaurant called Can on West Broadway in SoHo. Although I didn't know much about Vietnamese cuisine, it wasn't for lack of eating it, and this job seemed right up my alley. One of the items I fell in love with was something my wok cook made for staff meal: pork in caramel sauce. It was a clay-pot preparation redolent of lemongrass and fish sauce, sweetened with dark caramel, and cooked long and slow with fatty pork. This was served over rice and I couldn't get enough.

More than a decade later, I revisited my wok cook's Vietnamese pork and came up with this gentrified version that calls for ample veal stock instead of the classic choice, water, to create a reduction sauce in the French manner. In light of these countries' similar approach to caramel and, due to colonization, the influence each had on the other's food and culture, this particular recipe seems doubly resonant. The pickled carrots add a crunchy contrast and cut the richness of the pork while picking up on the cooked sugar's sweetness. The lotus provides additional sweet earthiness and crunch, and the rootlet, a Vietnamese jarred pickle, brings an extra burst of acid.

Make the pickled carrots: Stand the carrots, top end up, in a tall heatproof quart-size container. In a large pot over high heat, bring the vinegar to a boil with the peppercorns, garlic, and salt. Pour the liquid over the carrots, leaving the green tips unsubmerged to keep them bright green (the acid will turn them brown). Let sit overnight before using.

Make the pork cheeks: Season the pork cheeks with the salt and pepper. Heat a large straight-sided casserole (large enough so that laid flat, all the meat should fit in one pan without overlapping) over medium-high heat until almost smoking, add the oil, and swirl. Sear the pork cheeks in the pan, browning on all sides, then remove from the casserole. Pour off the oil but do not wash the casserole.

Make the braising liquid: Put the sugar and ¼ cup water in a small sauté pan and boil without stirring until the mixture is caramelized, a medium

SERVES 4

FOR THE PICKLED CARROTS:
- 20 baby carrots, peeled
- 2 cups rice wine vinegar
- 1 tablespoon whole black peppercorns
- 6 cloves garlic, smashed
- 1 teaspoon salt

FOR THE PORK CHEEKS:
- 3 pounds cleaned pork cheeks
- ½ teaspoon salt
- Black pepper to taste
- 1 tablespoon neutral-flavored vegetable oil

FOR THE BRAISING LIQUID:
- ½ cup sugar
- 6 cups veal stock (page 232), or equal parts chicken stock (page 231) and D'Artagnan demi-glace (see Resources, page 233)
- 3 tablespoons fish sauce
- 1 large stalk lemongrass, pounded
- 3 cloves garlic, finely chopped
- 2 shallots, sliced

FOR THE CARROT EMULSION:
- 1½ cups carrot juice
- ½ stalk lemongrass, pounded and cut into 1-inch lengths
- 1 teaspoon fish sauce
- ½ cup neutral-flavored vegetable oil

(CONTINUED)

FOR THE CARROT EMULSION (CONT'D):
Salt and black pepper to taste

FOR THE SAVORY CARAMEL GARNISH:
½ cup sugar

1½ teaspoons salt

¼ teaspoon black pepper

¼ cup water

TO SERVE:
2 sections lotus root

2 tablespoons lotus rootlets in brine,
  cut into rounds

This is obviously a restaurant dish and one you may want to try on a weekend or on a special occasion. If you omit the carrot emulsion or caramel sauce, it's not too bad, but those elements make it something memorable. Lately, the use of salted caramel in desserts has become quite popular, but people seldom think to apply the sticky substance to appetizers or entrées. Such a practice isn't uncommon. Vietnam isn't the only country that uses caramel in savory dishes. In French cuisine (where the caramel au beurre salé—*caramel made with salted butter—trend was born), it is used in gastrique, a mixture of caramel and vinegar that is the base for many sauces, including the famous* à l'orange *that accompanies duck; it's France's version of sweet and sour.*

amber color. (Do not stir during this process or it will crystallize; once the liquid has started to brown, you can gently swirl the pan to color evenly.) Remove from the heat and add 1 cup of the stock. The sugar will seize up and form a solid mass, but do not worry. Return the pan to medium heat and stir until the caramelized sugar and stock are thoroughly combined. Transfer to the large casserole in which the pork was cooked and add the pork, along with the remaining stock, the fish sauce, lemongrass, garlic, and shallots. Bring to a boil, then lower the heat to a simmer and skim off the froth and some of the fat. Simmer, skimming occasionally and adding water as needed to keep the pork covered, for 3 hours, or until the pork cheeks are tender. Remove the pork cheeks to a bowl. Pour the liquid through a fine-mesh sieve into a saucepan, add ½ cup of the strained liquid to the pork cheeks, and cover the bowl. Cook the remaining braising liquid over medium-high heat until reduced and thickened so that it just coats the back of a wooden spoon; it should be well flavored, but not too salty.

Make the carrot emulsion: Put 1¼ cups of the carrot juice in a saucepan and cook until it is reduced to a glaze. Put the remaining ¼ cup juice along with the reduced carrot juice in a food processor with the lemongrass and process until the herb is finely chopped. Let steep for 30 minutes, then strain through a fine-mesh sieve. Place in a blender with the fish sauce and process, slowly adding the oil to emulsify. Season with salt and pepper.

Make the savory caramel garnish: Oil a piece of parchment paper. Combine the sugar, salt, pepper, and ¼ cup water in a small sauté pan to make a savory caramel, following the same method used to make the caramel for the braising liquid (boil until the mixture is caramelized, a medium amber color). Continue cooking until the caramel is a dark amber, then drizzle the liquid onto the parchment, making lacy patterns for garnish.

To serve: Peel the lotus root and cut into ¼-inch-thick rounds. Cook in salted boiling water for 10 minutes over medium to medium-high heat, making sure the slices stay covered. Remove the pan from the heat, drain, and keep warm. Place 3 slices of lotus root in the center of each serving plate and top with a quarter of the pork cheeks. Use the pickled carrots to form a pyramid around the cheeks and dot the plate with the lotus rootlets. Spoon a ring of the carrot emulsion and another of the reduced braising liquid around the meat. In a very low oven, gently reheat the caramel garnish to soften, then form into three-dimensional, free-form shapes that can easily sit atop the pig cheeks and pickled carrots.

GRILLED BEEF TONGUE AND BRAISED CHEEK
WITH TOKYO TURNIPS

One night, over dinner with my friends Tim and Lisa, I discovered just how succulent tongue could be. They brought me to a little Japanese restaurant in the East 40s where we had grilled tongue—it was the back of the organ, which is really fatty, and it was incredible. Up until then, I'd only had it braised, unless you count the kind you find in delis. Tasting the dorsal side and having it prepared on the grill was a cool new experience that inspired me to try a similar method.

The cheek benefits from braising, so, while the tongue gets a quick turn on the grill, its counterpart stews on the stove in a rich broth. Each protein is treated individually according to its consistency. You end up with two different bits of meat—one meltingly tender and musky, the other lusciously unctuous and charred. Japanese accents like pungent mustard, sweet mirin, and glazed bitter turnips provide contrasting, vibrant flavors and unite the separate cuts of beef. This is a simple recipe, so it's a great opportunity to be adventurous and try something different.

Make the beef cheeks: Heat a casserole over high heat. Season the beef cheeks with salt and pepper. Add 2 tablespoons of the oil to the casserole and when just smoking, add the beef and lower the heat to medium-high. Brown on all sides, then remove to a plate. Add the onion and the remaining oil. Lower the heat to medium and cook, stirring, until soft and translucent. Add the mirin and stir to scrape up any browned bits. Cook over medium-high heat until reduced by two-thirds, then add the beef cheeks and any accumulated juices back to the casserole. Cover with the stock, bring to a boil, and skim. Lower the heat to a simmer and cook, skimming occasionally and adding more stock as necessary to keep the meat covered, for 3 hours, or until tender. Remove the beef cheeks to a plate and reseason with ¼ teaspoon salt and black pepper to taste. Cook the remaining braising liquid until slightly thickened—it should just coat the back of a spoon. Season with the soy sauce and pepper. Pour through a fine-mesh sieve into a bowl.

SERVES 4

FOR THE BEEF CHEEKS:
1 pound beef cheeks, trimmed
Salt and black pepper
3 tablespoons neutral-flavored
  vegetable oil
1 small onion, chopped
1 cup mirin
About 1½ quarts veal stock (page 232)
1 tablespoon soy sauce

FOR THE TONGUE:
4 (4-ounce) steaks beef tongue,
  trimmed (about 1½ inches thick),
  fatty back part only
1½ teaspoons salt
Black pepper to taste
1 tablespoon neutral-flavored
  vegetable oil

FOR THE GLAZED TURNIPS:
12 baby Tokyo turnips or pink radishes,
  trimmed, tops reserved
About ½ cup dashi (page 231) or water
1 tablespoon butter
1 tablespoon sugar
1 teaspoon salt

TO SERVE:
1 tablespoon dry mustard powder
  mixed with 1 tablespoon water

Make the tongue: Season the tongue with the salt and pepper and coat with the oil. Grill over high heat to desired doneness. Let rest for 5 minutes before serving.

Make the glazed turnips: Put the turnips in a sauté pan in one layer. Add enough dashi to come halfway up the sides of the turnips. Add the butter, sugar, and salt and bring to a boil. Cook until all the liquid is evaporated and the turnips are glossy but not browned, then add the turnip tops and cook until wilted.

To serve: Divide the beef cheeks among 4 serving plates and ladle the reduced braising liquid over the cheeks. Decorate with the turnips and tops and a few dots of the mustard. Slice the tongue and place on top of the cheeks.

Your butcher can always order these parts for you, but the cheeks can be replaced by short ribs or any other stew meat—chuck, for one. You can grill or broil the tongue; just make sure to serve it medium-rare. And if you want to make this really easy, you can serve either the tongue or the cheek instead of both.

BRAISED VEAL CHEEKS
WITH MEYER LEMON, BACON, AND CRISP SWEETBREADS

This is a straightforward example of contemporary American cuisine. Essentially, it's an elevated version of stew served over grits or polenta. The veal cheeks are cooked with smoked, cured bacon; after three hours, their collagen starts to break down and renders the meat supple, nearly molten. Floral, citrusy Meyer lemon—with its juice and zest—brightens the cooking liquid, which becomes a thick, hearty sauce. Enriched with chicken stock and mascarpone, polenta, the plate's nutty starch, soaks up the ragout. Simply sautéed sweet, earthy baby carrots provide a pop of color (and a vegetable).

The garnish that takes this from comfort food to something a bit more special is sweetbreads, the veal's thymus gland and a celebrated delicacy of French cuisine. I remember being in Paris with my mom, my sister, and my first college girlfriend, Deirdre; one night we had dinner at Au Petit Marguery, a well-known restaurant not far from my apartment. I ordered the duck with glazed turnips. Deirdre ordered the *riz de veau* (which translates, literally, to rice of veal), because she thought it was a classic French veal entrée. She didn't realize she had ordered sweetbreads. She ate them anyway. For this dish, after a quick poaching, the "supreme offal" is browned and crisped in butter; it's an unnecessary but rewarding last touch.

Make the veal cheeks: Heat a casserole over high heat and add the oil. Season the veal cheeks with 1 tablespoon of salt and pepper to taste. When the oil is just smoking, add the veal. Lower the heat to medium-high and brown on all sides. Remove to a plate. Lower the heat to medium and add the butter. Add the onion, garlic, bay leaf, and thyme and cook, stirring, until the onion is soft and translucent. Add the wine and bring to a boil, scraping the bottom to remove any browned bits. Cook until reduced by half, then, over medium-high heat, add the bacon cubes (reserve the lardons), the veal cheeks and any accumulated juices, and the stock. Bring to a boil and skim off any foam that rises to the top.

SERVES 4

FOR THE VEAL CHEEKS AND BACON:
2 tablespoons neutral-flavored vegetable oil
1 pound veal cheeks, trimmed
Salt and black pepper
1 tablespoon butter
1 medium onion, chopped
2 cloves garlic, smashed
1 bay leaf
1 sprig fresh thyme
1 cup white wine
1 pound slab bacon, skin removed, cut into 4 (1-inch-square) cubes, the rest cut into lardons
About 1 quart veal stock or chicken stock (page 232 or 231)
1 Meyer lemon, 1 long strip of zest removed (white pith scraped off) and julienned, the remainder zested, then juiced (or substitute 1 regular lemon, reserving ⅓ of the juice for another purpose)

FOR THE POLENTA:
2 cups chicken stock (page 231)
½ cup polenta
¼ cup mascarpone

(CONTINUED)

Lower the heat to a simmer and cook, skimming occasionally and adding more water as necessary to keep the meat covered, for 3½ hours. Remove the meats to a plate and keep warm. Cook the liquid over medium heat, skimming occasionally, until slightly thickened—it should just coat the back of a spoon. Season with 1 tablespoon of the lemon juice and a pinch of salt and pepper. Pour through a fine-mesh sieve into a bowl, then add the lemon zest.

Render the lardons: In a large frying pan, cook the bacon lardons over medium heat until all the fat is rendered and the lardons are crisp. Drain off the fat and set the lardons aside.

Make the polenta: Bring the stock to a boil in a small saucepan and slowly whisk in the polenta. Lower the heat to a simmer and cook, stirring often, until done, about 30 to 40 minutes (or 5 minutes if using instant). Stir in the mascarpone and season with the salt and pepper.

Make the sweetbreads: Heat a small sauté pan over high heat. Season the sweetbreads with the salt and pepper. Add the oil to the pan and when just smoking, add the sweetbreads. Lower the heat to medium-high and brown, then turn and brown the other side. Add the butter and baste the sweetbreads until golden.

To serve: Put the carrots in a sauté pan and just barely cover with water. Add the butter and salt, bring to a boil, and cook until tender.

Divide the polenta among 4 serving plates and top with one piece each of sweetbreads, veal cheek, and braised bacon. Top each sweetbread with a little lemon juice, then surround with the reduced braising liquid and garnish with the carrots, lardons, and julienned lemon zest.

FOR THE POLENTA (CONT'D):
1 teaspoon salt
A few grinds black pepper
FOR THE SWEETBREADS:
8 ounces veal sweetbreads, blanched, membranes removed, and sectioned into 4 equal pieces
½ teaspoon salt
A few grinds black pepper
2 tablespoons neutral-flavored vegetable oil
2 tablespoons butter
TO SERVE:
1 tablespoon Meyer or regular lemon juice 16 baby carrots
1 tablespoon butter
½ teaspoon salt
Black pepper to taste

You could use another part of the veal instead of the cheeks; just make sure it's a braising cut such as breast or shank of veal. The sweetbreads are also optional. Regular lemon in place of the Meyer lemon will still be good, if more tart.

ANNISA BEEF
"POT-AU-FEU"

SERVES 4

FOR THE BROTH:

2 pounds oxtail, trimmed

4 beef marrow bones, marrow
  removed (have your butcher do this)
  and reserved for below

About 1 gallon chicken stock
  (page 231)

1 small cinnamon stick

3 slices fresh ginger

3 cloves garlic, smashed

1 scallion

2 tablespoons soy sauce

A few grinds of black pepper

¼ teaspoon salt

FOR THE BONE MARROW:

4 pieces bone marrow (from above)

1 teaspoon salt

FOR THE MEAT:

2 tablespoons neutral-flavored
  vegetable oil

4 (3-ounce) Wagyu strip, hanger, or
  skirt steaks, trimmed

1 teaspoon salt

Black pepper to taste

4 baby Tokyo turnips, peeled, halved,
  and blanched in salted water

4 baby carrots, blanched in salted
  water

1 purple potato, cut into rounds,
  blanched in salted water

(CONTINUED)

Since its humble beginnings when it was cooked in a cauldron over an open fire, pot-au-feu, the French pot roast, or, translated from the French, "pot on the fire," has always been a peasant dish that can be magnificent when done properly. Magnificence is achieved when the meat is so tender it falls apart, the broth deep and heartily flavored. During one of my summers as a student in Paris, I had this dish at Chartier, which is among Paris's oldest restaurants. In France, when one orders this lowly pot, the broth is generally served first—sometimes with noodles, or with toast garnished with the bone marrow—followed by a platter of the beef and vegetables, plus a phalanx of mustards to cut the richness of the roast, cornichons, and prepared horseradish.

This is an Asian-influenced version with accents of cinnamon, ginger, and soy, wasabi switched out for the horseradish, and spicy Japanese mustard or *karashi* instead of the Dijon and grainy mustards usually served in France. To lend a third pastel color to the trio of condiments, I add pink salt—it's from Hawaii, which has a large Asian American population, and is useful for heightening the flavor of the unseasoned bone marrow and sliced beef. The baby vegetables offer bright hues as well—since they're small, they don't take long to cook and, therefore, don't dull in color or get mushy. Underscoring the Asian theme, the scallion replaces the traditional leek, and the baby Tokyo turnips stand in for the traditional purple-top ones. The carpaccio is a direct reference to the well-known Vietnamese beef-based noodle soup pho. Finally, there's the tonburi, the small, greenish-gray seeds of the brown cypress bush. In Japan, they're known as "land caviar," because their appearance and texture are similar to that of small fish roe. I like using them in this preparation since they're garnishing a land-based protein.

It's definitely not the sort of pot roast you'd find in a classic French restaurant. You can go to Chartier for that. It's still there.

Make the broth: Put the oxtail and hollow marrow bones in a stockpot and add the stock. Bring to a boil, skim any foam that rises to the top, then lower the heat to a simmer and add the cinnamon, ginger, garlic, and scallion. Simmer, skimming occasionally, for 3 to 3½ hours, until the meat is falling from the bones. Pour through a fine-mesh sieve set over a saucepan, reserving the oxtails. Season the broth to taste with the soy

sauce and pepper. Pick the meat from the oxtail bones, season to taste with the salt and pepper and set aside. This can be done up to two days in advance; keep the broth in an airtight container in the refrigerator. When you're ready to use, remove the solidified fat layer on top of the broth and discard the sediment that has settled at the bottom of the container.

Prepare the bone marrow: Cover the marrow with water and add the salt. Soak overnight in the refrigerator, then drain.

Make the meat: Just before serving, heat a sauté pan over high heat. When hot, add the oil and swirl. Season the steak on both sides with the salt and pepper and when the oil is just smoking, add the steak in one uncrowded layer. Lower the heat to medium-high and cook until browned. Turn and finish cooking to desired doneness on the other side. Let rest on a plate for 3 minutes.

Slice the bone marrow into rounds and set aside in a warm place. Reheat the broth. Reheat the vegetables in a saucepan with a small ladleful of the broth. Reheat the oxtail meat in the same manner.

To serve: Divide the oxtail meat among 4 large heated soup plates, keeping it to one side of the plate, then top with a slice or two of bone marrow. Place a slice of the beef carpaccio, loosely mounded, in another third of each dish, and top with a small spoon of tonburi (if using). Slice the steak against the grain and arrange in the remaining third of the dish. Put the turnips, carrots, potato, and scallions in the center of the bowl. Just before serving (we do it tableside at *annisa*, so the guest can see the light cooking of the carpaccio), pour hot broth over all. Serve with the Hawaiian salt, wasabi, and mustard on the side.

FOR THE MEAT (CONT'D):
4 scallion whites, blanched and shocked

TO SERVE:
4 slices beef for carpaccio (ask your butcher to slice and pound it for you)
½ teaspoon tonburi, or boiled kombu cut into tiny dice (optional)
1 tablespoon Hawaiian pink sea salt or any coarse salt
1 tablespoon prepared wasabi
1 tablespoon Japanese mustard mixed with 1 tablespoon water

FILET OF VENISON
AND YORKSHIRE PUDDING

SERVES 4

FOR THE MARROW BONES:

4 marrow bones, 3 inches thick (make
   sure your butcher cuts them so that
   there is a large enough opening to
   dip a small spoon inside)

3 tablespoons salt

FOR THE OXTAILS:

3 tablespoons neutral-flavored
   vegetable oil

3 pounds oxtail, cut into 2-inch-thick
   rounds, trimmed

Salt and black pepper

1 cup red wine

½ cup port wine

1 shallot, finely chopped

1 quart veal stock (page 232), or
   2 cups demi-glace plus 2 cups
   chicken stock (page 231)

FOR THE CARAMELIZED ONION:

3 tablespoons butter

1 medium to large onion, halved and
   sliced

½ teaspoon salt

A few grinds of black pepper

FOR THE YORKSHIRE PUDDING:

½ teaspoon salt

Black pepper to taste

½ cup all-purpose flour

¼ cup milk

1 large egg, beaten together with
   1 teaspoon water until very frothy

(CONTINUED)

Venison filet is delicious only when served rare or medium-rare.
Any more cooking than that will result in something dry. The reason is that
this game meat is extremely lean. It's full-bodied and succulent, but it's
not for anyone who prefers things in the medium to well-done range. If it's
off-season, you can replace the venison with a filet of beef, which is also
relatively low in fat. Either way, this is a cold-weather dish; the Yorkshire
pudding is proof. Traditionally, this beloved British side is made with the
drippings of the roast it accompanies. Since venison doesn't produce much
drippings, I supplement the renderings from roasted marrow bones, which
are, in turn, served alongside the venison.

In lieu of gravy, I slowly cook oxtails in a rich combination of red and
port wines, veal stock, and shallots. The resulting stew is almost like a jam—
thick and concentrated. It's an optional addition, because of the long cooking process it demands, but I think it's definitely worthwhile. At this point, it
might seem decadent to bring anything else to the plate, but caramelized
onions are crucial; their savory sweetness balances the pudding's fat, the
venison's gaminess, and the oxtail's unctuousness. Mustard greens are also
necessary, because they provide some green and a sharp bitterness that
cuts through all the other heaviness.

I'd definitely serve this for a celebratory occasion; it's a great way to
make a winter holiday meal special.

Prepare the marrow bones: Soak the bones in water to cover with the salt
in the refrigerator overnight to remove blood.

Make the oxtails: Heat a casserole over high heat. When hot, add the
oil. Season the oxtails with 1½ teaspoons of salt and pepper to taste
and add to the casserole when the oil is just smoking. Brown on all
sides. Add the red wine, port, and shallot and bring to a boil. Cook until
the liquid is reduced by half, then add the stock. Bring to a boil, skim
any foam that rises to the top, then lower the heat to a simmer. Cook,
skimming occasionally and adding more stock if necessary to keep the
oxtails covered, for 3 hours, or until the meat is falling from the bone.
Remove the oxtails to a plate and let cool slightly, then pull the meat
from the bones. Season the meat to taste with salt and pepper. Simmer
the braising liquid until well flavored and slightly thickened; it should
just coat the back of a wooden spoon. Taste and add salt and pepper if

necessary. Pour through a fine-mesh sieve and keep warm, or refrigerate and reheat when needed.

Make the caramelized onion: Heat a sauté pan over high heat, then add the butter. When it is melted, add the onion and lower the heat to medium. Cook, stirring occasionally, until golden brown. Season with the salt and pepper and keep warm, or reheat when needed.

Make the Yorkshire pudding batter: In a large bowl, combine the salt, pepper, and flour, then slowly whisk in the milk and ¼ cup of water. Add the egg mixture to the flour mixture and whisk until uniform. Set aside while you roast the marrow bones.

Roast the marrow bones: Preheat the oven to 400°F. Place 1 bone upright in each of 4 (4-ounce) molds, such as ramekins or custard cups, and roast until a toothpick is easily inserted to the center of the marrow bone through the opening in the top, about 15 minutes. Remove the bones to a plate, reserving the fat in each mold.

Bake the Yorkshire pudding: Swirl the fat from the roasted marrow bones to coat each of the molds in which the bones cooked, then divide the batter among the molds and immediately return the molds to the oven. Cook until puffed and browned around the edges, about 17 minutes.

Make the venison: While the Yorkshire pudding cooks, heat a sauté pan over high heat. When hot, add the oil. Season the venison with the salt and pepper and when the oil is just smoking, add to the pan and brown the first side. Lower the heat to medium-high and brown the other side. Remove to a plate and keep warm.

Make the mustard greens: Put the mustard greens in a sauté pan with the butter, ¼ cup of water, and the salt, bring to a boil, and cook until wilted.

To serve: Remove each pudding to a plate, and fill with a little of the caramelized onion, followed by the oxtail meat, topped with a pinch of mustard seeds. Sauce the plate with the reduced braising liquid and top with the venison, sliced if you like. Dot the plate with a little mustard and serve each with a marrow bone topped with a pinch of sea salt and a pile of mustard greens.

FOR THE VENISON:
3 tablespoons neutral-flavored vegetable oil
4 (6-ounce) portions venison filet
1 teaspoon salt
Black pepper to taste

FOR THE MUSTARD GREENS:
6 ounces mustard greens, washed and chopped
2 tablespoons butter
½ teaspoon salt

TO SERVE:
1 teaspoon yellow mustard seeds
1 teaspoon Dijon mustard
Maldon sea salt or any coarse salt

Yorkshire puddings are, like popovers, egg-based hollow rolls. Their batters are virtually interchangeable. What differentiates them is that the pudding is made with the fat that drips off a roast. When cooked in direct heat, the sides of the soufflélike rounds puff up first to create a cup shape. To utilize that form, I place some oxtail in the center of each airy pastry once it's out of the oven.

SADDLE OF RABBIT
WITH BACON, MUSTARD GREENS, AND CREAMED CORN

SERVES 4

FOR THE RABBIT LOINS:

2 (14-ounce bone-in) saddles of rabbit, racks Frenched, loins boned, bones and scraps reserved, including kidneys (which should be set aside separately)

1½ teaspoons salt

Black pepper to taste

1 tablespoon fines herbes: equal parts chopped fresh chives, tarragon, parsley, and thyme

3 cups loose mustard greens, leafy parts only

12 ounces bacon, thinly sliced

FOR THE SAUCE:

2 tablespoons neutral-flavored vegetable oil

Rabbit bones and scraps (from above)

½ cup white wine

1 quart veal stock (page 232), or 2 cups demi-glace plus 2 cups chicken stock (page 231)

2 cloves garlic, smashed

1 sprig fresh thyme

1 bay leaf

Salt and black pepper

FOR THE FRENCHED RACKS OF RABBIT (FROM ABOVE):

1 cup buttermilk, plus more to cover

3 slices onion

(CONTINUED)

Though it might sound trite, rabbit really does taste like chicken, albeit a cousin. In France, it's ubiquitous; you can find the meat sold in grocery stores there. When I studied abroad, my fellow culinary students and I would cook rabbit in mustard sauce in our tiny *chambres de bonne* (the Parisian equivalent of a studio, the term is French for "maid's rooms"); all we needed was a hot plate and a pot for this simple, delectable braise.

I've always thought that people who are concerned about sustainability should eat these animals, because they're so easy to breed. They're cute, yes, but also delicious, mild, and not gamy at all. Theirs is a lean flesh, which lends itself well to this Southern approach that entails wrapping the loin in bacon and serving it with creamed corn. To prepare the loin, bone it and tuck some mustard greens inside its outer flap, roulade style. To showcase more than one part of the rabbit on the plate, I also reserve its rack and deep-fry the chops as you would chicken. All the saddle's remaining bones and scraps go into a basic sauce that's flavored with veal stock, garlic, thyme, and bay leaf and deglazed with white wine. The kidneys are treated separately; they're simply seasoned with salt and pepper and given a quick sear. Placed, in half, atop the corn, the organs act as a final garnish. They're not necessary, but there's no point in wasting them, and they are tasty.

Prepare the rabbit loins: Season the loins lightly with the salt and pepper and sprinkle the flap with the fines herbes, then line with the mustard greens and roll into a cylinder. Make four squares of bacon that will wrap around each of the loins. Do this by slightly overlapping the long sides of the bacon slices; the squares should be just wide enough to cover the loins as you roll them. Place the loins to one end of each square and roll, surrounding with the bacon and overlapping the ends. Set aside.

Make the sauce: Heat a large saucepan over high heat. Add the oil and when just smoking, add the rabbit bones and scraps. Lower the heat to medium-high and brown on all sides. Add the wine and scrape up the brown bits with a wooden spoon. Cook until reduced by half, then add the stock and garlic. Bring to a boil, skim any foam that rises to the top, and lower the heat to a simmer. Cook, skimming occasionally, until the sauce is thick enough to coat the back of a spoon, 1 to 1½ hours. Add the thyme and bay leaf and cook for 2 minutes more, then strain. Season to taste with a pinch each of salt and pepper.

Make the racks: Put the racks in a bowl and add enough buttermilk to cover; add the onion, garlic, and thyme. In a small bowl, season the flour with the salt, pepper, and cayenne. In a heavy saucepan, heat 1 inch of oil to 350°F. Just before serving, remove the racks from the buttermilk, dredge the meat part in the flour, and fry until golden brown. Drain on paper towels.

Cook the loins and kidneys: Heat a large sauté pan over high heat. Add the oil and when just smoking, add the bacon-wrapped loins, seam side down. Lower the heat to medium-high and cook, turning to brown all sides until the bacon is evenly crisp all over. (This will result in medium to medium-rare meat, which is tender and juicy.) Remove from the pan and keep warm. Season the kidneys with salt and pepper and place in the same sauté pan. Increase the heat to high and sear both sides, about 30 seconds per side. Remove and keep warm as well.

Make the creamed corn: Heat a sauté pan over high heat, add the butter, and swirl. Add the chanterelles, lower the heat to medium-high, and sauté until slightly browned and cooked through. Add the corn and enough cream to cover. Cook until reduced and thickened, then season with the salt and pepper.

To serve: Put the mustard-green stems in a small sauté pan. Cover with water and add the salt and bacon fat. Bring to a boil and, when bright green, remove to a clean paper towel. Divide the corn among 4 serving plates and sprinkle with the chives. Slice the loins into 1-inch rounds and arrange over the corn, then top with the rabbit chops. Cut each kidney in half and place on the corn as well. Circle with the sauce and decorate with the mustard-green stems.

It's not too difficult to bone the saddle; you do want to cut off the area where the rib bones are, since that's what you'll be using for your fried racks. You can always ask an upscale butcher to order and prepare the rabbit for you. D'Artagnan sells saddles too and they usually—not always—come with the kidneys.

FOR THE FRENCHED RACKS OF RABBIT (CONT'D):
2 cloves garlic, smashed
3 sprigs fresh thyme
½ cup all-purpose flour
½ teaspoon salt
Black pepper to taste
Small pinch of ground cayenne
Neutral-flavored vegetable oil

FOR THE KIDNEYS:
1 tablespoon neutral-flavored vegetable oil
2 rabbit kidneys (reserved from the rabbit loins)
Salt and black pepper

FOR THE CREAMED CORN:
1 tablespoon butter
¼ cup chanterelle, black trumpet, or other wild mushrooms, cleaned (optional)
3 ears corn, boiled, kernels cut off
Heavy cream to cover
½ teaspoon salt
Black pepper to taste

TO SERVE:
¼ cup mustard-green stems, cut into matchsticks
¼ teaspoon salt
1 tablespoon bacon fat or butter
1 tablespoon chopped fresh chives

CHAPTER FIVE

DESSERTS AND DRINK

INSPIRATION: TRAVEL

Travel is one of the most obvious ways to expand your palate and integrate new flavors into your cooking. There are many ingredients that, after I experienced them in different places around the world, forced me to reconsider what I thought they were "supposed" to taste like or how they were intended to be served, and made me more respectful of their value.

The more you see and sample, the greater the potential for what you can create in the kitchen. One example is offered by a seemingly mundane staple, yogurt. When I was six, during a several-month-long world trip my parents took the family on, we stopped in Iran. We stayed in the Shah's palace (it has since been torn down), an ornate and immaculate sprawling structure with endless arched walkways and sparkling fountains that I always wanted—but was never allowed—to swim in. A big black car would take us to see the sights: the Blue Mosque, the local bazaar, a watering hole where women would wash their clothes and children would swim in the murky brown water.

I think it was outside the bazaar that I had the yogurt. It came in a thick, handmade glass bottle with a wide lip and was closed with some sort of wire. Sitting at a dusty, hot outdoor table, I sipped. It was icy cold, and I remember being excited to try it; I expected some Yoplait-type drink. I can even remember the way the rounded edge of the bottle felt on my mouth: solid, smooth, and cold. Then came the yogurt: watery with crunchy bits of ice, searingly acidic with a funky, earthy taste. To this day, I wonder if maybe the stuff isn't supposed to be chilled. I think I got most of it down. My mother had said it was a specialty in this country and I wanted to appear sophisticated. I pretended to enjoy it. Inside, though, I was dying for some honey with which I could sweeten the potion. Or, maybe some fruit on the bottom like you'd find in those creamy plastic cups my mom used to buy at the grocery store.

Since that incident, after trying it in a number of countries, I have learned to appreciate yogurt as a versatile and complex ingredient. I'll turn it into something savory, with lemon and salt. Or I'll use it in dairy-based desserts like panna cotta (page 207). Sometimes, if it's sweetened, I am happy to eat it just so.

For me, there's only full-fat yogurt, and I favor labne, which is a yogurt-cheese hybrid that comes from the Middle East. Labne is a lot like Greek yogurt in that it's strained; it's just fattier, thicker, and richer. That said, if labne isn't readily accessible, or is not to your liking, you can always use the Greek kind. At the restaurant, we use labne made in Los Angeles at Karoun Dairies. If you're going Greek, the Fage brand can be found in most grocery stores.

While travel may have introduced me to these distinct yogurts and other unique local products, we now live in a world where I can re-experience them at home. In America, people create artisanal versions of the delicacies they've tasted elsewhere and chefs incorporate those ingredients into our dishes. In this way, dining out and cooking can become their own forms of travel. At home, or a few blocks away, you can experience faraway flavors without a passport.

I. DESSERTS

CHILLED GRAPEFRUIT AND GINGER SOUP
WITH SWEET AVOCADO MOUSSE

SERVES 4 AS A PREDESSERT
PALATE CLEANSER OR A LIGHT
DESSERT

FOR THE SOUP:

2 inches fresh ginger, roughly
    chopped (about 2 heaping
    tablespoons)

1 tablespoon lemon juice

¼ cup sugar

½ teaspoon unflavored gelatin,
    softened in 1 tablespoon water

FOR THE GRAPEFRUIT RIND:

Rind of 1 grapefruit, cut into thin
    strips (white pith is okay)

1 cup sugar, plus more for coating

1 tablespoon lemon juice

FOR THE AVOCADO MOUSSE:

1 ripe Hass avocado, peeled and cut
    into pieces

2 tablespoons sugar, or to taste

½ tablespoon lemon juice, or to taste

3 tablespoons cold heavy cream

TO SERVE:

2 large ruby grapefruit, peeled and
    sectioned

4 large fresh mint leaves, sliced

Avocado is technically a fruit and often treated as such in tropical countries, where it grows best. In India, Brazil, and all over Southeast Asia, you'll find avocado shakes and ice creams. Its high fat content and smooth texture work well in those preparations, and you can indulge in such treats with the knowledge that avocados are proven to lower your cholesterol. The following recipe is inspired by the classic grapefruit-and-avocado pairing often featured in a savory salad of crabmeat. The bitter, tart grapefruit contrasts with the creamy green nuttiness of the avocado. If you omit the crab, bring in some simple syrup for sweetness, and incorporate spicy ginger and mint to control any residual richness and add complexity, you have a refreshing chilled dessert. At first, the idea of creamy mousse set in a liquid might seem unusual—it's two soft substances in one bowl—but panna cotta is often placed in a soup, and this idea is echoed by the airy, cloudlike whipped-egg meringues that sit on a sea of crème anglaise in the traditional French dish *l'île flottante* ("floating island"). I'm not even sure this avocado mixture counts as a mousse, as there's nothing aerated folded into it, but it is light nevertheless. The candied grapefruit rind adds two different textural contrasts—chewiness and, thanks to the granulated sugar in which it's rolled, some crunch.

Make the soup: Put the ginger and 2 cups water in a saucepan and bring to a boil. Skim any foam that rises to the top, then lower the heat to a simmer. Cook until strong-flavored and spicy, about 30 minutes. Season with the lemon juice and sugar, then pour through a fine-mesh sieve into a container. Add the softented gelatin and stir to dissolve. Chill. The soup should be slightly thickened but not set.

Make the grapefruit rind: In a saucepan, blanch the rind in boiling water for 2 minutes. Drain, then return the rind to the pan, along with the 1 cup of sugar, 1 cup of water, and the lemon juice. Cook at a simmer, the surface covered with a piece of parchment to stop evaporation, for 45 minutes to 1 hour, until the rind is clear, shiny, and cooked through. Drain, roll in sugar, and set aside to cool.

Make the avocado mousse: Put the avocado in a small food processor with the sugar and lemon juice and blend until smooth. Add the cream and process to incorporate. Taste and adjust the seasoning.

To serve: Place 5 sections of grapefruit in each bowl and cover with the ginger soup. Place a large spoonful of mousse in the center, top with two slices of candied grapefruit rind, and sprinkle the soup with the mint.

If you want an alternative to grapefruit, blood orange would certainly work; it's a citrus that, like the one it's replacing, is a little less sweet and more sour and bitter. Plus, you don't lose the ruby coloring.

PECAN AND SALTED BUTTERSCOTCH BEIGNETS
WITH BOURBON MILK ICE

I love the comfort food of the South. Not that I've spent much time there, but my mother went to college in Tennessee and picked up many of the region's recipes. Growing up, I also had several African American nannies who made us their own versions of soul food, so somehow Southern cuisine feels like a part of me. The following dessert starts with a French idea, pâte à choux, or little cream puffs. To give it a Southern touch, I've added bits of pecan to the dough, deep-fried the balls of batter, and stuffed them with salted butterscotch sauce. The result is a crisp doughnut hole with a liquid center. On the side, I serve Bourbon milk ice. It's based on a cocktail that Southerners bring frozen to tailgating parties. Once halftime rolls around, you have a cold, melted sweet alcoholic drink. I've left it frozen, as you would with granita.

SERVES 8

FOR THE MILK ICE:
3 ounces confectioners' sugar
2 cups whole milk
6 tablespoons Bourbon
1 teaspoon vanilla extract

FOR THE BEIGNETS:
½ cup (1 stick) butter, cut into pieces
1 teaspoon sugar
1 teaspoon salt
(CONTINUED)

FOR THE BEIGNETS (CONT'D):

6 ounces all-purpose flour

4 large eggs

¾ cup chopped pecans

FOR THE SALTED BUTTERSCOTCH SAUCE:

1 cup firmly packed light brown sugar

3 tablespoons butter

½ tablespoon salt

½ cup light corn syrup

½ cup heavy cream

TO FRY AND SERVE:

2 quarts neutral-flavored vegetable oil

Confectioners' sugar

Make the milk ice: Whisk all the ingredients together and transfer to a shallow rectangular plastic container. Seal and freeze until solid, overnight.

Make the beignet batter: In a large saucepan, bring 1¼ cups of water, the butter, sugar, and salt to a rolling boil over high heat. When the butter is completely melted, remove from the heat, add the flour all at once, and stir. Return to medium heat and stir just until the mixture becomes a ball and pulls away from the edge of the pan. It should be well mixed. Transfer to the bowl of a stand mixer fitted with the paddle attachment and mix on low speed for 1 to 2 minutes. Add the eggs, one at a time, fully incorporating each egg before adding the next. When all eggs are mixed in, add the pecans and mix.

Make the salted butterscotch sauce: Put the brown sugar, butter, salt, and corn syrup in a heavy saucepan and bring to a boil. Lower the heat to medium-high, stir once, and cook without stirring until syrupy. Remove from the heat and add the cream. Stir again until uniform. Let cool, then transfer to a squeeze bottle fitted with a small tip.

To fry and serve: In a large pot, heat the oil to 375°F. Working in batches, spoon ¾-inch balls of the beignet batter into the oil. Fry until golden, about 5 minutes. Puncture the beignet with the tip of the squeeze bottle and squeeze ½ tablespoon of the sauce into each one. Dust liberally with confectioners' sugar and put 5 on each serving plate, with the holes up so they don't ooze out. Serve the milk ice on the side in small dishes.

If you want to make the milk ice nonalcoholic, just leave out the Bourbon—the vanilla will be plenty flavorful. Or, if you're feeling lazy, a scoop of vanilla ice cream is also a fine accompaniment to the beignets. Any nut can be used, although I like the way the sweetness of the pecans works with the butterscotch. Those with nut allergies can skip that element entirely. Finally, when deep-frying, it's important that the oil be hot enough. It has to be 375°F, or it will seep into the dough before the latter gets crisp.

ALMOND MILK PUDDING
WITH KUMQUAT SAUCE

One of my favorite childhood desserts was almond float, a Chinese confection that sets the nut-flavored milk jelly into a mixture of canned fruits—lychees, mandarin oranges, peaches, and maraschino cherries. I remember having it once at my uncle's house in Shanghai. I don't know if this is a testament to my age or to the rate of the city's development, but his house had a dirt floor and no running water. The stove was outside. I recall the swelteringly hot day, and, perched on a table that reached to about my chin, this cooling antidote.

In Michigan, my mother would replicate it by using Knox gelatin packets and almond extract. She brought out her Pyrex liquid measure and, as the mold, her lasagna pan. I would help by stirring the bloomed gelatin into the hot, sweetened milk. My favorite part was having a sip of the warm liquid before it set.

This pudding derives from those memories of my uncle's house and my mother's kitchen at home. It is presented in a Western fashion, like a panna cotta or blancmange, surrounded by a single variety of fruit, and heightened by the Southeast Asian flavors of lemongrass and kaffir. The toasted sliced nuts, a fitting garnish to an almondine treat, add crunchy textural

SERVES 8

FOR THE ALMOND PUDDING:

2 cups milk

1 cup heavy cream

½ cup sugar

Pinch of salt

1½ teaspoons almond extract

1 tablespoon brandy

1 tablespoon unflavored gelatin, softened in 1½ tablespoons water (see sidebar)

FOR THE KUMQUAT SAUCE:

1 stalk lemongrass, pounded

3 fresh kaffir lime leaves

1 tablespoon brandy

½ cup sugar

1 cup kumquats, cut into thin rounds, seeds removed

1 tablespoon grated lime zest

TO SERVE:

¼ cup toasted sliced almonds

The tricks to getting a smooth panna cotta, which is essentially the Italian version of what we call pudding, are to use cream or something else highly creamy in nature—strained full-fat yogurt, for example—and to be mindful of your gelatin. In cooking school, we always strained anything to which we had added gelatin, just in case. Make sure it has properly bloomed; the granules should be translucent and stuck together in a rubbery mass. If you're using sheets, these should be duly softened; I generally soak the sheets in ice water until this happens. Feel them with your hands—there should be no hard, inflexible parts left. When you add the bloomed gelatin to the cooked milky liquid, you want the gelatin to dissolve completely, or else you can end up with unpleasant little chewy clumps. Finally, whatever you do, don't boil gelatin.

contrast. As I used to do, I still sample a bit of the hot milk mixture—sometimes a whole cup.

Make the almond pudding: In a saucepan, combine the milk, cream, ½ cup water, the sugar, salt, almond extract, and brandy. Bring to a boil, stirring, then remove from the heat and whisk in the softened gelatin. Pour through a fine-mesh sieve into a container with a spout and divide among 8 (4-ounce) molds. Refrigerate until set.

Make the kumquat sauce: In a saucepan, bring ½ cup water with the lemongrass, kaffir, and brandy to a boil, then remove from the heat and let steep for 15 minutes. Add the sugar and bring to a boil. Remove and discard the lemongrass and kaffir and pour the liquid over the kumquats and lime zest. Chill.

To serve: Unmold the puddings, surround with the kumquat sauce, and garnish with the almonds.

YOGURT PANNA COTTA
WITH DATES AND PEDRO XIMENEZ

Yogurt can transform a common dessert into something completely new. You could, for example, use it in lieu of the ricotta in an Italian cheesecake to get something lighter and smoother than the New York–style version, whose stronger cream cheese lacks the signature gentle tartness that is specific to yogurt. That same levity and subtle tangy flavor can transform a panna cotta, which can be on the bland side, into something refreshing and surprising. This one is paired with dates that are soaked in Pedro Ximenez, a sweet Spanish sherry.

Make the panna cotta: Heat the yogurt, cream, and sugar in a saucepan over medium to medium-high heat until piping hot but not boiling. (Milk boils at 185°F, so you don't want it to get that hot.) Remove from the heat and whisk in the softened gelatin, stirring to dissolve. Pour through a fine-mesh sieve, pour into 6 (4-ounce) molds or small Pyrex dishes, and chill until set.

Make the date sauce: In a saucepan, cover the dates liberally with sherry and simmer until the alcohol is cooked off and the mixture is juicy and syrupy. Let cool.

To serve: Unmold a panna cotta in the center of each plate. Circle with the date sauce and sprinkle with a few pieces of rock candy.

SERVES 6

FOR THE PANNA COTTA:

8 ounces full-fat yogurt such as labne or Greek yogurt

1⅓ cups heavy cream

¼ cup sugar

¾ teaspoon unflavored gelatin, softened in 1 tablespoon warm water

FOR THE DATE SAUCE:

1 cup pitted dates, julienned

About 1 cup Pedro Ximenez sherry

TO SERVE:

2 tablespoons rock candy crystals

Sherry's unique flavor is a result of its blending process, the solera method, which entails incorporating some of the current year's production into the previous year's batch. The first year's product is "laid down" (that's the proper wine jargon) in a cask, and then, the following year, the newest sherry that tastes most like its predecessor is laid down on top of the latter. And so on. Every time a recent batch is added, a bit of the older liquid is drained from the bottom of the cask. Every bottle contains years' worth of blending. This creates a consistent product and accounts for that particular funk that makes sherry special. Our beverage consultant at Mirezi, Steve Olson, suggested simply pouring the wine over vanilla ice cream. It's delicious. You could also pair it with roasted figs when those are in season.

WARM CARROT-MACADAMIA NUT CAKES
WITH GINGER AND CRÈME FRAÎCHE

SERVES 8

FOR THE CAKES:

1 cup flour, sifted

1 teaspoon baking soda

1 teaspoon baking powder

½ teaspoon salt

1 cup sugar

½ teaspoon ground cinnamon

⅔ cup neutral-flavored vegetable oil

2 eggs

½ teaspoon finely chopped fresh
   ginger

1½ cups grated carrots

½ cup macadamia nuts, crushed

FOR THE CHIPS (OPTIONAL):

½ cup sugar

3 slices ginger

1 large carrot, cut into long, paper-
   thin strips on a mandoline

FOR THE CARROT-BUTTER SAUCE
(OPTIONAL):

½ quart carrot juice

½ vanilla bean, split, seeds scraped

1 tablespoon heavy cream

1 cup (2 sticks) butter, cut into small
   cubes and chilled

FOR THE CRÈME FRAÎCHE (OPTIONAL):

½ cup crème fraîche, chilled

½ vanilla bean, seeds only

2 tablespoons sugar, or to taste

In wartime England, when there was hardly anything to eat except potatoes and carrots, the orange root vegetable was added to desserts in place of sugar. We have that historic famine to thank for carrot cake's popularity. There are other cases during World War II in which a vegetable was incorporated into cake baking: In the United States, when rations were limited, boiled beets were mixed into red velvet cake batters to intensify the layered treat's coloring, and a number of recipes for that cake call for some form of beet to increase the baked good's moisture. Cakes made with oil instead of butter often rely on an easier, faster technique and produce a moister crumb. There is, however, no substitute for the flavor of butter, so to accompany my oil-based carrot cake I created a warm carrot butter sauce. Reducing the carrot juice concentrates the vegetable's natural sugars and produces a sauce that needs no help from any refined substance. The tartness of the crème fraîche stands in for that of the more traditional cream-cheese frosting and gives you a slightly more elegant presentation. The ginger lends a touch of the unexpected and some exotic spice, while the macadamia nuts, a richer alternative to the usual walnut or pecan, add a crisp yet yielding texture.

Make the cakes: Preheat the oven to 375°F. In a large bowl, mix the flour, baking soda, baking powder, salt, sugar, and cinnamon together. Add the oil, eggs, ginger, carrots, and nuts. Fill greased cupcake molds or other 4-ounce baking molds three-quarters of the way full with batter and bake until a knife inserted in the center comes out clean, about 20 minutes.

Make the chips: Place the sugar, ½ cup of water, and the ginger slices in a small saucepan and bring to a boil. Remove from the heat and allow the mixture to infuse for 10 minutes. Dip the carrot strips into the mixture and place on a nonstick baking surface. Bake for 15 to 20 minutes in a 275°F oven (preferably a convection oven), until dry but not browned. Remove from the baking sheet immediately and set aside to cool. While still warm, twist into shapes, if desired.

Make the carrot-butter sauce: Add the carrot juice and vanilla bean and seeds to a small saucepan. Reduce until ½ cup juice remains, then add the heavy cream. While the reduction is simmering, whisk in the butter little by little to emulsify. When all the butter has been incorporated, turn off the heat. Keep the sauce warm.

Make the créme fraîche: Mix the créme fraîche, vanilla bean seeds, and sugar, and beat with a wire whisk until the mixture holds stiff peaks.

To serve: Reheat the carrot cakes and place on a plate decorated with a little of the carrot-butter sauce and a spoonful of the créme fraîche. Garnish with a carrot chip and serve immediately.

The batter could be baked as cupcakes: Try applying a traditional cream-cheese frosting; if you like, stuff them with the carrot-butter sauce after baking and cooling, so you have a bit of sweet butter in the center (unless you're feeling decadent, you can skip the frosting). Alternatively, you can serve the original without the crème fraîche as a coffee cake for breakfast.

When you cook the carrot chips, the vegetable's sugars caramelize and have a crisping effect. Don't worry if they're limp when you take them out of the oven—as with caramel, these chips will not harden until they come to room temperature. While they're still soft, you can twist them into any shape you'd like. This technique works for most vegetables.

POPPY-SEED

POPPY-SEED
BREAD-AND-
BUTTER PUDDING
WITH MEYER LEMON

In Greek mythology, poppies symbolize sleep and rebirth. Hypnos, the god of sleep, used a poppy potion to quiet Demeter, the goddess of the harvest, when her daughter Persephone was abducted to the underworld. While Demeter mourned, the world became barren. After her deep slumber induced by the drugged drink, she awoke refreshed and the earth became green again. I like to think of this story in conjunction with the following recipe, as the dish is, in essence, a "rebirth" for dry, old bread, in a new poppy-seed dress. As poppy seeds and lemon are a classic cake pairing, I serve this bread pudding with a Meyer lemon curd whose floral, elegant flavor makes it extra special. Although the recipe calls for a relatively short list of ingredients, the outcome yields a surprisingly complex textural contrast. The top of the pudding is crunchy with toasty brown crouton-shaped crags, while the base is soft, buttery, and custardlike. I put it on the menu at *annisa* when we reopened after our kitchen fire, and now I'm pretty sure I might not be able to take it off without starting a riot.

Make the bread pudding: In a large bowl, toss the bread with the butter and the 2 tablespoons of sugar and place in a 9-by-13-inch baking pan. In a large bowl, beat the eggs with the salt and the remaining 1¾ cups sugar until lightened. Add the poppy seeds. In a small bowl, combine the rum with the vanilla-bean seeds and stir to break up the seeds. Add to the egg mixture, along with the cream, and stir. Pour over the bread and stir so that the bread is coated. Cover and refrigerate overnight for the bread to soak up the custard. The next day, preheat the oven (preferably a convection oven) to 325°F and bake until browned and set. (You can make this a day or two in advance and reheat before serving—it is easier to cut when it is has been refrigerated.) Cut into serving-size squares.

Make the Meyer lemon curd: Beat the eggs together with the salt and sugar in a large stainless-steel bowl and add the 1 cup of lemon juice and the zest. Place the bowl over a saucepan of boiling water and heat, whisking constantly. Add the butter little by little, stirring constantly,

SERVES 12

FOR THE BREAD PUDDING:

3 quarts ½-inch cubed, day-old
  plain French baguette, hard
  bottom and top crusts removed

½ cup (1 stick) butter, melted

2 tablespoons plus 1¾ cups sugar

5 large eggs

Pinch of salt

1½ tablespoons poppy seeds

3 tablespoons rum

½ vanilla bean, split, seeds scraped
  (pod discarded)

1 quart heavy cream

FOR THE MEYER LEMON CURD:

4 large eggs

Pinch of salt

1½ cups sugar

1 cup plus about 3 tablespoons
  Meyer lemon juice or regular
  lemon juice

Grated zest of about 6 to 8 Meyer
  lemons (about 1 cup of zest)

¾ cup (1½) sticks butter, cut into
  pieces

FOR THE MEYER LEMON CHIPS
(OPTIONAL):

½ cup sugar

12 (1⁄16-inch-thick) round slices
  Meyer lemon

until it melts and the mixture is thickened. Transfer to a cool container and chill. Add more lemon juice to thin to sauce consistency after the mixture is chilled.

Make the Meyer lemon chips, if desired: In a small saucepan, combine the sugar and ½ cup of water and heat just until the sugar dissolves. Dip the lemon slices in the syrup and place in a dehydrator. Cook on the "fruits" setting, or at 150°F in a conventional oven, until dried and crisp. Alternatively, place on a baking sheet in a convection oven on the lowest setting and dry until crisp. The rounds will be a little flexible when warm, but will become crisp as they cool.

To serve: Reheat the bread pudding and place it in the center of warm serving plates. Ring with the Meyer lemon curd and if desired, top with Meyer lemon chips and a dusting of confectioner's sugar.

Be sure to use plain French bread—a baguette—for the best results. A sourdough would overpower the gentle poppy seeds and citrus. Brioche will make the pudding richer, but will probably yield a much less crunchy top. Pullman should also be fine, but I think a baguette will give the crispest crust.

When starting this dish, plan ahead. Although the prep time is only about an hour, the custard mixture should sit overnight before baking. After baking, it should cool down to room temperature. If you want to cut the finished dessert into uniform squares, refrigerate it overnight until firm. Reheat it when you're ready to enjoy it.

CRISP WARM SESAME MOCHI
WITH COCONUT CARAMEL

Mochi **is the Japanese word used to describe the savory or sugared snack** made from glutinous sweet rice that has been pounded into a paste. It's also the name of one of my dogs, so I guess it's safe to say I like it a lot. A celebratory delicacy, it is an official food of Japanese New Year and is responsible for a small but significant fatality rate. At that time, annually, so many old people die from choking on the treats—the chewy substance gets stuck in their throats—that the country's local newspapers tally and report deaths by mochi. There are even special instruments designed to suck out mochi that has become lodged in a windpipe.

One of my favorite versions of this mostly harmless item is something you find in Chinese cuisine—the fried sesame-coated rice balls on the dim sum cart. I've attempted to create a dish that shows them at the height of their deliciousness, when they're just out of the fryer. At *annisa*, we made them our own by adding a new element, various dipping sauces. I've introduced a few options—a pineapple-ginger syrup or, for Valentine's Day, a red fruit compote. My favorite accompaniment, a coconut-caramel sauce, was inspired by the old-fashioned Malaysian chews my mom always had. The coconut picks up on the undercurrent of nuttiness that is brought out when the mochi's sesame seeds get toasted in the deep-fryer.

Make the mochi: Put the rice flour, wheat starch, butter, sugar, and salt in a mixing bowl. Stir and add the boiling water. Stir, then knead with your hands to form a smooth paste. Wet your hands and form twenty 1-inch balls, then roll in the sesame seeds. Set aside.

Make the sauce: Put the sugar and ¼ cup of water in a heavy saucepan and stir. Place over high heat and boil, without stirring, until the mixture is a deep-brown caramel. Do not stir at any point after the pan is placed on the heat or the sugar will crystallize. Lower the heat to medium-high, add the coconut milk and salt, and cook until reduced by one-quarter. Keep warm.

To deep-fry: Heat the oil in a pot to 350°F and fry the mochi balls until golden brown. Drain on paper towels and serve with the warm caramel.

SERVES 4

FOR THE MOCHI:
7 ounces glutinous rice flour
⅞ ounce wheat starch
1 tablespoon butter, softened
3 tablespoons sugar
Pinch of salt
¾ cup boiling water
1 cup white sesame seeds

FOR THE SAUCE:
1 cup sugar
1 (13½-ounce) can unsweetened coconut milk
Pinch of salt

FOR DEEP-FRYING:
1 quart neutral-flavored vegetable oil

The coconut-caramel sauce can be used on other things, including a scoop of ice cream. It lasts for a long time, too, because the cooked sugars act as a natural preservative for the coconut milk. If you have a hard time finding the rice flour, your nearest Chinatown should have plenty of markets that stock it. A Japanese grocery store will also sell it.

GOAT CHEESECAKES
WITH CITRUS AND CANDIED BEETS

SERVES 8

FOR THE CHEESECAKES:

¾ cup sugar

3 tablespoons cornstarch

15 ounces cream cheese

15 ounces fresh creamy goat cheese
  (chèvre)

1 large egg, separated

½ cup heavy cream

½ vanilla bean, split, seeds scraped
  (bean pod reserved for below), or an
  additional 1 teaspoon vanilla extract

¼ teaspoon vanilla extract

Pinch of salt

FOR THE CANDIED BEETS:

1 cup sugar

½ vanilla bean pod (from above)

Pinch of salt

A few grinds of black pepper

2 small beets, peeled and cut into thin
  slices

FOR THE CANDIED ZEST:

1 cup sugar

Julienned zest of ½ grapefruit,
  1 orange, and ¼ lime, white pith
  removed

FOR THE CITRUS SALAD:

8 grapefruit sections

16 orange sections

8 lime sections

At Bouley, where I held my first professional cooking position in Manhattan, my initial job was at the canapé station. We made miniature terrines out of fresh goat cheese, roasted beets, and fresh herbs. It was a standard French combination, borrowed originally from Joel Robuchon, for whom David Bouley had worked. Each ingredient heightened the other: The saltiness of the chèvre was offset by the earthiness of the beets. We drizzled a vinaigrette over the top of the bite-size savory. Made with mushroom juice, sherry, and red wine, the sauce's acid balanced the fat of the cheese and accented the saccharine notes of the beets. This dessert relies on the same concepts, but focuses on different aspects of each ingredient: the cheese's creaminess and the beet's sweetness. Here, the idea is to borrow the beet's sugar—not to draw out its vegetal nature, but instead to use it as a sweetener for dessert. The citrus adds further complexity while providing the acid that the vinaigrette had in the savory version. It's an interesting compromise between a dessert item and a cheese course, although it is pretty sweet; in fact, it's very much like a New York cheesecake.

Make the cheesecakes: Preheat the oven to 350°F. Liberally spray 8 (4-ounce) molds with nonstick cooking spray. In the bowl of a stand mixer, combine the sugar and cornstarch and mix until the cornstarch is no longer clumpy. Add the cheeses, egg yolk, cream, vanilla-bean seeds, and vanilla extract and beat with the paddle attachment until soft and uniform. Using the whisk attachment and a clean bowl, whip the egg white together with the salt until soft peaks form. Fold the two mixtures together and transfer to the prepared molds. Bake until light golden brown on top. Let cool and refrigerate, covered, until use.

Make the candied beets: In a large saucepan, bring the sugar and 1 cup of water to a boil with the scraped vanilla-bean pod, the salt, and pepper. Add the beets to the pan and cook over high heat until tender and the syrup is reduced. Set aside.

Make the candied zest: In a saucepan over high heat, combine the sugar and 1 cup of water and bring to a boil. Add the zests and simmer for 4 to 5 minutes, until cooked through and glossy. Drain, reserving the syrup.

Make the citrus salad: In a bowl, combine the sectioned fruit together with the zest cooking syrup. Place on one side of each serving plate. Use the beet syrup as a sauce on the other side and top with an unmolded cheesecake, garnished with the candied beets and candied zest.

CHOCOLATE CHESTNUT CAKE
WITH CHESTNUT MOUSSE

When I was little, I spent lots of time alone with my nanny, Auntie Beth, and that was always something I looked forward to. One of the things we did was build a fire with chopped wood, score chestnuts, wrap them in foil, and throw them in the embers. When we took the chestnuts out, they were lovely. In America, that's how most people know this hard-shelled, meaty-centered entity, as something roasting on an open fire and being peddled by a street-cart vendor. Otherwise, it's a featured item in holiday stuffing.

With this dish, I wanted to make something easy. I also wanted to take a chocolate dessert in a slightly different direction. The chestnut mousse couldn't be lower maintenance, and it lends the cake elegance. As a flavor, the nutty tree fruit brings out the chocolate's natural earthiness.

Make the cake: Preheat the oven to 350°F. Butter an 8½-inch round cake pan. Melt the chocolate and butter in a double boiler over medium-high heat, stirring until fully melted and smooth. In a large bowl, whisk ½ cup of the sugar and the egg yolks together until lightened in color. Do not allow the eggs and sugar to sit together in the bowl before whisking, as small granules will develop. Add the chocolate mixture and stir.

In a separate bowl, whip the egg whites together with the remaining ¼ cup of sugar, the salt, and the cream of tartar until they hold firm peaks. Fold one-quarter of the whites into the chocolate mixture, then fold that back into the remaining whites. Finally, fold in the chestnut pieces. Pour the batter into the prepared cake pan and bake for 35 to 40 minutes, until just set. Let cool.

Make the chestnut mousse: Put the butter in a saucepan over medium-high heat and cook until dark brown and nutty smelling. Immediately add the cream and chestnuts and bring to a boil. Transfer to a food processor with the sugars and salt and puree until smooth. Taste and adjust the seasonings. If serving immediately, let the mousse cool only slightly, place in a pastry bag fitted with a star tip, and pipe onto the top of the cooled cake. If you won't be serving the cake immediately, set the mousse aside and warm it slightly and pipe it right before serving.

SERVES 8 TO 10

FOR THE CAKE:

8 ounces bittersweet chocolate, chopped

¾ cup (1½ sticks) butter

¾ cup sugar

6 large eggs, separated

Pinch of salt

½ teaspoon cream of tartar

½ cup peeled, roasted chestnut pieces

FOR THE CHESTNUT MOUSSE:

¼ cup (½ stick) butter

¼ cup plus 2 tablespoons heavy cream

6 ounces roasted peeled chestnuts

¼ cup granulated sugar

1 tablespoons light brown sugar

1 teaspoons salt

The rule for baking with chocolate is to buy the best quality you can get your hands on. I like Valrhona, specifically the 57% Caraque. It's not the highest cocoa percentage you can get, but it's an all-around solid, versatile choice. Perfect for the pantry.

MILLEFEUILLE OF FRESH FIGS AND RICOTTA

SERVES 4

FOR THE PHYLLO SQUARES:

¼ cup (½ stick) butter, melted

5 sheets phyllo dough

Sugar for sprinkling

FOR THE RICOTTA FILLING:

1 cup fresh ricotta cheese (preferably
   full fat)

¼ cup sugar

Grated zest of 1 lemon

½ tablespoon lemon juice

Pinch of salt

TO SERVE:

Fig-flavored or aged balsamic

Black pepper

8 ripe Black Mission figs, sliced

1 tablespoon toasted pine nuts

If fig-flavored or aged balsamic is out of reach, you can cook regular balsamic vinegar down until it gets sticky and sweet. It's not quite the same thing, but if you throw in some spices—a tiny piece of a cinnamon stick, peppercorns, a vanilla bean, or a clove—to lend complexity, you'll get something delicious and long-lasting.

Once again, the simpler the dish, the better—fresher—your ingredients need to be. This dessert was initially created around the black fig. In East Moriches, my neighbor Dorothy Kalins has two of the trees in her yard. I have planted one in my garden, but until it starts to yield anything edible, I will rely on Dorothy's generosity. Funnily enough, I'm actually allergic to most raw seeded fruits, including the fig. Unless they're dried or cooked, if I eat one, my throat gets itchy, and if I take it too far, my lips will swell up. That doesn't stop me from using them in the kitchen or, when I can't resist, tasting them.

Black figs have a distinct but delicate flavor—they're not as astringent as their green counterparts, yet they have a certain quiet tanginess beneath their sweeter, earthy top notes. A mild substance like fresh ricotta makes an excellent complementary partner. I chose phyllo because it's both crisp and light. To balance the ricotta's creaminess, aged balsamic infused with the central fruit is ideal; I add some ground black pepper to offset the sweetness and give the whole combination a surprising kick. Toasted pine nuts provide a softer kind of crunch and bring a bright nuttiness into the whole.

Make the phyllo squares: Preheat the oven to 325°F. Brush a baking sheet with butter and carefully lay one sheet of phyllo on top. Cover the remaining phyllo sheets with a damp cloth so they do not dry out. Brush the sheet liberally with butter and evenly sprinkle a healthy amount of sugar on top (about 1 heaping tablespoon per layer). Lay another sheet of phyllo squarely on top and press down to collate. Repeat this process until all sheets of phyllo are used, ending with the sugar on top. Cut the layered phyllo into 3-inch squares. (This will make a total of 12 squares for the sheets.) Lay another baking sheet on top to keep the phyllo from puffing up. Place in the oven and bake for about 15 minutes, or until the squares are golden brown and crisp.

Make the ricotta filling: In a bowl, mix all the ingredients together.

To serve: Cook the fig balsamic in a small saucepan over medium-high heat until syrupy and reduced. Set aside.

Place a small dollop of the ricotta filling on a plate. Place 1 phyllo square on top, then top with a heaping tablespoon of ricotta, then with slices of fig. Place another layer of phyllo on top and repeat so that you have 3 layers of phyllo with two layers of ricotta and figs sandwiched in between. Grind a little black pepper on top, drizzle with the reduced balsamic, garnish with the pine nuts, and serve.

The hardest thing about this otherwise easy recipe is dealing with the phyllo dough. Make sure it's completely defrosted before proceeding and don't let it dry out. On the other hand, you don't want to waterlog the pastry, so keep a damp—not wet—towel on it at all times. Finally, make sure you place ample butter and sugar between layers.

WALNUT TEA
WITH MALTED MILK AND WILD-RICE CRISPIES

I've hired many Filipino cooks and, through them, learned a lot about their cuisine. They refer to this, polvorón, as a milk candy because there's a substantial amount of milk powder in it. There are many variations to be found around the world, especially in Spain, where it originates, and Latin America. In those locales, it's considered a form of shortbread. You'll also see the treat in areas that were colonized by the Spanish; this explains how it got to the Philippines, although it doesn't account for the fact that, once there, the cookie took on a more candylike consistency. Both include toasted flour (the baking process accomplishes that), milk, nuts, and a lot of butter, which actually is browned. What differentiates the Filipino polvorón from its antecedents is the dried milk. Maybe that is what changes the texture into something less dense than shortbread and more comparable to a malted candy, crumbly and dry.

What I like best about this kind of polvorón is its just-baked flavor. I add walnuts to mine and pair it with a tea made from the same nut. This is a drink I've always loved and something that would be given at the end of a ten-course Chinese meal. Made from sugar water and ground walnuts, the beverage contains no actual tea leaves, but, like its namesake, it's a warm, comforting liquid that settles your stomach. Serve that with the Filipino specialty and you might consider this dessert a decaffeinated equivalent of coffee and biscotti.

Make the tea: Puree the walnuts with the sugar, salt, and 2¾ cups water. Mix with the strained rice liquid and bring to a boil, stirring, over medium-

SERVES 8
FOR THE TEA:

2 cups walnut pieces

1 cup sugar

Pinch of salt

Liquid from ½ cup raw white rice, soaked overnight with ¾ cup water, then pureed and strained through many layers of cheesecloth

FOR THE POLVORÓN:

½ cup (1 stick) butter

¾ cup all-purpose flour

4½ tablespoons milk powder

4½ tablespoons Ovaltine powder (malt flavor, not chocolate)

Large pinch of salt

4 tablespoons sugar

½ teaspoon vanilla extract

¼ cup small walnut pieces, toasted

FOR THE WILD RICE (OPTIONAL):

2 tablespoons wild rice

½ cup neutral-flavored vegetable oil

high heat until the raw rice flavor is cooked out, tasting as you go. Keep hot.

Make the polvorón: Lightly brown the butter over medium to medium-high heat in a small sauté pan. Toast the flour in the largest sauté pan possible over low heat until light brown, constantly moving the flour with a heatproof spatula, about 10 minutes, being careful not to let the flour burn. Let cool. Add the milk powder, Ovaltine, salt, and sugar and stir well. Add the browned butter and vanilla extract and stir until no clumps remain and the mixture just stays together when packed. Fold in the walnuts.

Make the wild rice, if desired: in a small sauté pan, deep-fry the wild rice in hot oil until it puffs.

Serve the molded polvorón (about 3 tablespoons per person, packed into any type of small mold on a small plate), and topped with the fried wild rice (if using) with a cup of walnut tea on the side.

> *The fried wild rice is optional, but if you're a fan of extra crunch, I suggest you try it. And you don't have to use walnuts in the tea; any nut that purees nicely to yield a creamy texture will suffice—peanuts, cashews, or even pistachios are good; even almonds will work, if boiled long enough to become soft. Because it's crisp and breaks up so easily, the Filipino polvorón is also a wonderful garnish for a dense chocolate cake and a perfect topping for ice cream.*

NAPOLEON OF KABOCHA AND MASCARPONE
WITH GINGER

Kabocha is my favorite gourd. I used it as a savory ingredient initially (see page 71), and, coincidentally, prepared it with something you usually associate with dessert, chocolate. Here I'm doing the opposite. I started cooking with the plump, hearty squash in the 1990s when it was only available in health food stores. At the time, I was the chef at Mirzei and thought it would be appropriate to use a Japanese pumpkin in that pan-Asian context. There's no reason you can't use it in a sweet or Western-influenced preparation.

This dish is as effortless as the starring squash is accessible, which is to say it's pretty damn easy (kabocha is no longer obscure here). The focal point is a puree of the pumpkin sweetened with dark brown sugar, enriched by heavy cream and spiced with ginger. A tuile is applied for buttery crunch and helps to enhance the napoleon, or tower, effect. Mascarpone—less demanding than custard and denser than whipped cream—has a silky texture and acidity that balances the kabocha's starchy earthiness. A green pepita (pumpkin-seed) sauce not only offers a bold color contrast against the puree's orange hue, it also adds a nutty dimension to the overall flavor profile; plus, it's a nice extension of the pumpkin theme.

The only challenge to this otherwise facile dessert is the tuile. It's not hard, per se; it just takes technique. What we do in the kitchen at *annisa* is cut a 3½-inch circle from a thin-walled—⅛-inch-thick is ideal—plastic container (like a large plastic lid, for example) and use that as an elevated shape on which to spread the batter.

Make the tuiles: With a mixer fitted with the paddle attachment, cream the butter and sugar together. Add the egg whites, a little at a time, until incorporated, then add the flour in batches and mix until smooth. Preheat the oven to 275°F. On a nonstick baking sheet, make 3½-inch rounds with a heaping tablespoon of the batter spread evenly, to make thin cookies, then decorate four of them with 5 pumpkin seeds each. Bake until evenly golden brown and crisp, about 12 minutes. Turn halfway through baking to ensure an even crisp.

SERVES 4

FOR THE TUILES:

½ cup (1 stick) butter

⅔ cup sugar

½ cup egg whites (about 3 large egg whites)

¾ cup plus 2 tablespoons all-purpose flour

20 pumpkin seeds (for 4 of the tuiles)

FOR THE KABOCHA PUREE:

2 cups skinned and cubed kabocha squash, steamed

¼ cup packed dark brown sugar

3 tablespoons heavy cream, heated

1 tablespoon butter

¼ teaspoon salt

⅛ teaspoon ground cinnamon

1 teaspoon grated fresh ginger

FOR THE MASCARPONE:

1 cup mascarpone cheese

3½ tablespoons sugar

⅛ vanilla bean, seeds only

Pinch of salt

FOR THE PUMPKIN-SEED SAUCE:

½ cup toasted hulled pumpkin seeds (pepitas)

¼ cup simple syrup (1 part sugar plus 1 part water, boiled)

(CONTINUED)

¼ teaspoon salt
⅛ vanilla bean, seeds only

FOR THE GINGER CHIPS (OPTIONAL):
1 hand ginger, peeled and sliced very
  thinly on a mandoline
Simple syrup (1 cup sugar plus 1 cup
  water, boiled)

Make the kabocha puree: Let the steamed kabocha dry a little, then put it in a food processor with the remaining ingredients and process until smooth. Chill and transfer to a piping bag.

Make the mascarpone: Mix the mascarpone, sugar, vanilla-bean seeds, and salt together and transfer to a piping bag. Keep chilled.

Make the pumpkin-seed sauce: Puree the pumpkin seeds in a blender with the simple syrup, salt, and vanilla-bean seeds. Add water (about 2 tablespoons) until the sauce is smooth and spoons easily.

Make the ginger chips, if desired: Dip the ginger slices in the simple syrup and place on a nonstick baking sheet. Bake at 275°F until golden brown, preferably in a convection oven, 10 to 12 minutes. Remove to a cold sheet pan immediately to cool.

To serve: Place a small dollop of the kabocha puree in the middle of a plate and place a plain tuile on top. Make alternating dots of mascarpone and kabocha puree on top, with kabocha in the center as well. Top with another plain tuile and repeat. Top with the pumpkin-seed tuile and place a small dot of mascarpone on top, then garnish with the ginger chips (if using). Surround with the pumpkin-seed sauce and serve.

If you can't find kabocha, buttercup squash, butternut squash, or yam can be substituted, and if mascarpone isn't on hand, whipped cream won't disappoint.

CHILLED COCONUT-FRUIT SOUP
WITH MINT

The first time I saw jicama presented as anything other than a root vegetable was in Thailand, at a cut-fruit cart in Bangkok, when I traveled there alone in my early twenties. I didn't recognize it as the round, light-brown tuber with a white interior that I had eaten in savory Mexican salads, because it was peeled and sitting among cubes of mango, pineapple, pink crunchy pear-shaped rose apples, and a myriad of other more typical tree and vine fruits. Of course, since I couldn't identify it, I had to buy a piece. Crunchy, and faintly sweet, it was a bit like an Asian pear without the fruity soft acidity; plus there was a very slight earthy nuttiness.

Jicama is found all over Central America and Southeast Asia, but is versatile in any cuisine. Most major grocery stores now carry it. With its mild, sweet crunch, it can be used in any recipe that calls for water chestnuts. Like the latter, jicama works with almost any flavor and can be used to provide textural contrast in countless dishes. Here, it does just that, and plays the role it did when I had it in Thailand—a refreshing, crisp treat.

Like jicama, coconut is found anywhere tropical, and is often paired with dairy (think of a coconut cake, or an Almond Joy). For this soup, cow's milk is the right choice, because it thins the coconut liquid out without making it watery. For the topping, any seasonal fruit will do. I recommend tropical ones since they're more typically matched with coconut. Mint adds freshness and contrast to the dense coconut milk; it brings an extra layer of flavor. This is certainly a summertime dessert, but the tropical fruits are usually in season in winter, and, surprisingly, the soup has enough intensity to hold up in colder weather.

Put the coconut milk, milk, sugar, and salt in a saucepan and heat just until the sugar dissolves. Remove to a bowl and put in the refrigerator until chilled. Mix with the fruit and jicama and divide among 4 bowls. Garnish with the mint and serve.

SERVES 4

1 (13.5-ounce) can unsweetened coconut milk

2½ cups milk

½ cup sugar, or to taste

Pinch of salt

3½ cups diced fresh seasonal fruit

¾ cup finely diced jicama

8 large fresh mint leaves, chopped

II. COCKTAILS

SAKE PEAR ELDERFLOWER COCKTAIL

In suburban Michigan, where I grew up, you wouldn't expect there to be too many wild-growing foods. But there, in the backyard of my split-level, aluminum-sided home, we found a cornucopia of free edibles—dandelions, wild blackberries, rhubarb, and tons of black elder bushes that produced both the fragrant flowers and the elderberries that my Slovenian neighbors, the Kaples, made into jam once a year. They sealed it with white wax to preserve it. I never would have known that these ingredients were there for the picking if it weren't for my Hungarian nanny or the Kaples. In front of all the elderberry bushes was a lone small pear tree. It didn't get much sunlight. It once produced a single, tiny pear, which, in our excitement, my brother and sister and I picked way too early and ate anyway.

The following drink has nothing to do with that old backyard. We never were taught to use the elderflowers, only the resulting berries. The former are frequently employed to flavor cordials, which, once diluted, become refreshing drinks, and the French have a liqueur called St. Germain that is made with the flower and is quite popular right now. While I think of it as a European flavor, when its floral notes combine with the mild sweetness of the pear, the result seems very Asian to me. Coincidentally, both are fragrances often found in sake. The pairing was serendipitous, just like this childhood memory, and the result—at once Asian and European—a bit like me, minus the boozy part.

In a cocktail shaker, muddle one of the slices of pear by crushing it with a sticklike bar tool known as a muddler. Add the remaining ingredients and ice. Shake and strain into a chilled martini glass and garnish with the remaining slice of pear.

2 slices ripe pear

3 ounces sake

½ ounce Poire Williams

½ ounce elderflower cordial

MARGARET LO
ON THE ROCKS

FOR THE BASE:

2 parts lime juice

1 part simple syrup (1 part sugar to
   1 part boiling water, cooled)

½ part kaffir lime leaves pureed until
   very smooth, then semi-strained,
   leaving a little pulp

FOR THE CHILE-SALT MIXTURE:

1 cup coarse salt

1 cup Korean chile powder

1 tablespoon ground cayenne

FOR EACH DRINK:

Cut lime

3 ounces tequila

1½ ounces triple sec

2 ounces base

It is easy to find similarities among the flavors of tropical countries, regardless of what part of the planet they come from. This adult beverage was named for my sister Margaret, who lives in Southeast Asia, and it was the most popular drink at bar Q, my Asian barbecue restaurant on Bleecker Street that, tragically, closed within a year of opening. Aptly, Margaret's namesake is a classic margarita with a Southeast Asian twist (pun intended) or two—the addition of fragrant, floral kaffir lime leaves to the shaker and chile to the traditional salt rim. Wendy Louie, the general manager at Mirezi, a pan-Asian spot where I was the chef in the mid-'90s, created the base concept, and over a decade later I decided to heat things up with the chile. Cheers, or, as they say in Thai Mexico, *Choc-tee, salud!*

Make the base: Combine all the ingredients.

Make the chile-salt mixture: Combine all the ingredients in a bowl and mix well.

Make the drink: Rim a rocks glass by rubbing the lip with cut lime then dipping in a plate of the chile-salt mixture. Put the remaining ingredients in a cocktail shaker over ice. Shake and pour into the prepared glass.

The best-known Korean chile is usually found in the form of a paste called gochujang *and is made from fresh peppers. For the edge of the cocktail glass, I use the* gochu garu, *which is a ground dried chile that can be coarse or fine in texture—it's sweet, mildly spicy, and available in Korean markets. (Gochu means chile, garu ground, and jang sauce.) Espelette comes close, but is almost as difficult to source and incredibly expensive. Perhaps taking red chile flakes and pulverizing them in a spice grinder with a bit of sweet paprika would do.*

JAPANESE PICKLETINI

In the American South, the pickle is an important everyday ingredient and is made of many different items, from cucumbers to okra, watermelon rind to peaches. When served batter-fried, it is, at base, a vinaigrette—the oil in the crisp exterior complements the acidity of the pickle. Pickles and pickle juice even turn up in bar culture; you'll find a Texan shot of whiskey with a briny back, or a pickletini—a martini made with pickles instead of olives. I created this version of that 'tini for short-lived bar Q. This rendition made sense, since barbecue is also a Southern phenomenon. Hendricks, a gin infused with cucumber, among other flavorings, is paired with a Japanese cucumber tsukemono (pickle) to create an East-Asian version of the American classic. At the restaurant, we garnished the finished product with cucumber ice in popsicle form; it was frozen on a bamboo twist skewer so you could stir and keep your drink icy while adding more cooling cucumber as you sipped.

Put the gin, vermouth, and pickle juice in a cocktail shaker with ice. Shake and strain into a chilled martini glass. Garnish with the pickle slices and the cube of cucumber ice (if using).

NOTE: If you're including cucumber ice, only use an unwaxed cucumber.

5 ounces Hendricks gin

1 ounce dry vermouth, or to taste

1 tablespoon pickle juice

3 slices Japanese cucumber pickle

1 cube cucumber ice (cucumber juiced, with skin on, then frozen with a pinch of salt; optional; see Note)

CELERY-DILL MARTINI

With its many herbs, botanicals, and spices, gin is a complex beverage that pairs well with fresh, simple flavors. The word *gin* is derived from the French *genièvre* or the Dutch *jenever*, both words for juniper, the drink's dominant aroma. I created this drink during my nine-month hiatus from restaurant work when *annisa* burned down in July 2009. Along with a sommelier, a mixologist, and a perfumer, I was invited to be part of a focus group for one of the high-end gin companies. Mostly, we talked about food preferences and trends, and why people drink what they do. At the end of the session, we were asked to play with flavors, namely those of the gin and some other ingredients provided for us. That improvisation led, eventually, to this martini. The fresh, slightly saline, green flavors of the celery, and the dill's sweet, herbal notes blend well with the piney, citrusy gin. As juniper, dill, and citrus are the standard ingredients used to cure gravlax, the salmon is an obvious garnish choice here. Originally created by the Dutch, but popularized by the Brits, gin is now dressed in Nordic attire.

Break the celery into 1-inch pieces and muddle with the dill in a shaker. Add the gin, lemon juice, simple syrup, and ice; shake, and strain into a chilled martini glass. Garnish with the gravlax bread stick and dill sprig.

1 (5-inch) celery stalk

6 sprigs fresh dill (about ¼ cup loose)

6 ounces gin

2 teaspoons lemon juice, or to taste

1 tablespoon simple syrup (1 part water to 1 part boiling water, cooled)

1 (4-by-1-inch) slice gravlax or smoked salmon wrapped around a thin bread stick (grissini)

1 dill sprig or celery stalk

GREEN TEA BUBBLE TEA

FOR THE GREEN-TEA SIMPLE SYRUP:

1 cup sugar

¼ cup green-tea powder

Pinch of salt

1 cup boiling water

FOR EACH DRINK:

2 tablespoons black bubble-tea
  bubbles, cooked, strained, and
  rinsed according to package
  instructions

Splash of amaretto

2 ounces vodka

1½ ounces green-tea simple syrup, or
  to taste

2 ounces milk

Here is another bar Q cocktail I created one particularly drunken night— a sort of green-tea ice cream crossed with bubble tea and enhanced by vodka. My general manager likened it to an Asian White Russian, which I hadn't thought of. We immediately renamed it a "Light Lussian," but then rethought that moniker once sober. Originally, I made it with black sesame and almond "caviar," which was formed using Ferran Adrià's spherification method. This technique, invented at his restaurant El Bulli, is based on a chemical reaction between calcium chloride and sodium alginate that creates a thin, jellylike shell around a liquid such as pea juice or oyster water, for example. It proved to be too labor intensive for a barside endeavor; the bubbles had to be conjured to order or they would become hard and lose their flavor. A good substitute, premade Chinese "bubbles," or wheat-starch balls, are what is added to sweet teas to brew "bubble tea," a popular drink first conceived in Taiwan. They make this an apéritif you can literally chew on.

Make the green-tea simple syrup: Whisk the sugar with the green-tea powder and salt until no clumps remain. Slowly add the boiling water, whisking constantly until dissolved. Strain if necessary to remove clumps. Let cool.

Make the drink: Combine the cooked "bubbles" with the amaretto in a rocks glass and fill with ice. Put the vodka, green-tea simple syrup, and milk in a cocktail shaker with ice. Shake and strain into the rocks glass. Serve with a wide straw.

BASIC STOCKS

CHICKEN STOCK

Makes 3 quarts

- Bones from 2 chickens
- 1 onion, roughly chopped
- 1 stalk celery, roughly chopped
- 1 small carrot, roughly chopped
- 1 large clove garlic, smashed
- 1 sprig fresh thyme
- 1 sprig fresh parsley
- 7 whole black peppercorns
- 1 bay leaf

Put the bones, onion, celery, and carrot in a pot with enough water to just cover them and bring to a boil. Skim off the foam and scum that rise to the top, then lower the heat to a simmer. Add the remaining ingredients and simmer, skimming occasionally, for 2 hours, or until well flavored, adding cold water as necessary to keep the ingredients covered. Remove from the heat and let sit for 30 minutes to allow maximum gelatin to release from the bones into the stock. Pour through a fine-mesh sieve and discard the solids.

DASHI

Makes 2 quarts

- 1 (4-inch) square kombu
- 1½ cups bonito flakes

Rinse the kombu in cold water to remove dust. Put the kombu in a pot with 2½ quarts cold water. Bring to a boil. Remove from the heat and add the bonito flakes. Let steep for 15 minutes, then pour through a fine-mesh sieve lined with a clean kitchen towel or cheesecloth.

LOBSTER STOCK

Makes 2 quarts

- 1 tablespoon oil
- 1 small onion, roughly chopped
- 1 large clove garlic, smashed
- 1 cup roughly chopped carrot
- ½ cup roughly chopped celery
- Shells and heads of 4 lobsters
- 1 sprig fresh thyme
- 1 sprig fresh tarragon
- 1 sprig fresh parsley
- 1 bay leaf
- 7 whole black peppercorns

In a large pot, heat the oil and add the onion, garlic, carrot, and celery; cook over medium heat to sweat for about 5 minutes, until the vegetables are softened and the onion is translucent but not browned. Add the lobster shells and heads and stir. Cover with cold water and bring to a boil. Skim off the foam and scum that rise to the top, then lower the heat to a simmer. Add the remaining ingredients and simmer, skimming occasionally, for 1 to 1½ hours, until well flavored, adding cold water as necessary to keep the ingredients covered. Pour through a fine-mesh sieve and discard the solids.

VEAL STOCK

2 gallons

- 20 pounds veal bones
- 1 quart roughly chopped onions
- 3 cups roughly chopped carrots
- 3 cups roughly chopped celery
- 4 cloves garlic, smashed
- 1 quart peeled (see page 24), seeded tomatoes
- 2 bay leaves
- 2 sprigs fresh thyme
- 2 sprigs fresh parsley
- 15 whole black peppercorns

Preheat the oven to 400°F. Put the veal bones in a large baking pan in one layer and roast, turning once, until nicely browned, about 30 minutes. Add the onions, carrots, and celery, stir, and roast until the vegetables are soft and browned, about 25 minutes. Transfer the bones and vegetables to a large stockpot. Cover with cold water and bring to a boil. Skim off the foam and scum that rise to the top, then lower the heat to a simmer. Add the remaining ingredients and simmer, skimming occasionally, for about 6 hours, adding cold water as necessary to keep the ingredients covered. Pour through a fine-mesh sieve and discard the solids.

RESOURCES

Black Bubble-Tea Bubbles
BOBA TEA DIRECT,
www.bobateadirect.com

Black Mustard Seeds
KALUSTYANS, 800.352.3451;
www.kalustyans.com

Black Onion Seeds
KALUSTYANS, 800.352.3451;
www.kalustyans.com

Black-Truffle Butter
D'ARTAGNAN, 800.327.8246;
www.dartagnan.com

Bonito Flakes
(the shavings from dried smoked
skipjack tuna or bonito fish)
KALUSTYANS, 800.352.3451;
www.kalustyans.com

Bottarga di Muggine
(dried, cured mullet roe)
IGOURMET, 877.igourmet;
www.igourmet.com

Burdock Root, pickled
MITSUWA, www.mitsuwa.com

Caperberries
KALUSTYANS, 800.352.3451;
www.kalustyans.com

Caviar
PETROSSIAN, 800.828.9241;
www.petrossian.com

Chinese Sausage
VERYASIA, 888.424.8379;
www.veryasia.com

Hon Dashi
(a powdered substitute for dashi,
a broth derived from kombu)
MITSUWA, www.mitsuwa.com

Daikon, pickled
(Japanese radish)
MITSUWA, www.mitsuwa.com

Demi-glace
(reduced veal [or duck] stock)
D'ARTAGNAN, 800.327.8246;
www.dartagnan.com

Duck Demi-glace
D'ARTAGNAN, 800.327.8246;
www.dartagnan.com

Duck-Liver Mousse
D'ARTAGNAN, 800.327.8246;
www.dartagnan.com

Duck Fat
D'ARTAGNAN, 800.327.8246;
www.dartagnan.com

Fig Balsamic
KALUSTYANS, 800.352.3451;
www.kalustyans.com

Foie-Gras Mousse
D'ARTAGNAN, 800.327.8246;
www.dartagnan.com

Guinea Hens
D'ARTAGNAN, 800.327.8246;
www.dartagnan.com

Kaffir Lime Leaves
VERYASIA, 888.424.8379;
www.veryasia.com
You can often find these, frozen, at
Asian grocery stores.
Substitute: lime zest, although it's not
as aromatic

Kombu
(Japanese sea kelp)
MITSUWA, www.mitsuwa.com

Naengmyun
(Korean buckwheat noodles)
HMART, 877.427.7386;
www.hmart.com

Labne
(a Middle-Eastern hybrid of yogurt
and cheese)
Substitute: strained Greek yogurt

Lamb tenderloin
D'ARTAGNAN, 800.327.8246;
www.dartagnan.com

Mentaiko
(marinated pollock roe)
MITSUWA, www.mitsuwa.com

Mushroom Soy
VERYASIA, 888.424.8379;
www.veryasia.com

Nigella Seeds
KALUSTYANS, 800.352.3451;
www.kalustyans.com

Pink Salt (Hawaiian coarse)
KALUSTYANS, 800.352.3451;
www.kalustyans.com

Rabbit Saddle
D'ARTAGNAN, 800.327.8246;
www.dartagnan.com

Salted Egg
VERYASIA, 888.424.8379;
www.veryasia.com

Sansho Peppercorns, pickled
MITSUWA, www.mitsuwa.com

Shichimi Togarashi
(Japanese Seven-Spice)
MITSUWA, www.mitsuwa.com

Squid Ink, frozen
LA TIENDA, 800.710.4304; www.
tienda.com
Substitute: jarred squid ink

Tonburi
(broom cypress seed or "land caviar")
MITSUWA, www.mitsuwa.com

Umeboshi paste
(Japanese salted plum paste)
MITSUWA, www.mitsuwa.com

Unagi
(freshwater eel)
MITSUWA, www.mitsuwa.com

White Soy Sauce
MITSUWA, www.mitsuwa.com

White-Truffle Butter
D'ARTAGNAN, 800.327.8246;
www.dartagnan.com

INDEX

Page numbers in *italics* refer to illustrations.

ACKNOWLEDGMENTS

I'd like to thank all of my teachers—those who can be called teachers in the traditional sense, as well as my friends, colleagues, immediate family, and extended family of employees, past and present, whose influences can be found throughout this book. To Anna, who helped me write the elusive introduction and who, along with my staff at *annisa* (Greg! Danny! Suzanne! Michael! The Vidals! et al.) supported me through all the late nights and long hours. To Jennifer, who helped create *annisa* and nearly a decade of culinary memories and who meticulously tested the bulk of these recipes. To Jerry and Neil, whose waterfront home decorates many of these pages and who brought *La Famiglia*, both literally and figuratively, into my life. To Laurie, who named both of my restaurants and with whom I've explored many of the exotic locales mentioned here. To Charlotte, who wrote most of this book and made me a better (if imperfect) writer for the rest of it, and who, along with my agent, Laura Nolan, believed in the concept when it seemed no one else would. To my editor, Natalie Kaire, who tirelessly helped see the project through its final stages.

A human being is the sum of her experiences, and you all have made mine much richer.

Published in 2011 by Stewart, Tabori & Chang
An imprint of ABRAMS

Library of Congress Cataloging-in-Publication Data:
Lo, Anita.
Cooking without borders / Anita Lo, with Charlotte Druckman.
p. cm.
ISBN 978-1-58479-892-7 (hardback)
1. International cooking. 2. Cookbooks. I. Druckman, Charlotte. II.
Title.
TX725.A1L59 2011
641.59—dc22
2011008281

Editor: Natalie Kaire
Designer: Alissa Faden
Production Manager: Tina Cameron

The text of this book was composed in Gotham.

Printed and bound in the U.S.A.

10 9 8 7 6 5 4 3 2 1

Stewart, Tabori & Chang books are available at special discounts when purchased
in quantity for premiums and promotions as well as fundraising or educational use.
Special editions can also be created to specification. For details, contact
specialsales@abramsbooks.com or the address below.

THE ART OF BOOKS SINCE 1949

115 West 18th Street
New York, NY 10011
www.abramsbooks.com